DANGEROUS CHILDREN

DANGEROUS CHILDREN

On Seven Novels and a Story

KENNETH GROSS

The University of Chicago Press * CHICAGO AND LONDON

The University of Chicago Press, Chicago 60637
The University of Chicago Press, Ltd., London
© 2022 by The University of Chicago
Published 2022
Printed in the United States of America

31 30 29 28 27 26 25 24 23 22   1 2 3 4 5

ISBN-13: 978-0-226-81977-8 (cloth)
ISBN-13: 978-0-226-81978-5 (e-book)
DOI: https://doi.org/10.7208/chicago/9780226819785.001.0001

The University of Chicago Press gratefully acknowledges the generous
support of the University of Rochester toward the publication of this book.

Library of Congress Cataloging-in-Publication Data

Names: Gross, Kenneth, author.
Title: Dangerous children : on seven novels and a story / Kenneth Gross.
Description: Chicago : University of Chicago Press, 2022. | Includes
    bibliographical references and index.
Identifiers: LCCN 2022009996 | ISBN 9780226819778 (cloth) | ISBN
    9780226819785 (ebook)
Subjects: LCSH: Children in literature. | Children and adults in literature.
Classification: LCC PN56.5.C48 G76 2022 | DDC 809.3/93523—dc23
    /eng/20220421
LC record available at https://lccn.loc.gov/2022009996

♾ This paper meets the requirements of ANSI/NISO Z39.48-1992
(Permanence of Paper).

for LIZA

CONTENTS

PROLOGUE

TO CALL THEM by name, child by child: Alice, Pinocchio, Maisie, Peter, Odradek, Emily, Portia, Lolita. Some of these names can conjure up an entire world. All become signs of a larger life, a life unknown and familiar.

I look here at the ways that certain writers have imagined childhood. I'm curious about how these imagined children catch hold of us, often in scary or painful fashion. What do these dangerous children have to do with what we are and were? What do they ask of me? What is my part in these children?

The writings I've focused on are Lewis Carroll's *Alice in Wonderland* (1865)—with glances at *Through the Looking-Glass* (1871)—Carlo Collodi's *Pinocchio* (1883), Henry James's *What Maisie Knew* (1897), J. M. Barrie's *Peter and Wendy* (1911), Franz Kafka's "The Cares of a Family Man" (1919), Richard Hughes's *A High Wind in Jamaica* (1929), Elizabeth Bowen's *The Death of the Heart* (1938), and Vladimir Nabokov's *Lolita* (1955). The fascination of these stories' imagined children lies in their unsettling energy, their playfulness, their willfulness, their capacity for survival and transformation, their bluntness and violence. It lies in their unpredictability, in a fierce curiosity about the adult world joined with a refusal to readily accommodate to its rules.

These dream children invade our milder dreams of childhood. They enlarge and test our inherited pictures of innocence, and its loss. They

make innocence at home within unexpected forms of knowledge, pleasure, and craft. They create paradoxical alliances between weakness and
strength, seriousness and jest, sense and nonsense, the human and the
nonhuman.

These children's voices—by turns wounded, comic, questioning, ecstatic, and cruel—can summon a world of listeners. They may speak
with terrible plainness. Or their words may sound unrelatable, half-
articulate, not like words at all. ("Learning to speak, the child has either
too few or too many words.") Ordinary language may struggle to keep
up with them. All of these children are storytellers, but their way with
stories is often at odds with that of the adults around them. The children often fall into silence, or into conversations that drive them, and
those they're talking with, a little mad.

These children are given bodies that move with strange energy, that
fall weightlessly, run without tiring, or suddenly fly up, bodies that burrow, dance, float, stretch out or collapse upon themselves, survive burning and drowning, sometimes starving, sometimes filling themselves
with the most uncanny food.

They find unexpected occasions for play, they find games in places
where games shouldn't be, games whose rules keep changing, or that
change what we think of as the aims of play, that shift the grounds of
winning and losing, taking sides, what it means to cheat. Games that are
violent or that do violence to games, played on a broken or a twisted
playing field, or in places where games are prohibited, with equipment
that has a life of its own—hedgehogs for balls, flamingoes for mallets.
Games that can only be lost, you may think, even if *"everybody* has won,
and *all* must have prizes." Such play can intensify the children's solitude,
or draw them into a more anarchic community.

Theirs is a schoolroom that is no longer a schoolroom. These children are caught in schemes of education gone awry, deformed, abrupt,
impoverished, or insane, in lessons more wildly free, a schooling that
asks for more eccentric, more dangerous teachers, a schooling that
feeds minds unsettlingly precocious or luminously obtuse.

All of them become wanderers, nomads, explorers, forced or willing
exiles, sometimes squatters, possessed of at best uncertain and temporary homes.

They become companions of animals, beasts ordinary and unheard of, odd, silly, sad, mad, and wise, some with human faces, some given the power to speak—rabbit, pig, donkey, bear, griffin, cat, caterpillar, cricket, mouse, monkey, and goat, minnows and worms and cockroaches.

Their books tell odder stories about the ways that children share their lives with made things, with toys and dolls, with shoes, candles, books, teacups, watches, thimbles, and bottles. Often undergoing metamorphosis, animation and deanimation, these things are the children's riches and their poverty, generous and desperate tools for probing the world, gifts that can yet be charged with violence. One of my children makes her imaginary babies out of broken rope ends and iron spikes.

You often can't fix their ages. They can seem preternaturally old, archaic creatures, child-adults, or children suspended in time, who age, if at all, according to a line of days you cannot count or count on.

These children keep company with the dead, they are creatures who return to us out of a distant past, out of a dead life, a dead and unknown childhood, secretive, hard to lay hold of. They can seem like ghosts who need to be laid to rest or banished, or like ghosts we must welcome, make a home for, shades with whom we need to take up stranger conversations.

They do not die. They offer an unsettling vision of continuance, even immortality, a vision of an early life that also resists time, stops time or overgoes it, a child life killed, mourned, and continually resurrected. ("And who then was ever cured of his childhood?" asks the poet Lucie Delarue-Mardrus.) By this they draw us into a richer sense of our own life in time.

These fictive children, again, ask us to think differently about innocence, how innocence gets lost or stays in place, how it takes up changed forms. In their speech and gestures, their sensory worlds, their pleasures and fears, their games, their acts of violence, they test simpler ideas of innocence. Theirs is an eroticism that is both distant from the *eros* of an adult world and perilously close. They thrust us back into stranger beginnings and stranger continuities, aspects of childhood that subsist within us, that we might have difficulty remembering, or might not want to remember, and can now only imagine. There is more in these children than any adult has been able to keep. They may show us, as Gaston Bachelard writes, "moments in childhood when every child is the astonishing being, the being who realizes the *astonishment of being*." They invite us to open ourselves to invisible, forbidden, unfinished, or unlived childhoods, impossible childhoods, childhoods "insolent and remote." They speak of a past that might give us the face of an unknown future. As with the wildly various images of play in Pieter Bruegel's painting *Children's Games*, the play of these children can hold within itself "the present, the almost-past, the not-yet, the about-to-be, the held-in-abeyance, the imagined-away, or the permanently translated."

I CALL MY subjects *dangerous* children. What is dangerous in them is no one thing, and keeps on changing, like their forms of play. The danger may lie in something the children see with terrible clarity, or something they're blind to. It lies in the danger they pose to adults, to adult passions, imaginations, words, to adult silences, in how the children deform or mock those things. Some of these children irritate adults simply by refusing to allow their souls to be stolen. The dangerousness can also come from ideas that adults impose on the children, out of fear or envy, even love, from a way of seeing that these children can't help but collide with. It emerges simply in the ways adults speak of and to these children, how they call the child by other names, call it "monster," "horror," "serpent," "idiot," "traitor," "thief," "demon," "lunatic," "spying common," "awful baby." Starkly imagined as they are, these children task us with imagining how others imagine them, and how they imagine themselves, even as we may find their minds and hearts beyond imagining.

My dangerous children are very often endangered children. The dangers they face, the wounds, are at times only half-visible, at times all too naked, emerging from the outside world and from within the children's own passions and acts. They are dangers belonging to the present, past, and future, dangers we're continually asked to see and acknowledge in new guises. We are set to be these children's minders as well as their imaginers. "Our children," writes Marina Warner—great mythographer of ogres, of their fright and charm—"can't be better than we are."

These dangers, as I've suggested, include the ways that adults, for their own purposes, make these children strange, the ways they invent both the children's innocence and their menace (as does the governess in James's *The Turn of the Screw*). The very unreadability of these children can make them more inimical than endearing. Their vulnerability can make those who face them feel unexpectedly vulnerable. Their play may come to seem, as Joe Moshenska frames the relentless paradox, something "at once utterly insignificant and charged with demonic danger." It's a relation in which adults may turn their own ghosts into scarecrows or bogeys to threaten children, rather than facing those ghosts themselves—adults who, in Giorgio Agamben's words, "literally play dead and prefer to entrust their own phantoms to children and children to these phantoms." "The child," James Kincaid reflects, "carries for us things we somehow cannot carry for ourselves, sometimes anxieties we want to be divorced from and sometimes pleasures so great we would not, without the child, know how to contain them." Yet it's hard to give up imagining the child, however liable this is to distort things, to feed dangerous projections. Adam Phillips, thinking about the task of listening to child speech, including our own, writes that "if the child, and stories about childhood like psychoanalysis, have acquired a quasi-religious significance, have become our most convincing essentialism, it is perhaps because children are, as their parents always say, impossible. They want more than they can have. And, at least to begin with, they are shameless about it." We have these stories to help us reenter that shamelessness, to see what we can make of it.

THREE OF MY subjects—the *Alice* books, *Pinocchio*, and *Peter and Wendy*—were written with child readers in mind. Carroll's and Barrie's fables indeed took their origins in games of make-believe and improvised storytelling with beloved child-friends—child-muses even—before being translated to the page. The stories invite children to imagine themselves inside doubles of their own worlds of discovery and doubt, fear and pleasure, to place themselves inside an imagined child's career of play, transgression, impersonation, entrapment, and metamorphosis—or simply learning to use a language. They allow

a child to take up conversation with myriad forms of other life, creatures who may offer curious mirrors of the adult life and speech around
them, or who catch at, even reshape, the hidden life in the child's head.
At the same time, and for many of the same reasons, these books have
never ceased to keep a powerful hold on adult readers. Part of their continuing power lies, indeed, in how they ask us to redraw any boundaries
we set between the two audiences, revising our sense of how fictions
can be intended toward them, how each speaks to the other. They offer measures of an imagined innocence, also new dimensions of knowledge in an uneasy alliance between innocence and experience. There
are always darker threads of longing and sadness, eroticism and irony,
hidden in the web of childish play and nonsense, as you can feel in
Alice's endless changes of form and troubled conversations with beasts
and mad persons, in Pinocchio's relentless motion and hunger, in the
rage and sorrow that fill Peter's thoughts of lost mothers.

My five other stories—*What Maisie Knew*, "The Cares of a Family
Man," *A High Wind in Jamaica*, *The Death of the Heart*, and *Lolita*—
were written for adult readers. You feel this in the greater demands of
their language, in their more bluntly sexual themes, in a sense of guilt or
shame missing in the other three. These books know things that might
make adults want to keep them from children (granting that adults
have wanted to ban children from reading *Alice in Wonderland*). Death
is a starker presence in these five texts, both physical death and what
Bowen calls "the death of the heart." They probe more sharply the cruelty and compulsion at work in the world. The element of the fantastic in them is framed more ironically, if it's there at all. Nor are any
of these, like *Pilgrim's Progress*, *Robinson Crusoe*, or *Gulliver's Travels*,
books written for adults that child readers have possessed for themselves, works that—often in abridged, adapted forms—they've made
mirrors of their own reading life, of their imaginative lives *as* books, as
one scholar finely describes it. These five are "books without pictures,"
such as Alice complains of in her grown-up sister's reading, though
none of them is "without conversation."

Yet for all that they direct their words to adults, the power of these
five fictions lies in how they continue to enter, or try to enter, the child's
perspective, how they lodge the imagined child in the midst of an adult

world, make the child a presence at once charismatic and questioning, the source of uncanny speech, its own unknown book or teller of stories, translating continuously. Here the child who wonders is itself a wonder. Such texts invite a continual dialogue between voices of childhood and adulthood. They suggest that part of our business as adults is to measure the degree to which we "never grow up."

"When I was a child, I spake as a child, I understood as a child, I thought as a child: but when I became a man, I put away childish things." That is Saint Paul in his first letter to the Corinthians, speaking of our souls' task as we mature in spirit, as the spiritual world reveals itself to us, as we come to inhabit and look into it, to look *after* that world, assume its gifts. Drawing such lines isn't simple or without cost. The poet John Hollander spoke memorably about the awful parody of maturity you can feel in a world where people have "put away the wrong childish things," an adult world of overgrown and undergrown children, creatures with more than a child's power to do harm—especially through elements of childish thinking disguised as reason and truth. (And then, as the philosopher Stanley Cavell wrote, "childish things can be put aside vengefully, which is not giving something over.") One gift of these books is that they keep the mind open to the right childish things, which may be close enough to the wrong ones. They keep the claims of childish things always in flux. They ask what we've learned, or think we've learned, in growing up, what conversations we can still have with our childhood. What kind of child or adult do I become in reading these stories? The place of childishness is inevitably hard to mark. It breaks through in unexpected places. You can feel in these books, indeed, an insistent doubling of child voice and adult voice. Each seeks out the other and plays with the other, each mirrors and invades and seizes the other, collaborates with and tests the other. Each also may hide away from the other, or disguise itself as the other. If this mutual contamination of child and adult languages opens up a space of shared sympathy, a bridge across an abyss, it just as often splits apart child speaker and adult speaker, sets each the more strongly in their cut-off, self-enclosed worlds of thought and imagination. Each has its own complicity in the chaos that ensues.

Part of the singularity of my eight elected children is that each of their fictive careers comes to an end *before* they become adults. Their lives as children don't run forward into a larger life story, though not, save in one case, because they die. It's their child life, an interval stretched out and at play, that claims us. You rarely get more than a brief glimpse of the child grown old, looking back on the past. These children come (if at all) just to the threshold of adulthood, and so make uncertain the nature of that threshold itself, what crossing it begins or brings to an end. Floating free of their adult lives, these children acquire a weird sufficiency, something elemental. This is part of their power to stand against time and change, part of how they survive in *our* minds as images of childhood. If it's difficult to imagine their adult lives, one yet keeps wondering about their part in the world of adults, as well as their part in the world of other children, and of various nonhuman and half-human creatures. These children are inside time and yet outside it, crying to us from a mysterious place, from a realm of possibility and play whose scope is hard to fix. That's one reason perhaps why we keep reading these stories, why we want to claim these children for ourselves, even if they disown us, or draw a circle around themselves.

THIS IS A kind of memory book of reading. My choice of subjects is in the end a personal one. I've tried to seize each of my stories whole, as they seize me, as page by page they've become things to live with. Each chapter is a self-sufficient essay. Each seeks to catch the energies of a particular tale and of the child figure at its center. No single thesis binds these essays together, no one theory, rather a shifting constellation of thoughts, recurring questions. I've held back from fixed interpretations. I am not trying to write a chapter in a history of the child in literature, or tracing particular traditions of writing *for* children. Others have done these things better than I could. I've tried to evoke the poetry of these stories, to keep faith with some gesture of life in the language of each. My imagined wholes will be, for some readers, merely fractions.

Other children clamored for attention as I wrote. There is, for one thing, an older genealogy of stories barely touched on. I think of ancient myths that give us child-gods born in full strength, who come into the world solitary, orphaned or raised by surrogate parents, infant trickster and thief like Hermes, or like Dionysus a rebellious child threatened with death yet keeping command of his own life and powers, always changing shape, a child dismembered and devoured but in the end reborn. Hindu sacred texts give us stories of the guileful child Krishna, a destroyer of ogresses who would nurse him on poison, an eater of dirt who holds the cosmos in his mouth. Even the young Jesus, in one ancient apocryphal gospel, is a dangerous child—he violates the Sabbath by making clay birds and then animating them, blinds his accusers, and kills with a curse teachers and children who mock or strike him, only some of whom he restores to life. Such dangerous divine children often take shape in myths of origin and creation, they're embodiments of some chaotic energy at the heart of nature or human life, sustained by elemental forces that might otherwise consume them—as in a Finnish fable Carl Kerényi recounts, about an infant-god born from and living in flames, "a little boy: / Fire for hair, and fire for beard, / And his eyes were suns," a Promethean child-giant who sets fires that destroy and purify, conquering the dark. A version of such an originary child lurks within a saying of the Presocratic philosopher Heraclitus, evoking the uncertain nature of our being in the world: "*Aion* [time, or the life force working in time] is a child moving counters in a game. The royal power is the child's."

Close to the world of myth, many traditions of fairy tale give us dangerous children facing danger, orphaned and abandoned children, children who are wise fools or cunning tricksters, or both at once, who are both victims and thieves of magic. Touching only on European examples, I think of clever Hansel and Gretel, who manage to burn up the witch who's entrapped them, and would have eaten them; of the dead boy in "The Juniper Tree" who, changed into a fiercely singing, enchanted bird, takes revenge on the stepmother who killed him; of gentle Red Riding Hood, who in one early version of the tale unwittingly drinks her grandmother's blood and eats her flesh. Like the lost child Mamillius in Shakespeare's *The Winter's Tale*—himself a strong teller of tales "of sprites and goblins"—such figures evoke more hidden powers and fears in both children and adults. They suggest some of the ways in which fairy tales may "speak the unspeakable," or speak for the unspeaking.

Certain poems by William Blake and William Wordsworth have come repeatedly to mind. These give us startling, potent, yet fragile, sometimes ghostly children, objects of love and fear, figures whose child life admits of passions and knowledge, even a kind of self-destructive energy, that trouble simpler ideas of innocence, of its loss and survival. Crucial precursors of later imagined children, especially in British and American literature, these figures suggest just how richly ambiguous, how self-aware, the "Romantic child" is in its beginnings. I think here of the children who cry out in Blake's *Songs of Innocence and Experience*— Infant Joy and Infant Sorrow ("Helpless, naked, piping loud; / Like a fiend hid in a cloud"), the little boy or girl lost or appalling churches with their cries of pain. Such voices reflect Blake's revision of the fall story, in which any curse on human life is a thing invented by the human mind itself, partly as a way to give shape to its fears of such childish energies. I think of Wordsworth's fascination with the "little maid" in "We Are Seven," counting together the dead and the living in a way that so troubles her adult questioner; of the poet's child-adults, like Margaret in "The Ruined Cottage," cleaving to her place and thought; and of his visions of his own child-self moving through the natural world as sacred thief and "fell destroyer," dangerous and endangered, alien and open, "listening to sounds that are / The ghostly language of the ancient earth."

Among nineteenth-century novels, to mention just those in English, I've not taken up Mary Shelley's dark child-creature in *Frankenstein*, that "phantasmagoria of the nursery." I've said nothing about the demanding, bleeding child-ghost of Cathy Earnshaw in Emily Brontë's *Wuthering Heights*, seeking the wild child Heathcliff. There's nothing about Charles Dickens's child criminals and suffering orphans, children prematurely aged, made lurid, even monstrous in their relentless piety and forbearance. Nothing about Thomas Hardy's "Little Father Time" in *Jude the Obscure*, weird, unpredictable, murderous, and suicidal. Nothing about the uncanny children of Victorian fairy stories by George MacDonald, Charles Kingsley, Jean Ingelow, and Christina Rossetti, children wandering through menacing worlds, earthly and fantastic, endangered creatures lent their own mysterious powers of survival.

The twentieth century gives us the conspiratorial sister and brother of Jean Cocteau's *Les enfants terribles*, orphans whose ruthless games demand "victims, summary executions, human sacrifices." There are the lost schoolboys of William Golding's *Lord of the Flies*, who, in what seems an island paradise, change into adultlike savages, mirrors of a violent order within the larger world. For the civilized listener in Nathalie Sarraute's *Do You Hear Them?*, the laughter of unseen children changes from innocent noise into a sound that "babbles, skips, rolls, sprawls, leaps, nibbles, squanders, bungles, destroys, mocks." There's fierce, vulnerable Louie in Christina Stead's *The Man Who Loved Children*, turning against an oppressive father his own invented language. In *The Fifth Child*, Doris Lessing creates a domestic monster, a child whose energy, hunger, and seemingly source-less aggression conjures the fear and corrodes the love, the deepest life sympathies, of those who live with it. Lessing draws into the ordinary world an older line of stories that give us demonic or evil children. About such fables Joyce Carol Oates asks, "Do we secretly yearn to hate that which we have been obliged to love?"

There are also novels whose dangerous children become witnesses to a larger, more frightening history, actors within a grimmer sort of adult fairy tale. The child Oskar in Günter Grass's *The Tin Drum*, born in the Free City of Danzig in 1923, stops himself growing at age three, like a weird Peter Pan, disgusted by the grown-up world. By turns clown, trickster, paranoid plotter, refugee, possessive lover, and accused murderer, his prolonged childhood is marked by his relentless drumming and by his glass-shattering shriek, anarchic sounds that invade the mad historical Neverland which grows up around him with the rise of Nazism, a world war, and the Soviet invasion at the war's end.

I think also of the noisy, invasive child-ghost that Toni Morrison imagines in *Beloved*. It's the ghost of a "beautiful, magical best thing," a form of innocence who dies in a frightening act of love, a terrible witness to the death-in-life of slavery, that human negation whose poisoning of love, life, thought, and hope the novel traces so starkly. If this wounded and wounding ghost speaks for the continuing power of that poison, Morrison late in her novel gives the ghost-child words that, for a moment, claim an ownership in love that might undo the brute obscenity of ownership in the slave world.

Then there are the strange games of David Grossman's Momik in *See Under: Love*, a nine-year-old boy living in a poor Jerusalem neighborhood in the 1950s, a place full of survivors of the death camps. Momik's games attempt to conjure and defeat an elusive, hearsay enemy, "the Nazi Beast." They end up inflicting pain on innocent animals and on already suffering adults, as well as on the child himself, as he comes to hear in his own throat the cry of that Beast.

Readers will have other names to add to this idiosyncratic list. Of my own choice of stories I will only say that, as this book evolved, I felt these works' peculiar power to challenge my vision of both child and adult worlds, my feeling for how these worlds cross or fail to cross, their invitations to revise our histories of growing up. There was also the increasing sense of a pull of gravity between these eight stories, the hint of what wondering Maisie shows us about wondering Alice, what wooden Odradek shows us about wooden Pinocchio. The stories have become a house of thought.

I cannot easily imagine my eight children speaking to one another, much less playing a game together. I do not imagine them sharing the space of a nursery or a schoolroom. Still, they form in my mind a kind of family.

ALICE

"DOWN, DOWN, DOWN, would the fall *never* come to an end?" The madness of *Alice in Wonderland* starts with a falling. The child finds herself falling almost before she knows it. It is a slow fall, without fear or panic, almost without surprise. It's a fall stretched out, shaped by a different gravity from that of earth, a fall that lasts long enough that there's time for thinking over spell-like questions or riddles—"Do cats eat bats? . . . Do bats eat cats?"—words like lullabies for her entry into a waking dream. There is time for the child to worry about the danger of a dropped, sadly empty jar of marmalade falling on heads below, creatures she knows nothing about. There is time to wonder whether you might fall through the earth and into the "antipathies," and how you will talk with the people *there*. The fall endows a new world. It is a little like falling asleep, a thing that happens to you before you know it's happened, a falling that you pursue, even if you can't quite will it.

Down, down, down. A long fall through unknown space. "She tried to look down and make out what she was coming to, but it was too dark to see anything." That falling never does end. The falling is part of the being of this child, even when she walks on the ground, moving through this new world. We fall into such a world, and into such children. And the children fall into us. We fall into the flood made of our own tears, likely to be drowned in punishment for weeping so much, a flood that threatens other creatures as well, animals commonplace and exotic, even extinct, though they all survive the flood and afterward run an impossible race. Drinking an unknown liquid, we shut up like a tele-scope. Fanning our faces, we shrink again, almost to the point of going out like a candle. Or we collapse down suddenly onto our own feet, our chins sharply hitting our shoes.

Down, down, down. And then we shoot up again, exiled from our feet, bidding them farewell, our necks stretched out high and twisting so madly that an angry pigeon mistakes us for a snake ready to eat her eggs. Falling and rising work by a shifting logic, the laws of gravity and the laws of human growth operate strangely. You almost *fall upward* in this world, possessed of a grave lightness. It is like the motion of the body in thought, in dreams, more free and more compelled. Such flight suggests a power in Wonderland to make real those things that the child at play only imagines for itself, also the child's loss of the power to con-trol such play. Growing in Wonderland is never quite a growing *up,* even for a child, partly because growing larger is always involved with growing smaller. It makes you dangerous to yourself and others. Grow-ing large, you find yourself crammed inside the walls of a house, folded up on yourself like a rag doll or fetus, though still able to reach out your hands and feet in violent ways, making one animal fall to the ground and another fly up into the air, kicked out of a chimney. There is a con-tinual sound of breaking glass. The changes are unpredictable, they fall upon you, though you try to calculate them in advance, or to control them by nibbling on one or another side of a giant mushroom.

Down, down, down. It is an innocent fall, the fall of what remains innocent. You do not fall into hell, like Milton's Satan, or into a world of pain, labor, and death. You fall into a world that can seem homely enough, full of ordinary objects, rituals, and work, yet these ordinary things are transformed, they turn unreadable, or mad, animated by the intrusion of an alien (sometimes just *slightly* alien) life. A new world of play falls back into Alice. We follow this child as she wanders, calmly enough, from place to place, without a map, without boundary mark-ers or clear horizons, with barely a thought of the home she's left be-hind. There's an effect of "serene seductive discontinuity," writes Wal-ter de la Mare. In moving to each new spot, Alice the quester may find a momentary place of rest, a refuge, a chance (like that of Odysseus) to tell her story to those she meets. But crossing the threshold isn't always easy, and each new resting place may become a place of chaos, a trap she must escape. The creatures she meets might terrify her—gigantic caterpillars, angry pigeons. Yet she faces them as an equal, with surprising composure, like that of our dream encounters, and with conscious, liberating curiosity. None of the creatures seems to recognize her *as* a child, save perhaps in the freedom they take to criticize her manners and language, to face her with questions, lessons, and morals, though they often seem quite ready to ignore her.

And as you read, some odd turns of speaking, inadvertent remarks, keep opening up the unknown histories of the creatures themselves— an impossible beast's nostalgia for his peculiar schooling, a mad hatmaker's humiliation by angry Time, a mouse's unjust trial—pasts that can yet feel improvised, arbitrary, and incomplete.

There is no magic in the place, or no singular magic. There's no Prospero in Wonderland to organize its changes of scale, shape, and seeing, no hidden order of spiritual powers, benign or harmful, to do one's bidding. There's no designing God, as in Dante's *Divine Comedy*, who creates this fantastic world as a system of rewards and punishments, imposing on surviving souls forms of mockery and delight, freedom and compulsion, forms that symbolize the souls' true or erring desires (six-footed serpent, bleeding tree, speaking fire, dancing star, luminous cloud). The changes in *Alice in Wonderland* have something in them of game, something of accident, something of practical contrivance, something of law (I'm reminded of the play of change in Ovid's *Metamorphoses*). The magic may be keyed merely to what seems a foolish pun. Each turn of the story changes the conditions of the world, including the conditions of what the world understands as nonsense. Bodies in space are as mutable as words in a sentence, run through by all the unpredictable tricks of language, twisted, turned, emptied out. Alice wishes for "a book of rules for shutting people up like telescopes." She will not find such a book, though this doesn't keep her from trying to find the rules, or to apply those she believes she already knows, even if these prove treacherous. Of the creatures she meets, only the Cheshire Cat seems wholly in control of its changes, of how much of itself appears and disappears, though we're never wholly certain about the Cat's reasons for doing one or the other.

In Wonderland, the rules that shape our play, the energy of play by which our soul and imagination and reason improvise or extend themselves into new forms, by which minds and bodies rehearse their freedom and test its limits—these rules become radically unpredictable. The rules of play are always being reinvented, challenged, broken, perverted, made unintelligible, though in ways that sustain rather than kill the work of play. The power that ruins play is indeed aligned with what creates it, in part because Carroll's creatures seem to set against organized games some earlier, more idiosyncratic, more unstructured impulse to play. Or else, these creatures set themselves to odd activities that seem so like games, that seem so much to evoke what is impractical and unconventional in play, even if such play is pursued with a kind of vexing seriousness or solemnity—a power to wound, to provoke fear or sadness—that we might hope is alien to play. (Melancholy Bill the Lizard, in the jury box, keeps writing with his finger on his slate after Alice, unseen, takes away his squeaking pencil; later he uses the ink trickling down his face after the Queen of Hearts, without reason, throws an inkstand at him.)

"If we decided that from now on chess pieces could only be used to play checkers with, what would the word 'chess' refer to? Chess would lose its grip on our imaginations, as if by magic. It would seem like a vestige of something—quaintly old-fashioned." So writes Adam Phillips, thinking about the necessary quality of our trust in certain rules, their pragmatic truth, what we stand to lose in giving them up. In Carroll's world such a disenchanting magic, such an undoing of the rules of play, creates its own grip on our minds. The ruined games of Wonderland are just as likely to lead us on to fresh revelations of what play can be, hints of the other passions or powers that play channels—Phillips himself knows just how sharply the improvised games of children and adults can link them back to otherwise lost, inarticulate sources of knowledge and pleasure. We're caught up as we read in a more potent kind of quaintness, by turns progress and regress, both opening into new possibilities and arcane entrapments. Such a toying with rules shifts along the threads of all our talk, all our desire, all our work.

Before her fall, Carroll tells us, "this curious child" sometimes played croquet with herself, cheating at the game and then boxing her own ears for cheating, as if both the cheating and the punishment were parts of the game, close to its heart. Alice's experiences in Wonderland give richer shape to these early games, suggesting how so idiosyncratic a style of play can open up and animate a whole world. When she finally enters the garden of the Queen of Hearts, a glimpse of which had stirred her first attempts to change her shape, Alice is set to play croquet on a field where everyone cheats. Here the croquet hoops are living playing cards—entities belonging to a different game world—that keep wandering from their places. It's a playing field full of troughs and humps, where Alice's mallet and ball are intractable living creatures, each with a will of its own, the exotic flamingo and the more earthbound, though sufficiently uncanny, hedgehog. As Alice complains bitterly to the Cheshire Cat, kindly avatar of Wonderland's madness, "They don't seem to have any rules in particular: at least, if there are, nobody attends to them—and you've no idea how confusing it is all the things being alive." And one after all *should* know, if only for the sake of the game, what is dead and what is alive.

"*You've no idea how confusing it is all the things being alive.*" If they address the Queen's loony game, Alice's words also speak for a more primal bafflement and wonder structured into Carroll's books. It places you in a world in which the conditions of life itself—life in things and persons—are essentially confusing, always crossing boundaries or breaking some primal taboo, spilling out in some unknown form. Life itself is a trickster here. In this the *Alice* books seek to cultivate in us an anarchic competence or a "flaunted, a *skillful*, incompetence," as Susan Stewart writes of play and nonsense both, a readiness to violate and reinvent the rules that define play itself, incorporating disorder into new forms of order. Carroll's books remind us that all too often we don't truly know what the life of things or the life of words is, or how they die—and the fright in becoming aware of that lack of knowledge. Alice's cry might be the cry of any of us complaining about a world in which objects, persons, games, and words don't function with the regularity or transparency that we want and need—when ordinary objects of use and play (spoon, pencil, top) don't work in our hands, fall from our hands, out of clumsiness, haste, weariness, or chance. Her cry also invites us to consider the uncanny life that objects acquire when we look at those objects outside of their conventional uses. It reminds us of how, as the novelist Helen Oyeyemi writes, "the dangers of childhood and the relationship to the inanimate in which childhood often places us persist into adulthood, just as the objects themselves may persist, silently refusing to confine their meanings and functions to the names we've assigned to them, but becoming more and more alive the more we listen to what they can't, don't, or won't say."

One of the few moments of outright laughter we hear in the book comes when Alice's flamingo, refusing to keep its head to the ground and do its malleting work, keeps turning about to look Alice in the eye. Just why the bird's glance makes Alice laugh we're left to imagine for ourselves.

ALICE IS A form of motion. That is her claim on us. Foundling, orphan, and exile (at least within Wonderland). The guarantor of both our freedom and our entrapment. We learn the sound of her truth. The "wonder" of Wonderland takes its fundamental shape in our hearing Alice murmur so often to herself, "I wonder..." The *Alice* books trace continually the uncertain threshold between the adult and the child, in Alice herself and among the creatures she meets, creatures by turns affectionate, troubled, frenzied, obsessed, clownish, servile, resentful, gentle, and needful. Such creatures can seem themselves children in disguise, or belonging to a child's fantasy of the adult world, even as they resemble adults who have put away the *wrong* childish things. It is the fearlessness, the imperturbability of Alice in the face of that confusion, the sense in her of what Willian Empson calls "a sort of reserve of force," an independence of mind, that makes of this madness a kind of lucid enchantment, a lesson in survival. "Alice has become our mentor and is at no one's mercy," writes Marianne Moore. We are drawn to this child whose company and mind we rarely leave in the *Alice* books, who never sleeps (unless it is *all* sleep and dream). We are drawn to the energy of exchange she puts into motion, drawn to her place in this world, her ways of moving through it, her ways of provoking and animating its words. She takes these words into her capacious, acute, often troubled ear, even as she finds her own voice less recognizable to herself. The world outside of Alice has something of the mutability of an interior world. It's as if she is at once traveling inside her own thoughts and looking at them from the outside, realizing how little she owns them, both hero and monster in the mind's labyrinth. In Alice's encounters in Wonderland, you can sense the isolate mind pressing back against its limits, finding a power to shape and break its limits, to question the nature of limit itself, the madness and necessity of that.

Virginia Woolf wrote that Carroll's own childhood lodged within him as "a perfectly hard crystal... whole and entire." This hard crystal, suspended within its "untinted jelly" (she's thinking of a Victorian dish of molded aspic), starved the adult man of the nourishments of maturity; the fixed crystal or stone of childhood became for him both impediment and parasite, she thought, making the man as ungraspable to *us* as to himself. And yet, "since childhood remained in him entire... he could return to that world; he could re-recreate it, so that we too become children again" in reading him.

As a subject for biography, I find the author of *Alice in Wonderland* as ungraspable as Woolf does, despite having the help of fierce accounts of his life and mind by Morton Cohen, Gillian Beer, Robert Douglas-Fairhurst, and others, their pictures of a complex, self-knowing and self-questioning person, deeply reserved, at times a mystery to himself, yet aware of what in his nature was idiosyncratic, haunted, even obsessional, and always open to larger if still gamelike conversations with the world—a maker of riddles who had a rare capacity to trust children, and was trusted by them. Thinking of Carroll's fiction, though, I would want to turn on Woolf's forceful image. For in the *Alice* books, that hard crystal of childhood is not simply fixed and dead. It has its own curious life, it changes its shape or takes multiple shapes. There are ideas of childhood there that survive metamorphosed, or in disguise, or thrown into such alien contexts that they never seem purely childlike. Any idea of innocence is so transformed that it's hard to give it a simple or singular meaning. The fictive Alice embodies something childish that we might ask for ourselves as an adult endowment, something knowingly playful, realistic, deliberate, impatient, skeptical yet open to wonder. It's something that Carroll knew to treasure in himself. It works to challenge both what the adult world has made of itself and what it has made of childhood, its narrower images of innocence, also the childish masks of maturity, made visible in an endlessly changing looking-glass.

Alice is a "curious child"—"curiouser and curiouser" she finds the world, and we find *her*. That curiosity, mixing appetite and pleasure, often harks back to something infantile, it's a link to more archaic, animallike hungers, a will to seize, to devour, to consume the world and its creatures, to challenge their possession of real and imaginary food (even talking food). The small girl-child in this finds her affinities with the cat and the snake, also the smiling and seductive crocodile, creatures uncanny, secretive, predatory. Such early appetites mingle with that in Alice which is humanly eager to know and name the world, also with what in her is humanly despotic, prim, pedantic, obtuse, and reckless. What in her is inarticulate or infantile (from Latin *infans*, speechless) also feeds her *speaking*, her way with questions, answers, and stories.

Reading the *Alice* books, you're caught by an arcane courtesy of manner, a tone "like Proust's: at once formal and intimate, utterly without patronizing (a rare gift in writing for children)." That tone shows itself most strongly in an exquisite fascination with shapes of *dis*courtesy, with images of courtesy baffled or hardened, made mad. Here a Victorian book of manners—for both children and grown-ups—is turned into a chaotic and lucid dream. All that Alice takes for granted about polite conversation loses its grip, its truth, its apparent naturalness. We keep encountering breeds of courtesy that obey stranger laws, suffused with the anarchic and yet deeply human energies that courtesy tries to organize, subdue, and ritualize, or convert into witty play. (Taking *both* Tweedledee's and Tweedledum's extended hands so as not to hurt either's feelings, she finds herself instantly dancing in a ring. "This seemed quite natural... and she was not even surprised to hear music playing.") Our almost metaphysical attachment to social convention is put to the test. Carroll's games of conversation remind us, Kenneth Burke wrote, of what remains unknown or unmapped in officially marked differences of social status, even as those games question differences between youth and age, weakness and strength, educated and ignorant, human and inhuman, animate and inanimate, differences full of their own "complications and reversibilities." (For Burke it puts the *Alice* books "in the same bin" as *The Castle* and *Lady Chatterly's Lover*.)

Courtesy is a hard game in Wonderland, just because the readiness of its inhabitants to take offense seems structured into this world, the occasions for offense being endless and unpredictable. Discourtesy seems inevitable, essential to how the creatures try to teach Alice, how they seek to question, challenge, test, and educate her into the irregular logic of Wonderland. "I wish the creatures wouldn't be so easily offended!" There is no telling, she finds, what will or will not cause offense to one of those creatures, even mistakes or mis-speakings she claims as innocent. The possibility of offending is a kind of glue, a magnetic field that holds the atoms of this world together even as it divides them, sends them apart, flying off into spaces of ever-stranger isolation. Offense turns out to be generative and clarifying as well as wounding. It's a promise, a pathway to the hidden histories, memories, and appetites through which these creatures make themselves present to us, take on visible shape and claim their own names, or claim our *care*, the means by which they grip us with their peculiar magic, with questions about our own language, spirit, and forms of being.

Offense in Wonderland aligns itself closely with nonsense. The play of nonsense indeed emerges most grippingly *within* these troubled conversations, these trials of courtesy. Antonin Artaud, imaginer of a "theater of cruelty," deplored Carroll's nonsense as heartless, unmarked by suffering, too much a matter of polite surfaces and afraid to excavate buried fear and disgust. Artaud did not see (as his admirer Gilles Deleuze *does* see) how that nonsense is sparked by sharp, mysterious, and playful violations of such surfaces. You feel the nonsense emerging in sudden interruptions and angry corrections, moments when Alice's words are seized by a forced or inadvertent pun, by willful or misplaced literalism, by idle or aggressive non sequiturs, by impossible questions, or by inadequate or arbitrary explanations which yet claim to be final. Each such turn leads on to other confusions of talk, or more baffling silences.

Alice wants to trust the words she knows, wants them to be adequate to negotiate the world in which she finds herself. Instead, she finds words taken out of her mouth by odd theft. Her plainest questions get turned by another creature into riddles, never answered as she asks them to be—"What tremendously easy riddles you ask!" says

Humpty Dumpty in *Through the Looking-Glass*, when Alice has asked, sympathetically you'd think, "Why do you sit out here all alone?" and "Don't you think you'd be safer down on the ground?" Or else her words emerge within her own mouth altered by some process she does not understand. A familiar rhyme comes out "wrong from beginning to end," spoken in a voice "hoarse and strange" to her, as if she were a medium for alien powers—powers aligned with that "little bat" that replaces the twinkling star, or with that sly crocodile that replaces the hard-working bee. Alice is often, against her will, a clown, and at the same time Wonderland's perfect straight man, perpetrator and victim of a comic freedom she cannot own. Carroll's nonsense is transitive, endlessly evolving, collaborative and competitive, hungry and vulnerable. It's a prehensile, almost a Darwinian nonsense.

Some of the nonsense games have a curious gentleness, even in their blunt literalism. When Alice protests to the Cheshire Cat, "I wish you wouldn't keep appearing and vanishing so suddenly: you make one quite giddy!" it vanishes "quite slowly," such that "the grin . . . remained some time after the rest of it had gone." Other occasions are more intrusive, aggressive, moments when nonsense speaks for something more dangerous within language, and within speakers of a language. We can see this when some Wonderland creature seizes on a word, making it alien to how Alice had meant it: "'Really, now that you ask me,' said Alice, very much confused, 'I don't think—' 'Then you shouldn't talk,' said the Hatter." These games of seizure and marring Carroll would have learned from the mournful, aggressive-defensive wordplay of Hamlet and the grave, pained wit of Lear's Fool. Words acquire their own life, perversely and cruelly her own words are turned against her, as if she never properly knew her own language. Such turns of word can urgently enwrap us as well, even in their mockery: the Mad Hatter's challenge to Alice to think while talking is a real one, after all, especially in a world where words too often do your thinking for you.

Crucial to the drama of nonsense in Carroll are occasions when Alice or another shouts out "Nonsense!" "Nonsense!" can be a cry of rational clarity, a way of protesting a settled, authorized madness, a way to answer its darker childishness, as when Alice cries "Stuff and nonsense!" to the Queen of Hearts's "Sentence first—verdict afterwards." To say "Nonsense!" also puts away the face of something you don't understand. It's a defense against a real or imagined threat. You cry out "Nonsense!" in response to a nasty, overgrown child who insists that you'll disappear like a blown-out candle when the king who dreams your existence wakes up, as if you're already a flame-like phantom. "Nonsense!" keeps at bay the thought of death, ghostliness. Indeed, much of Carroll's nonsense seems like a mind at once embracing and pressing back against the apparent senselessness of being, even as it sets itself against the lunacy or violence of nonsense disguised as sense, reason, and fact.

Alice encounters words she thinks she knows that suddenly become the source of confusion, turned into weapons or stumbling blocks. After she has eaten a piece of the Caterpillar's mushroom, the word "serpent"—used first by the narrator—names Alice's solitary experience of pleasure when her neck suddenly stretches up above the trees, freely curving about, able to twist back on itself so she can see lost parts of her body. But "serpent" quickly turns into a word of bitter accusation in the mouth of a mother-pigeon who spies Alice moving about at such a height, threatening the space she's made safe for her eggs. After a sharp hiss, snake-like herself, the bird screams "Serpent!" The pigeon is astonished, indeed frenzied at finding a snake "wriggling down from the sky" as well as climbing trees. The accusatory label is something Alice refuses to accept: "I'm *not* a serpent! . . . I—I'm a little girl." Yet she's reduced to mute confusion by the pigeon's insistence that the words "serpent" and "girl" are closer than she had before imagined, not in the shared experience of an inhumanly flexible life but in the homelier fact that both serpents and little girls eat eggs. Here the life of words becomes as mobile and intractable as the life of Alice's newly serpentine body.

Alice must learn to trust words differently as well as distrust them, to question how others trust them and make use of them, what it is they name. You see the eerie poetry of this in her conversation with the Mock Turtle about his time at school. In place of "History, ancient and modern," the weeping creature boasts that he was taught "Mystery, ancient and modern." It's a joke about the empirical ambitions of history itself. It also reminds you that mystery *has* a history, even as it mocks any attempt to categorize and teach mysterious matters. The Mock Turtle's basic arithmetic wasn't Addition, Subtraction, Multipli-

cation, and Division, but "Ambition, Distraction, Uglification, and Derision." Those words sound like pretentious malapropisms, as Empson
suggested, or like the deformations of dreams, or like those humorous
mistakes created in the party game called "Telephone," where you pass
a whispered phrase secretly from ear to ear, and wait to see the monster that emerges at the end. Yet the Turtle's words invite us to think
more about how we learn certain things, to think of ambition and derision, or of our power to make things ugly, as fundamental skills that
we learn as children, things that adults *teach* to children, rather than
being instinctive, unlearned. What lessons in pleasure, sickness, and
self-dramatization come from an art master who teaches not "Drawing, Sketching, and Painting in Oils," but "Drawling, Stretching, and
Fainting in Coils"? And in what school, within what version of Classics
(or Mystery), do children learn not "Latin and Greek" but "Laughing
and Grief"?

"Why is a raven like a writing-desk?" Alice responds to the Mad
Hatter's sudden riddle with the happy cry, "I believe I can guess that."
She's relieved to find herself on familiar ground, in a game where mad-
sounding questions most likely *will* make sufficient sense once the secret of the riddle is revealed. "Do you mean that you think you can
find out the answer to it?" asks the March Hare. "Exactly so," she says.
"Then you should say what you mean," he shouts back. The Hare has
set Alice up, you could think, seizing pedantically on a narrowed sense
of "mean" in his own question, something that Alice might take for a
simple paraphrase of what she had said (though it's not a trivial matter to pry apart believing you can guess a thing from thinking you can
find it out). Caught off guard, Alice tries to regain ground: "I do ... at
least—I mean what I say—that's the same thing, you know." This only
moves the mad tea drinkers to remind her of more visceral differences
in the shape of our experience, differences that small but fundamental
shifts of usage and syntax attempt to sort out:

"Not the same thing a bit!" said the Hatter. "Why, you might just as
well say that 'I see what I eat' is the same thing as 'I eat what I see'!"
"You might just as well say," added the March Hare, "that 'I like what
I get' is the same thing as 'I get what I like'!"

"You might just as well say," added the Dormouse, which seemed to
be talking in its sleep, "that 'I breathe when I sleep' is the same thing as 'I
sleep when I breathe.'!"

"It *is* the same thing with you," said the Hatter.

Hatter, Hare, and Dormouse press distinctions that are urgent enough,
reminders of the world we live in and the words we live *by*. And yet part
of their madness is to suggest a limiting condition or horizon of nonsense. The mantra of "you might just as well say" invites you to imagine a condition of life in which meaning what you say and saying what
you mean, getting what you want and wanting what you get, might co-
incide as readily as, in the Dormouse, breathing and sleeping, sleeping
and breathing, a dreaming life and life of dreams.

The power of such play lies in its lightness, and in our not quite
knowing how light or weighty it is, how closely it touches our ordinary
speaking. Even in Carroll's *Symbolic Logic: Part I, Elementary* (1896)—a
work of demanding, if still playful instruction—the sample syllogisms
suggest how arbitrary, self-enclosed, comical, even dreamlike the struc-
tures of logical thought can be, the surreal worlds they generate.* *Wonderland* plays with the game of syllogism more nakedly. To prove its
part in a world where "we're all mad," the Cheshire Cat puts Alice's
logic to the test. Having gotten her to agree to the premise that "a dog's
not mad"—being a creature who growls when angry and wags its tail
when pleased—the Cat proves its own madness by pointing out that,

---

* I'll quote just one example from *Symbolic Logic*, a set of propositions that form
premises in a chain of nested syllogisms, composing what in formal logic is called a
"sorites," from the Greek word for "heap":

(1) Animals are always mortally offended if I fail to notice them;
(2) The only animals that belong to *me* are in that field;
(3) No animal can guess a conundrum, unless it has been properly trained in a Board-
School;
(4) None of the animals in that field are badgers;
(5) When an animal is mortally offended, it always rushes about wildly and howls;
(6) I never notice any animal, unless it belongs to me;
(7) No animal, that has been properly trained in a Board-School, ever rushes about
wildly and howls.
Conclusion: No badger can guess a conundrum.

contrary to the dog, it growls when pleased and wags its tail when angry. "Therefore I'm mad." "*I* call it purring, not growling," Alice protests. "Call it what you like," it responds, to which Alice has no answer.

The Cheshire Cat's words, idle as they seem, have a strange force. They hint that Alice has freedom of will where, as a speaker of English, she might feel she has none, or none she knows how to take responsibility for. The Cat's "Call it what you like" is as wild as the rule of that giant egg Alice meets later, in *Through the Looking-Glass*: "'When *I* use a word,' Humpty Dumpty said, in rather a scornful tone, 'it means just what I choose it to mean—neither more nor less.'" Lewis Carroll, or the Reverend Charles L. Dodgson, would have known how Jesus Christ challenges human speakers in the Gospel of Matthew, promising that for "every idle word that men shall speak, they shall give account thereof in the day of judgment. For by thy words thou shalt be justified, and by thy words thou shalt be condemned." There's no such day of judgment in Wonderland, and the final trial we do witness only makes it harder to know which words to justify and which to condemn, which are "important" and which "unimportant."

For all its disorder and strangeness, the temptation to break off talk, such conversation ties Alice more closely to the creatures she meets, even as it shifts her within herself. Conversation in Carroll works at the threshold of contact between inner and outer, revealing the unknown side of both. It lives between will and compulsion, free play and mechanism. Conversation is the shared skin of language, charged with sensitivity to inward and outward touch; it's like the shared element of air that flows between us. The smallest turn of speech becomes a rabbit hole into which we fall, a chasm opened by a "very small earthquake," as if we had to learn language again from the ground up. ("'You see the earth takes twenty-four hours to turn round on its axis'—'Talking of axes,' said the Duchess, 'chop off her head!'") Conversation in Wonderland sends forth unknown nerves of thought, discovering curious points of contact among very different speakers. For all its being a matter of polite surfaces, conversation becomes intimate, tactile, it acquires an erotic or erogenous character, giving to "just words" a power to touch or call to a place within us that stirs up a strange combination of need, pleasure, hunger, and irritability. ("All adults have been children," Beer writes. "They are in dialogue with their past, which is also lost to them. Much of Alice's conversation is conducted within this nimbus of the irrecoverable.") Nonsense talk becomes a place where bodies and souls, and the words they need to survive, rub up against one another, moving along surfaces whose sensitivity they may not have known before. Words come alive unexpectedly, even as they turn their familiar faces away from us.

One of the final pieces of nonsense in *Wonderland* is that poem which the White Rabbit offers in evidence against the Knave of Hearts for his theft of the Queen's tarts, verses discovered in a letter addressed to no one and written in an unknown hand. Here are the last two stanzas:

> My notion was that you had been
>   (Before she had this fit)
> An obstacle that came between
>   Him, and ourselves, and it.

> Don't let him know she liked them best,
>   For this must ever be
> A secret, kept from all the rest,
>   Between yourself and me.

If they prove nothing about the Knave (despite the King of Hearts's insistence), these verses do offer evidence of *something* central to this world. With their continually shifting pronouns, the verses confide a story about stories gone awry, about dangerous, even divisive messages straying into the wrong ear. They evoke obscure fits, breakings of language, that *remove* an obstacle to talk. They speak of acts of conversation that can make listeners obscure to themselves ("An obstacle that came between / Him, and ourselves, and it"), listeners both divided and bound together by the words, suspicions, and secrets they must urgently keep, creatures made powerful by those secrets, even if they seem like childish secrets, childish pacts of silence ("A secret, kept from all the rest").

SILENCE GIVES A crucial edge to the play of nonsense in Wonderland. The shifting rhythms of words, familiar and unfamiliar, are shaped by countless intervals when there are no words. We fall into silence as we fall into space and into nonsense. These silences come unpredictably, at the start of the conversation, or in the middle, or they can bring it suddenly to an end. They can be calm silences, echoing the silence of the child at play, puzzling over an enigma, wondering at some new object. The silences may also be bound to frustration and anger, bafflement and embarrassment—including a fear of "talking nonsense." There are calculated silences and silences that are spontaneous, silences by turns weighty and light. The silences of Wonderland settle into bodies, invite you to feel what in these creatures, human and inhuman, is mute, alien, unseen in its motions. Some characters hold silence in a way that seems essential to them, like the Cheshire Cat, smiling with its human teeth. For others, like the Queen of Hearts, keeping silent feels more like an accident, or a wound, a sign of offense. Some silences are shared, they bind creatures together, if only in mutual uncertainty, or in the shared hope of finding something to say. Such silences have a generosity about them, even in their mystery. More often the silences speak of an intensified solitude. They speak of what's unknown, blocked in oneself, or what sits in the space between oneself and others. Carroll makes you feel silence as part of the madness of all speaking.

The Mad Hatter's watch has stopped, its works full of crumbs and butter, unfixable despite being dipped repeatedly in tea—that's the result of Time's anger at the Hatter for "murdering" time in a song he once sang. (Thus it is always teatime for him and his friends, a condition at once entrapping and liberating.) If you hear the ominous sound of time in Wonderland, it's not in the ticking of the Hatter's watch or any other clock, but in the silences. The silences evoke time remembered and time foreseen, or a present moment uncannily stretched out. These silences can last "a minute or two," "a while," or "a long time." In practice, all such spaces of time are left for you to imagine, to expand or contract, to let work on you as you will. Time is disordered as a function of the world of play, but also as part of an adult world that doesn't recognize its own madness, how mad and broken attempts to control time can become.

Silence in the *Alice* books is often "transitive," as Paolo Valesio describes it in his book *Ascoltare il Silenzio* (Listen to the Silence). It is a silence shaped by *acts* of silencing, intentional or unconscious. There is the silencing of your own speech that comes from being amidst so many creatures speaking all at once, or the silencing of sense when an articulate cry becomes a shriek like the sound of a train engine. There is the silence that comes from suddenly discovering a word's opacity, or its stranger resonance—moments when words get up and silently follow you from the places where you thought they belonged. There's the silence that comes of being suddenly interrupted by another person's words, and the silence that comes from another person's failure to respond to yours. Alice is often, even against her will, silenced, or she willfully holds her tongue, silencing herself. In both cases she's thrown back into the condition of an infant (*infans*), even as this silence opens up your sense of her mind, her unspoken negotiations with herself. "Alice said nothing: she had never been so much contradicted in her life before, and she felt that she was losing her temper."

This silenced child also, in time, learns to silence others: "'Nonsense!' said Alice, very loudly and decidedly, and the Queen was silent." Precariously balanced Humpty Dumpty, commanding words to mean what he says they mean, is also trying to silence the clamor of other senses that we may hear in those words. (Even his authoritative decipherings of "portmanteau" words in "Jabberwocky" leave many associations unspoken, as readers have been at pains to show.) The sharp-chinned Duchess relentlessly improvises a series of opportunistic, arbitrary morals in response to Alice, often mistaking or twisting her words, though seeming eager to agree with her. ("'The game's going on rather better now,' [Alice] said, by way of keeping up the conversation a little. ''Tis so,' said the Duchess: 'and the moral of that is—"Oh, 'tis love, 'tis love, that makes the world go round!"'... There's a large mustard-mine near here. And the moral of that is—"The more there is of mine, the less there is of yours."'") The Duchess keeps talking, not so much to silence Alice's words as to silence her *thought*, while Alice stands pondering those very morals, trying to parse the slips of logic or language that give them birth: "You're thinking about something, my dear, and that makes you forget to talk."

The silences of the *Alice* books build on one another, weave together and provoke one another, as do their games of nonsense. Hearing and not hearing, speaking and silence dance together. Words emerge *out* of silence in a way that's unpredictable, making that silence the stranger, silence becoming the impish shadow of speech. Carroll lets you feel how a spoken word can carry with it shreds and remnants of the silence from which it's been plucked:

> "Your hair wants cutting," said the Hatter. He had been looking at Alice for some time with great curiosity, and this was his first speech.
>
> "You should learn not to make personal remarks," Alice said with some severity: "it's very rude."
>
> The Hatter opened his eyes very wide on hearing this; but all he *said* was, "Why is a Raven like a writing-desk?"

The Hatter's silent gaze makes a wonder of Alice herself, even as it makes *his* wonder more opaque. What goes on behind the Hatter's wide-open eyes is the more mysterious because the narrator's "all he *said* was" implies that so much is left *un*said. In breaking in as he does, perhaps the Hatter is just curious to see how Alice will respond, to see how her mind works. If rudeness is ordinarily something to be controlled or silenced by courtesy, here it's part of a different order of courtesy. If you must learn not to make personal remarks, you must learn also just how and when to make them. (Can you imagine any form of love behind the Hatter's mad eyes?)

Like cats in the ruins of Rome, silences turn up everywhere in the *Alice* books once you start to see them, curled up in odd corners, in the gaps and shadowed spaces of the text, making themselves at home. Here are a few more instances of many from *Alice in Wonderland*:

> "I don't believe it," said the Pigeon; "but if they do, why, then they're a kind of serpent: that's all I can say." This was such a new idea to Alice, that she was quite silent for a minute or two.

> The Caterpillar and Alice looked at each other for some time in silence: at last the Caterpillar took the hookah out of its mouth, and addressed her in a languid, sleepy voice.
>
> "Who are *you*?" said the Caterpillar.
>
> This was not an encouraging opening for a conversation.

"Then the words don't *fit* you," said the King, looking round the court with a smile. There was a dead silence.

"It *is* the same thing with you," said the Hatter, and here the conversation dropped, and the party sat silent for a minute, while Alice thought over all she could remember about ravens and writing-desks, which wasn't much.

"Once," said the Mock Turtle at last, with a deep sigh, "I was a real Turtle."

These words were followed by a very long silence, broken only by an occasional exclamation of "Hjckrrh!" from the Gryphon, and the constant heavy sobbing of the Mock Turtle. Alice was very nearly getting up and saying, "Thank you, Sir, for your interesting story," but she could not help thinking there *must* be more to come, so she sat still and said nothing.

In that last example, visceral noises break into and intensify the silence. You may hear unspoken meanings implicit in the Gryphon's incomprehensible, vowel-less "Hjckrrh," or hiding beneath the surface of the Mock Turtle's "constant heavy sobbing," a sobbing that seems both automatic and, as the Gryphon claims, unreal ("What is his sorrow?" asks Alice. "It's all his fancy, that: he hasn't got no sorrow, you know"—though the double negative betrays some doubt). Other unspoken words are implicit in the "more to come" that Alice thinks *must* be coming, words that her own silence waits on—since Alice's hunger for conversation is never dulled by her finding out just how impossible conversation in Wonderland can be.

Some kinds of silence are harder to hear in the *Alice* books (though less hard, perhaps, if you imagine Emily Dickinson, Henry James, or Sigmund Freud listening in). In *Through the Looking-Glass*, Alice broods silently over the all-too-common death of "Bread-and-Butterflies," but the terrible muteness of the dead is barely hinted at in Carroll. You hear the silence of a child plotting some mischief, or the silence of a child's canny or angry withholding of answers to a grown-up's questions. But you don't hear the silence of the spy at work in the shadows, the silence of the murderer stalking some prey, or the silence of the paranoid lunatic imagining himself the victim of both. You don't hear the silence of the enslaved person in chains, the silence of the prisoner gagged, or the silence of the prisoner who *wills* silence, who holds her tongue, refusing to respond to an interrogator. You don't hear the vengeful, slightly childish self-silencing of Shakespeare's Iago: "Demand me nothing. What you know, you know. / From this time forth I never will speak word." You don't hear the bitterness of Timon of Athens rejecting all human speech before he dies: "Lips, let four words go by and language end." Spectral as some Wonderland creatures are, you don't hear the silence of ghosts, as at the start of *Hamlet*, or the more mysterious and resolute quiet with which Hamlet's life ends: "The rest is silence."

While curious, unknown fears gather around Alice, I rarely hear the silence of great terror, or only at a distance, mingled with a comic note ("Mind the volcano!"). I do not hear the silence of sublime awe. I do not hear the silence of deep contemplation, or the silence that helps to heal the sick. I do not hear the silence of the sacred, the silence of a worshipper in a temple or of a priest at sacrifice. Do you ever hear the silence that can sit between lovers? No silence of the gods makes itself heard in the *Alice* books. I do not hear the silence of the uncreated world before the divine Word speaks. Nor do I hear the silence of a God who offers no response to human prayers, as in George Herbert's "Denial": "When my devotions could not pierce / Thy silent ears."

You may hear in the *Alice* books the silencing of more unsettling, more visceral human impulses. There are moments when, clamoring below the surface of a pun or piece of nonsense, an inarticulate scream, you can hear more fiercely infantile wishes, rages, and fears (things that hark back to "that noisy silence, before language joined in"). Such feelings may belong variously to the domain of the child and to that of the adult, or to some place where the child and adult cross paths. Yet in Carroll such silences and silencings feel humanizing, generative rather than restrictive, neither signs of some repression in the author nor evasions of some more extreme or primal cry, or some more absolute silence. The silences are elusive, moving from place to place and disappearing, yet they also build on one another, creating an irregular rhythm, punctuating the play of speech, shaping its drama. Learning to be at home in the nonsense of the *Alice* books, you learn to be at home in their silences, a strange home, also a nursery of the world.

THERE ARE SCENES in these books I can scarcely stop reading over again and again. In *Wonderland*, there's that wood haunted by the smiling disappearing cat, that tea party frozen in time, that increasingly anarchic game of croquet. In *Through the Looking-Glass*, there's the battle of those always-falling chess knights, the unfolding of the White Knight's song, that shop of "things" that always crowd *another* shelf, and then vanish quietly through the ceiling. The words on the page fire the nerves in my fingers' ends, behind my eyes. They evoke a dream of life that keeps awakened wonder in play with a sense of darker possibilities, a childishness of lucidity and danger. Carroll's books let the most ordinary objects, while remaining ordinary, look back at you with a new face, new eyes. Reading in them, I know better the marmalade jar, the pocket watch, the teacup, the comfit, the letter, the pencil, the slate, the playing card, the croquet mallet, the railway ticket, and the rosebush (as I know the thimble better when Peter Pan mistakes it for a kiss). Carroll does the same with the most ordinary words.

There's a thrill in Alice's final, categorical cry in *Wonderland*: "Who cares for *you*? ... You're nothing but a pack of cards!" It's a cry of enlightened recognition, a sudden breaking through of the texture of a dream, whether the dream is her own or another's. It's a cry of power, a giving up of her long-held patience and politeness. She thereby silences the increasingly aggressive nonsense of the trial—in which so many of the creatures we've encountered are called back to participate, as witness, judge, audience, or member of a jury—a trial that demands literalizing a nursery rhyme, in which whim and will harden themselves into something as Kafkaesque as it is comic. Alice, a momentary Prospero, oversees the shutting down of such a game.

Yet Alice mistakes the creatures at the trial in calling them "nothing but a pack of cards." We've seen how complex a life takes shape from those cards, those tokens of game, and how much that imaginary life touches the texture of the real. We know how much there is in those cards to care for, how much care cards ask. (Latin *cura*, care, is the root of "curious.") And Alice's disenchanting cry works its own kind of magic: it gives the cards the sudden power to join together, to fly up into the air and then fly down upon her, now not a pack of cards but a pack of animals, provoking her scream of fear and rage.

Alice awakens from the dream to find that the dangerous cards are fallen leaves that her older sister brushes from her face. Even this gentle return to the real doesn't quite banish the dream. After Alice runs off, sounds from Wonderland invade her dozing sister's ear, sounds that ring changes on the more common sounds of an English countryside. She quickly contains this reverie, makes it again unreal, a witness mainly to "the simple and loving heart of her childhood" that she hopes Alice will keep when she grows up into a woman, and tells her tale to others. We can yet wonder about such a hope, having seen that the heart and mind of this child are anything but simple, her loves vexed, and the domain of childhood a place with wider and more ambiguous borders, a different kind of hope, than we might have thought.

The sister's reflections on Alice's future self serve as a prose epilogue to *Wonderland*. It echoes the book's prefatory poem, as it does the verse prologue and epilogue to *Through the Looking-Glass*. Carroll sets these poems in place to frame our reading of the tales. The poems speak, like Alice's sister, in the voice of a grown-up, conjuring the wondering eyes of the dream child, her innocence and vulnerability. They repeatedly call up the scene of his tale's first emergence on a summer boating trip, tying the authority of the published story to that original moment of spontaneous oral invention, a gift of Carroll to his child-friends, whom he always recalled as innocent, rapt, and demanding listeners. These poems speak for the hope that such innocent speaking will survive in time. Yet as you move from poem to poem, that scene of storytelling is present more and more purely *as* a memory. There's a gathering sense of loss, a sense of nostalgia for a vanished origin, a past that is now dead. In the prologue to *Wonderland*, the not-yet-started pages of the tale are already a "pilgrim's wither'd wreath of flowers / Pluck'd in a far-off land." In the verse prologue to *Through the Looking-Glass*—a book more consistently haunted by nostalgia, including that of the grown-up Alice—a storm rages outside the house, and sadness reigns within. The girl-child has grown older, she's now a "melancholy maiden" awaiting an "unwelcome bed" (marriage or death bed, each a version of the other). In the book's verse epilogue the writer's mood passes from sentimental longing to something ghostlier. Alice survives there as specter, a "she" who is severed from the living child: "Still she haunts me, phantomwise, / Alice moving under skies / Never seen by waking eyes." There's something vampirish in those beautiful lines, as if that child herself had never lived, had always been a ghost.

Such notes of self-wounding, even vengeful nostalgia rarely enter the tales proper, as if those framing verses helped Carroll to isolate such feelings and siphon them off. The tales are so fiercely present to the consciousness of the child Alice, which is also Carroll's own consciousness, what survives in him of a child, and more than a child, madly articulate and madly playful. A very different vision of the child's innocent life emerges there. Fear and sorrow, rage and self-pity, these can enter the prose tales and their more nonsensical poems, you sense these emotions hovering in the books' silences, in their oblique references to death, in Alice's frustrations, in the continual flight or vanishing of desired things, like those dream rushes she gathers in the stream where she sculls with a chess queen turned sheep and shopkeeper. But these darker strains are also always lightened, freed up, crossed with wilder and more curious games of language. There's an appetite for living in time as well as a fear of time, a readiness to mock the self in the face of its own losses and those of the world. At any moment we can find ourselves back at a place of emergent possibility, a beginning, not just a vanished place of origin or a dead past that infects the present. The remembered face of the "aged aged man" in the White Knight's song—Carroll's earnest, clownish avatar as storyteller and inventor—this face is "distracted with his woe." Yet the old man has eyes of fire, "eyes, like cinders, all aglow," and an eager voice that "snorted like a buffalo," with a stammer like Dodgson's own. Within the tales, a relentless, undying sense of play rings clearly, fearlessly, shamelessly. There "Alice moving under skies" is not the phantom of a lost listener but a lasting motion of life. And those skies are still ours.

PINOCCHIO

THE FISH ARE eating the donkey. They've swarmed to the beast thrown alive into sea and sunk to the bottom. The animal's owner wants to make a drum of its skin and he's drowning the donkey since he's too soft-hearted to cut its throat—he'd bought the lamed creature cheaply, because it couldn't any more dance or jump through hoops of flame in the circus. The man has tied a rope around the donkey's leg so he can pull it back to shore when enough time has passed.

"Greedier than children," the fish eat all that there is to eat: hide, hooves, muzzle, ears. "One among them was even kind enough to eat my tail." They eat the body down to the bone, but it isn't bone. What the fish find is no skeleton, or only a stranger kind of skeleton. They get to the hard wood of another being sealed mysteriously inside the donkey's skin, a wood that for this being is body and bones at once, a core that survives both drowning and the teeth of carnivorous fish. These frenzied eaters turn away in disgust from this "indigestible food." Stripped by these fish of the weight of living flesh, the living wood that had sunk down now rises to the surface.

This scene from Carlo Collodi's *The Adventures of Pinocchio: Story of a Puppet* (the original Italian book was published in 1883) shows one of an endless chain of surprising escapes for this creature. Without any pain that we're told about, he's returned by the devouring fish to his puppet life. Pinocchio is released from the donkey body into which he had been translated when he gave himself over to a world of complete, anarchic play in Toyland, an ultimately infernal place, the capital of noise, where this child-toy-demon had turned into a beast enslaved by others. As with Ovid's metamorphoses, that change had been a form of death, also a conversion into a satiric emblem. Nothing in Collodi's account of this transformation had hinted that the puppet's wooden body remained intact within the donkey's fleshly one. Yet we shouldn't be surprised. We've already in the book seen this body as an uncanny thing, a body always in motion, running with mad energy, always in flight or in pursuit, moving with the speed of a rabbit or goat, surviving impossible falls, hangings, and burnings, capable of violence of its own. This creature is now restored to life by the very childlike appetite of those imagined fish, animals whose avid hunger mirrors the appetite of Pinocchio himself.

Hauling up what he thinks is a dead animal, the donkey's owner gets a talking wooden puppet afloat on the surface of the sea, that sea which so often comes into this story, a realm full of hidden dangers and yet the puppet's very element. When the astonished man asks how the change from beast to puppet came about, Pinocchio first quips, "The salt water must have done it. The sea plays funny tricks." The puppet then tells what happened below the surface, how the fish devoured his "donkey rind" (*buccia asinina*). He laughs in childlike triumph as he swims away, leaving his former owner in a rage over the loss of the poor commodity of a donkey's skin, angry even over the loss of the wood that, at the least, he might have sold for a little money. "Goodbye, master. If you ever need a hide to make a drum, think of me.... Goodbye, master. If you ever need some seasoned wood to start a fire, think of me"—so the puppet taunts him, one poor thing abandoning another. Pinocchio's wood, though always at risk of being burned, is seasoned by a stranger history.

THE VITALITY THAT Collodi lends his creation is at once elemental and mysterious. It belongs to Pinocchio as a creature with a foot in the worlds of both the animate and the inanimate, the living and the dead. He is at once the wooden top and the child who spins the top, and then the pebble on which the top stumbles, wobbling its way to rest in a battle between momentum and gravity. The book continually invites us to say yes to powers we don't comprehend, that hide themselves in the most ordinary objects and creatures. Pinocchio lives at once in an enchanted world and one stripped of enchantment, a world where there are real magical forces at work even as magic gets revealed as an illusion, matter for opportunistic tricks and con games, like that of the Fox and the Cat with their promise of trees that sprout gold coins.

At its most basic, Pinocchio's vitality mirrors that of a child, a being at once hungry and playful, vulnerable and imperious, free yet very ready to be influenced. Pinocchio is a child by turns willful, brave, fearful, spiteful, kind, loving, and violent, resiliently gullible, a child who refuses instructions yet always calls out for help, who breaks and animates toys, a spirit of play that always breaks the rules of play. He's the victim of endless accidents, accidents that rhyme with his acts of willed disobedience, as well as his intense, unpredictable acts of devotion. He's a child life not easily educated, rejecting some lessons and madly embracing others. There's a *dream* of childhood in him—he's the image of some hard core of childhood that can survive poverty and violence, a childishness at once given and unknown. Pinocchio's career might show you how a child imagines its own life and energy, its own invulnerability. Pinocchio also gives you an image of how adults imagine what a child sees and thinks, what they suppose a child both thinks and doesn't think, an image of a thoughtlessness in children that adults find by turns charming and frightening.

Pinocchio's is a childishness that springs out from its embryonic log already gifted with speech, often mocking, insolent speech, as if its words had been lying a long time sealed in that wood from which he's carved. ("Could someone be hidden inside it?" asks the carpenter Master Cherry, who first brings it home.) It's a child life orphaned, exiled, at sea, a childishness awakened to life in a world of childish adults, always confronting the adults' guile and need and cruelty, their forms of kindness. Such child life may be something we've lost in our growing up, or something we feel still hidden within us, skeletal yet buoyant. The Italian actor and director Carmelo Bene, who staged his own dark, manic version of Collodi's tale, saw in Pinocchio "the spectacle of a prematurely buried infancy reawakening, and kicking at its coffin." Bene heard in him an infant voice backed by some "terrible and inaudible Injury that unearths the human, its chattering, its breathing."

This childlike vitality in Pinocchio is joined by some primal glue to his being a puppet, that archaic, often creepy theatrical creature. The connection is plain enough, even as Collodi puts the state of being a child and the state of being a puppet into endless dialogue. Despite Pinocchio's jointed wooden form, Collodi calls him not a *marionetta* but a *burattino*, the word also used in Italian for a simple glove puppet, the puppet closest to the energy of the hand that makes, holds, strikes, and begs, the hand that itself speaks, that gives shapes to gestures of love and need, of glee, contempt, and rage. Puppet theater was in Collodi's day a popular form of entertainment, a theater provocative of childish things, perhaps, but never a theater just for children. While it could show romance and tragedy, its most famous characters were devoted clowns, figures at once clever and foolish. These puppet-clowns lived especially in the freedom with which they could give and survive blows, blows both verbal and physical, figures who indeed found themselves energized rather than disabled by blows. What one scholar describes as "the dry shadow-light" of such arrogant quips and blows made these puppets innately satirical beings, implicit realists, even as this theater drew for its plots on fairy tales such as those which Collodi himself translated, tales full of magic objects and talking animals. Such a theater works by drawing our sympathy for creatures who remain bound to the world of inanimate matter, their life at once compelled and free. It's a theater in which poor, crude objects, things like toys or dolls, become instruments of generosity and discovery. Survival is again key. Puppets are dead figures that, for all the violence they suffer, cannot die, becoming rather producers of new life.

A puppet without strings, Pinocchio proves himself ill adapted to any actual puppet stage. Early on, Gepetto tells his friend Master Cherry about his dream of making a "really amazing" puppet—able to dance, fence, and do somersaults—with which he can travel the world, "earning my crust of bread and cup of wine." That ambition vanishes as he sees the unruly thing he has made from the log that the carpenter has passed along to him. Pinocchio is no better suited to act in the "Great

Puppet Show" of the monstrous puppet master Mangiafoco ("Fire-eater"), the show that draws Pinocchio away on his first day of school. Mangiafoco's marionettes—all clown characters out of the Italian *commedia dell'arte* tradition—somehow know the newborn Pinocchio by name when he enters their tent, and they embrace him as a brother, as a fellow wooden actor in this *compagnia drammatico-vegetale*. But Pinocchio's arrival also disrupts the show, provoking a revolt of the puppets, whom the puppet master in turn threatens to destroy. Throughout the book, Pinocchio indeed shows himself as a puppet with unmasterable, even suicidal impulses, mad flights of will and pleasure. You could say he has too many as well as too few strings, being continually seized, moved, and transported by other creatures, other forces, momentary puppeteers who make of Pinocchio their toy, servant, clown, and pawn. He's always pulled into plays not of his own making, and then abandoned to his own uncertain devices.

So much worked on by others, Pinocchio yet has power to make those around him fall into puppetlike motions and gestures, even as he suggests the human passions behind them. At the story's very beginning, the small voice of the log makes Master Cherry gape in archaic fear, such that he looks "like those grotesque faces carved on fountains." Later, the log's taunts provoke Gepetto and Master Cherry to fight like puppets, not just exchanging insults but biting each other's noses and taking each other's wigs in their mouths. It's Pinocchio's disruption of Mangiafoco's puppet show that brings forth the puppetlike master with his vast beard, mouth like an oven, eyes like red lanterns, carrying a whip braided of snakes and foxtails—a man for whom, by some puppet logic, sneezing is a sign of pity. The mere sight of Pinocchio with his head in the mud and scampering legs is enough to make a giant serpent laugh so hard his heart explodes.

Along with his life as uncanny child and uncanny puppet, Collodi traces Pinocchio's life, his destiny, as simply a thing of wood. The book begins:

> Once upon a time there was…
> "A king!" my little readers will say at once.
> No, children, you're wrong. Once upon a time there was a piece of wood.

"The nonexistent king is infinitely necessary and frightening," writes Giorgio Manganelli, whose *Pinocchio: Un libro parallelo* tracks so many shadowy doubles and hidden itineraries in Collodi's tale. The necessity and fright come into play because that nonexistent king, the face of power, remains an aspect, however hidden, of this sovereign piece of wood.

Collodi gives this wood no fairy-tale genealogy. No god or witch has sent this difficult log to Master Cherry as a treacherous gift, it does not come from a tree that was once a nymph pursued by a god or a person who committed suicide, or a tree that grew from the grave of a murdered child. But this log has something in it that frightens the carpenter as soon as it turns up in his workshop, hence he happily gives it to his friend. Ugly wooden eyes (*occhiacci di legno*) glare at Gepetto the moment he carves the face, a mocking tongue sticks out from the newly carved mouth, the nose grows long before any lie is spoken, and the figure runs off with fantastic speed the instant it has feet.

Such magical life remains bound, nonetheless, to the ordinary facts of wood, to the gifts and costs of his being a creature of wood. This shows itself in Pinocchio's hardness, his density, his power to give and survive blows, to break the knives of assassins and resist the teeth of fish. It's there in his readiness to be shaped, broken, and repaired. If his wooden being makes Pinocchio vulnerable to burning, it also saves him from pain: a carpenter's plane merely tickles him, and his feet burn off "as if they were someone else's feet." This woodenness lends him his lightness, his ability to float on the sea or to be carried great distances by a bird. It also binds him to the world. Collodi might have known that the ancient Greek word for matter, *hyle*, can also be the word for "wood" or "forest." Pinocchio's wood is the substance not just of puppets but of chairs, tables, shacks, carts and cartwheels, it's the wood of stage platforms, boats, and cages. It's the wood out of which, in Collodi's time, the paper of the book we read might have been made.* It's

---

* Collodi fixes the likeness in a late episode, where a school of fish finds the paper of books, which they first take for food, as indigestible as the puppet's wooden limbs inside the drowning donkey. Pinocchio's schoolmates persuade him to go with them to the seacoast to catch a glimpse of a "shark as big as a mountain." Rushing there avidly, he finds no shark, only the knowledge that he's been the victim of a practical joke (though one in its way prophetic). A rapid exchange of insults and threats turns into an actual fight. Un-

the wood that feeds the fire to cook the food he's hungry for, the wood of the windlass that he will toil at like a donkey. He's made of the same wood as the carpenter's mallet that he throws in rage at the ancient cricket, smashing it against the wall after the insect has mocked him for being a foolish puppet with a wooden head. His substance is also like the living wood of the "Great Oak" that moves so violently in the wind, the tree from which Pinocchio will be hung by his enemies, the Fox and the Cat, and left to die.

That last episode reminds you of how much the puppet's vitality remains bound to death, shapes of death. This is crucial to any sense of his wood being, as Benedetto Croce wrote, the wood of our humanity. We see this link to death not only in the puppet's closeness to inanimate matter, but in the destructive forces that emerge from both inside and outside him, murderous and suicidal. Death pursues Lewis Carroll's dream child too, of course. Yet for her the threat most often comes obliquely, set at a distance—as when Alice, falling down the rabbit hole, thinks how brave the fall has made her: "'Why, I wouldn't say anything about it, even if I fell off the top of the house!' (Which was very likely true)." Or when, in shrinking, Alice imagines, with more curiosity than fear, "going out altogether, like a candle." The career of Pinocchio calls up starker, more savage images of mortality. Burning, drowning, starvation, being skinned alive, being cooked and being eaten, all these threaten the puppet in the course of his story. He is always running through shadows of death and darkness. Yet death in Collodi's book is not simply a loss, a destruction, it gets joined to a strange energy, a desperate appetite and desperate play, a search for new forms of play, often ghostly play. There's a drive in the story, and in Pinocchio, that exposes him to death even as it keeps him alive, makes death animate him, transform him. He's always at once running away from death and running toward it, always surviving what would kill

---

able to match with fleshly blows the puppet's hard wooden fists and feet, the boys hurl schoolbooks at him, missiles that he dodges and that end up falling into the sea. We're told that among the books whose paper the fish spit out in disgust are "a couple ... by a fellow named Collodi"—though which books by this prolific journalist, satirist, fabulist, translator, and lexicographer (whose real name was Carlo Lorenzini) the narrator does not say.

him, saved by luck, guile, magical intervention, or something harder to specify—perhaps simply the author's love of his own creation. The hanging of Pinocchio ended Collodi's story in its original form, published in 1881 as a serial tale in the first Italian magazine for children, *Il Giornale per i Bambini*. The puppet is described as dying for hours and hours, and even at the close of the story is never assuredly dead. Readers would not let him die either, and Collodi was persuaded to continue the story in later issues, and then to gather the episodes into a book.

IN HIS EPIC tale of this death-haunted and never-dying child-puppetlog, Collodi always keeps us close to the world of the poor, close to its forms of labor, pain, and pleasure, its acts of charity and theft, truth telling and lying. Beginning to tell his story in 1881, Collodi for one thing reminds his readers of the still intractable, impoverished underworlds of the Kingdom of Italy, the unified nation established two decades earlier, for which he himself had fought as soldier and writer. He regards these worlds with sympathy, but also distanced irony and humor, making them the occasion of some of his strangest poetry—vying with poverty of a more fantastical sort.

At the very start, Gepetto selects the puppet's name to mark his future place in this world, its wealth of poverty: "I think I'll call him Pinocchio. That's a lucky name. I once knew an entire family by that name: the father was Pinocchio, the mother was Pinocchia, and the kids were all Pinocchio Juniors, and they got on just fine. The richest one was a beggar." In his small, one-room dwelling place, Gepetto's only hearth is a painting on the wall of burning logs, an imaginary fire that heats an imaginary pot, with painted clouds of steam from an imagined *minestra*. Preparing his wooden child for school, Gepetto clothes him in the stuff of his poor world, reusing what's cast aside: Pinocchio's hat is made from crumbs of bread, his coat of old pieces of flowered wallpaper, and his shoes of bark. Poor as they are, such fragments of the made, material world can have mysterious affinities with other parts of this world. You can think that the bark of those shoes has been stripped from the very log of which the puppet was carved. His wallpaper coat recalls those other paper images pinned to the wall. His hat crowns him with the sign of that world's scant nourishment. Mad King Lear, sitting among cast-off objects and cast-off persons, cries out: "The art of our necessities is strange / And can make vile things precious."

It is *hunger* that most sharply troubles this poor life in Collodi's book, a hunger of many shapes, by turns concrete and fantastic, general and peculiar. Thin and stick-like in the original illustrations, the image of a starved body, Pinocchio is always in search of food, food that is most often scant, unappealing, unreal, and likely to vanish. On his first night in the world, Pinocchio is left alone in Gepetto's house, after his maker has been put in jail on suspicion of wanting to harm the puppet-child he's been chasing through the streets. As a storm rages outside, he feels a "wolflike hunger—a hunger you could have cut with a knife." That hunger makes him madly yawn, "so wide that the corners of his mouth met his ears," a "yawning to death," as Collodi later describes it (a yawn that mirrors the mad smile that breaks out the moment he's made, also running from ear to ear). Gazing at the painted pot makes Pinocchio's nose grow "at least four inches longer," though he soon realizes it's only an image. Pinocchio ends up searching the house from top to bottom, looking for "a little bread, even stale bread, a crust, a dog's bone, a little moldy corn mush [*polenta*], a fish skeleton, a cherry pit." That cherry pit recalls the red nose of Master Cherry, while the moldy polenta recalls the mocking name by which the children call Gepetto, "Polendina," after his corn-yellow wig—as if to suggest that Pinocchio is ready to eat his own makers along with the rest of the world (making him a double of the monstrous Shark who later swallows both the puppet and his father). In the end, Pinocchio finds nothing but a solitary egg sitting on top of a rubbish heap. He cracks the egg to fry it—in water rather than oil, since there is no oil—and out comes a bird who thanks Pinocchio for sparing him the work of breaking his shell, and who quickly takes his leave. "The omelet flies out the window" says the brief plot summary at the head of the chapter.

The next morning, when Gepetto returns home from his night in jail, Pinocchio demands the three small pears that Gepetto has bought for his own breakfast. He asks that his father peel them and core them, but then devours first the peelings and after that the core he'd rejected. In a later episode, during a pause in his flight on a pigeon's back—

carrying him, as he hopes, to find his lost father—the starving puppet happily fills mouth with vetch, a cheap bean crop that served for fodder in nineteenth-century Italy but could also make a bread for the poor (Pinocchio says he hates it). In a yet later moment, fainting with hunger at the door of his protector, the Blue-Haired Fairy (*Fata Turchina*), he is brought an elegant meal by the infinitely slow-paced Snail, a sign of the Fairy's forgiveness. But the food turns out to be made of painted plaster, cardboard, and stone. Pinocchio seems only once actually to lose his appetite. That is when, at the Red Crawfish Inn, he watches the Cat and Fox devour a desperate sounding dream goulash of "partridges, quails, rabbits, frogs, lizards, and paradise grapes," a feast bought with one of the puppet's own gold coins.

Painful as he finds it, there's a gift in the puppet's hunger. Perhaps because it binds the puppet to the world, this hunger never saps his vitality, never wears him away. It's rather like a fuel, linked to deeper sources of life in him, deeper sources of need and pleasure. Pinocchio's hunger feeds him, nourishes his fantasy, his inventiveness (think of the smile that mirrors his yawn of hunger), it drives his motion through the world, provokes his discovery of new powers and relations. Eating and the need to eat are often the real things that educate Pinocchio, more than learning to read and write, more than the moralistic mutterings of his minders, father, cricket, and fairy. If nothing else, Pinocchio's hunger has given him a preternaturally strong mouth. He can bite off the hand of a ghostly assassin—the Cat in disguise—who tries to rob him, and lock within his mouth his pieces of gold, refusing to open it even when his attackers try to pry it open with a knife.

Pinocchio turns his hunger toward the world. As it is in infants, his hunger is part of his way of knowing the world, of finding it out, giving it shape in his mind, falling in love with it, with what the world has and does not have. The world is in turn hungry for Pinocchio. From the start, this mad eater is in danger himself of being eaten (his name, after all, means "pine nut," he's at once food and the seed of wood), though he often proves to be uneatable. The world's hunger for the puppet indeed seems part of the condition of his being. Images of devouring mouths proliferate on all sides in *Pinocchio*. When his feet have been burned off by coals, the puppet imagines an analogy between devouring flame and hungry cats—"They've eaten my feet," he cries, as Gepetto pounds on the door, himself threatening to eat Pinocchio if he doesn't let him in. When Pinocchio disrupts the puppet show, "Fire-eater" decides to punish him by using his wooden body to feed the fire that's cooking his dinner. Later the swimming puppet is snared in a net with fish of many sorts, taken for a fish himself (a rare "puppet-fish"); he finds himself soon rolled in flour and almost thrown into a cauldron of hot oil by a hungry monster with hide and hair of green (color of the sea, color of leaves). It's telling that, when he arrives at Busy-Bee Island, he asks a sympathetic dolphin, "Would you be so kind as to tell me if there are villages on this island where one might get something to eat, without the danger of getting eaten?"*

As with Pinocchio's own hungers, the world's hunger for Pinocchio proves generative as well as murderous. It can be an occasion for a new, stranger freedom, the entryway into a stranger life.

The saving power of hunger is often merely circumstantial. On the verge of being cooked by that green-haired fisherman, it's the smell of frying fish—a smell that Pinocchio, close to death, can't help finding as delicious as the snuff of a candle flame—that attracts the dog who rescues him. It's the greedy hunger of that school of fish that releases the puppet from donkey flesh, and hunger that drives the thousand woodpeckers who shorten Pinocchio's nose, freeing him from the room in which that vast appendage had trapped him. At the climax of the fable, however, the energies of hunger work in more mysterious ways. One form of hunger weaves itself together with another.

Released from his donkey body and searching the seas for the father who's been lost in searching the seas for *him*, Pinocchio is swallowed

---

* In its vision of the life of hunger and poverty, *Pinocchio* might be set beside Giovanni Verga's *I Malavoglia*, also published in 1881. The novel traces the ways that poverty shapes the lives of a family of Sicilian fishermen named Malavoglia (meaning "ill will" or "reluctance"). Much as it is grounded in historical and economic fact, Verga's book has its own fantastic, hallucinatory aspects. For one thing, his language evokes a sense of how poverty becomes for these fishermen a hungry, devouring monster, a monster that seems by feeding on their lives to gain an ever-more-unshakeable life of its own—partly nourished by the desperate shape of the family's attempts to overcome it. The larger, often wild dreamscapes of famine among the poor in preindustrial Italy are the subject of Piero Camporesi's *Bread of Dreams: Food and Fantasy in Early Modern Europe*.

by the Great Shark. The monster eats him up "as if he were sucking up a raw egg." He's left in a vast darkness, like that of "a brimming inkwell," as if this interior darkness shares the substance of the fluid with which Collodi writes his tale. It is just this being swallowed, and this voyage through darkness, that brings Pinocchio into the presence of his lost father, in a scene whose images of an eating life mingle strangely loss and gain, starvation and animation.

He walks toward the pit of the Shark's stomach through puddles that "smelled so strongly of fried fish that it reminded him of the middle of Lent." Tracking a small bit of light he sees in the distance, Pinocchio comes upon an old man "so white he might have been made of snow, or whipped cream," sitting at a small wooden table with a candle in a green-glass bottle. This food-like man is himself at the point of starving to death. He's a man who, having eaten his last crumb of civilized food, is now "champing absentmindedly on some live minnows—so live they occasionally jumped right out of his mouth as he chewed." In those minnows that we see escaping from the old man's unthinking, devouring mouth—fish that are ordinarily bait for catching other fish, here turned into desperate food—Collodi shows us something in the life energies of Pinocchio himself.

The unedited, uncontrollable life of mouths in *Pinocchio* shows itself even more sharply when the puppet tells his history to the father he's found so wondrously in the belly of the Shark. Pinocchio at first "whimpered confusedly and stammered out a few broken and incoherent words." When his tale finally does spill from him—running on for almost two pages, with no punctuation but commas—it seems made up of words madly swallowed, madly digested, and madly disgorged, words that feed him and starve him as he speaks:

> ...I ran off to see the puppet show, and the puppet master wanted to throw me on the fire to help roast his ram, and he was the one who ended up giving me five gold coins to bring to you, but I ran into the Fox and the Cat, who took me to the Red Crayfish Inn, where they ate like wolves, and when I left alone that night I ran into murderers who started chasing after me, and I ran and they chased, and I kept running and they kept chasing [e io via, e loro dietro, e io via, e loro sempre dietro, e io via],

until they hung me from a branch of the Great Oak, where the Beautiful Girl with the Sky-Blue Hair sent a little carriage to fetch me, and when the doctors visited they said at once, "If he's not dead, it's a sign he's still alive," and then a lie slipped out of my mouth and my nose started growing and wouldn't fit through the door, which is why I went with the Fox and the Cat to bury the four gold coins, one of which I had spent at the inn, and the Parrot started laughing, and instead of two thousand coins I found none, causing the judge when he heard I'd been robbed to send me straight to jail, to reward the thieves, and as I was leaving I saw a nice bunch of grapes in a field, but I got caught in a trap...

The story is at once confession, explanation, and evasion. It's a vision of wonder, and a vision of a perfectly ordinary life. We catch from the puppet's mouth a retrospective glimpse of his adventures, the tricks and trials and accidents, the games and catastrophes that have led him to this meeting, the pieces of his history all strung together as in a Bible story, "everything only connected by 'and' and 'and,'" as Elizabeth Bishop puts it. Pinocchio's words at once reshape the past and make it emerge alive in the moment of telling. You might wonder whether his nose is growing as he speaks. Even in such a childlike, ecstatic rush of words, you're aware of things that Pinocchio leaps over or leaves out, whether from forgetfulness, cunning, or shame. He also invents curious chains of cause and effect to connect events in this history. So, for example, "then a lie slipped out of my mouth and my nose started growing and wouldn't fit through the bedroom door, which is why I went with the Fox and the Cat to bury the four gold coins." The odd causal logic recalls a moment in an earlier tale Pinocchio tells, when he explains to Gepetto how he had his feet burned off: "Since I was still famished I put my feet on the brazier to dry them." This is Pinocchio's nonsense, his version of the logic of Wonderland, a riddling means to explain a riddle. And as with Odysseus's tale-telling in Homer's epic, Pinocchio's words take you inside Collodi's own way of telling a story. You see his way of shaping a tale whose causes keep chasing and stumbling on one another, always giving you too many and too few explanations for the ways we move from moment to moment. The motion of Pinocchio's story feels like the relentless motion of the puppet's own body. (Geoffrey Brock's English translation, quoted throughout this chapter, sharp and fluent as it is, can't convey how Collodi's vivid Italian fills one's mouth and makes it move, making one a puppet of his words.) The story gives us the voice of wood and the voice of the fire that burns the wood (releasing the sunlight within it), the voice of the child who is made of wood and the voice of the sea that tries and fails to drown that child.

THE TALE PINOCCHIO tells Gepetto has not been worked through first in his mind or memory. He seems rather to call up, create, and devour his memories in the immediate flood of his speaking. The story may remind you that, for all his mad, even dreamlike vitality, there's no sustained sense of an inward life in this puppet, a life hidden inside his head. He lives too much in the moment, in the impulses of his body and will. He has little time for reflection. Everything happens too fast. You can't imagine Pinocchio, like Alice, brooding in silence on a maddening conversation, holding back his anger, or pausing in thought to find his balance in a world of mad creatures and garbled rules of play. You can't imagine him wondering to himself about whether he is dreaming what happens, much less worrying over whether his own life is nothing but another person's dream. Collodi's book is stitched together with night scenes, moments of flight, uncertainty, and isolation, as when Pinocchio finds himself inside the Shark's mouth, or when he leaps out of that mouth into the starlit sea. But darkness for him is not a place of reverie. Part of Pinocchio's mystery is that he is never a mystery to himself. He can show sharp surprise at what happens to him, at the failure of his own plans and plots, and at the baffling intentions of those he meets. This dream puppet can himself dream for brief moments, as when he imagines the library of the great house he wants to build for his father, the shelves filled not with books but with "candied fruit, cakes, dessert bread, almond cookies, and wafers topped with whipped cream." But Pinocchio mostly leaps instinctively into his actions, with little thought of past or future.

Many figures in the book try to lend this puppet the orderly inward life he lacks. They try to make him think and remember and plan for the future in a world of time, to shape his conscience, his powers of choice, and in this to help him contain his more anarchic impulses. They ask him to internalize the forms of proper behavior, those commitments to work, study, obedience, and selflessness that will convert him into a "proper boy," *un ragazzo perbene*. Sometimes they do this through ironic lessons, sometimes through the reciting of old proverbs, vivid pieces of shared wisdom: "Hunger's neither picky nor greedy," "One good turn deserves another," "There are two kinds [of lies], lies that have short legs and lies that have long noses," "Children are quick to make promises, but they're often slow to keep them," "Strange things happen." Even the green-haired, ogre-like fisherman has a proverb ready for the terrified puppet-fish: "It's always comforting to be fried in company." Yet it's hard to know how any of these lessons lodge in that wooden head, how Pinocchio owns them. Some of these sayings prove true enough. None, though, is ever adequate to sum up the turns of the tale we are reading, to lend a clear moral to its motions of loss and gain, pain and pleasure. Pinocchio finds some of those old proverbs to hand when, late in the tale, he meets again with the Cat and the Fox, who beg his help, the Cat now truly blind after having so long pretended to blindness, the Fox ragged and moth-eaten and tailless. "Stolen money never bears fruit," says Pinocchio. "He who steals his neighbor's cloak will die without a shirt.... The devil's flour turns out to be chaff." But he uses the proverbs mainly to taunt his old enemies, sounding like the cricket at its most smug. His words remind you how blind and opportunistic, how *mindless*, the pointing of morals can be.

One commentator, tracing the anarchic, carnivalesque energies of *Pinocchio*, finds the book a perfect "graveyard of good purposes" and of good advice. There are moments when this unruly puppet-child seems to conform to the rules that others set down, moments when he acts out of virtuous impulses of love, charity, gratitude, regret, or obedience, drawing other creatures to himself, provoking their return of love. At such times, he proves himself *not* merely one of those typical children "with thick skulls and hard hearts." Pinocchio is even ready—though it can seem a theatrical gesture—to sacrifice himself for another, asking Mangiafoco to burn him in place of Arlecchino. For all of the puppet's willfulness, there's indeed a strong if irregular rhythm of rule follow-

ing in Pinocchio, something that's wound together with the relentless rhythm of rule breaking that shapes his history, those moments of
transgression and suffering that are so often followed by self-reproaches
and resolves *not* to disobey. Yet the puppet's impulses to obey the rules
can feel as arbitrary and unreflective as his impulse to break them. He
both follows and violates the rules with incorrigible and often self-
destructive energy, an energy that belongs to him as a child, and as
something beyond mortal childhood.

How you judge Pinocchio's relation to rules depends partly on what
you make of those who frame and enforce those rules, the ones who try
to pull the puppet's moral strings and to moralize his errors. The book
plays odd games with anyone who assumes the mantle of ethical, legal,
or scientific authority.* They belong to "a world portrayed by Collodi
from the very beginning as an insane world."

Gepetto, Pinocchio's maker and father, is by turns angry and indul-
gent, manipulative and self-sacrificing. For all his loyalty to old proverbs, he's content to leave Pinocchio's education to schoolrooms that
we as readers rarely see. The talking cricket is not the kindly insect of
the Disney film, but often cruelly mocking, never shaken from his dire
wisdom about the fate of puppets, and the worse when, after Pinocchio
squashes him, he returns as an eerie ghost. There's the gorilla judge who
throws Pinocchio in jail for having been swindled out of his money, and
the jailers who let him out of jail with scarcely a thought. There are the

---

* Suzanne Stewart-Steinberg, in *The Pinocchio Effect: On Making Italians, 1860–1920*,
suggests that Collodi's puppet gives us an ever-changing image of how, as humans, we
find ourselves pulled back and forth, sometimes suspended, between the claims of inward impulse and the claims of outward convention, influenced and influencing at once.
It's a picture of the self moved or caught between something prior to what we call ideology, often refusing or exceeding it, and the self's uncertain, often costly capture *by* the
forces of ideology. Somewhat like Freud's "death drive," Pinocchio is both "an irresistible,
moving urge and the expression of a fundamental inertia." This picture sustains Stewart-
Steinberg's broader account of how Pinocchio could become—for Italian reformers and
educational theorists in the years during and after the struggle for unification—an image
of a *national* body, a body always needing to be educated and yet remaining to some degree anarchic, ineducable, resistant to influence. As she knows, her history cuts off just
before the moment when Pinocchio found himself transformed into a hero of Italian
Fascism, put to work as a darker kind of "influencing machine," on which see Luciano
Carreri's *Pinocchio in Camicia Nera: Quattro "Pinocchiate" Fasciste.*

cops who arrest him for killing a friend he was in truth trying to save. There's the ironically punitive farmer who, finding the puppet stealing grapes to stave off hunger, chains him up in lieu of his dead watchdog to protect his chickens from weasels. (Pinocchio does the work well, in truth, and even exposes the former watchdog's conspiracy with the weasels.) No just god or punitive devil oversees the darkest lesson of Pinocchio's history—that moment in Toyland when he's turned into a donkey, and sold into the slavery of a circus. Here, in lieu of some grander master of punishments, there's only that tiny, whispering, and weird coachman, *l'Omino*, "the little man" round and unctuous as a ball of butter, a never-sleeping creature who gleefully bites off the ears of a child-donkey who tries to warn Pinocchio of the danger he's in. It's the little man who later sells the donkey Pinocchio to the circus ringmaster, linking the puppet's infernal metamorphosis to the world of commerce and entertainment.

Then there are the self-important doctors, Crow and Owl, who minister to Pinocchio after his hanging: "'When a dead person cries, it's a sign that he's on the mend.' ... 'It grieves me to contradict my illustrious friend and colleague ... but I believe that when a dead person cries, it's a sign that he doesn't like dying.'" Their words, even as they mock the portentous certainties of physicians, also hint at a stranger wisdom about the life of sorrow.

The most potent authority figure in the book is the most equivocal: the Blue-Haired Fairy. She's the closest thing to a puppet master or major magician in Collodi's tale, the one who seems most to guide and shape and test the puppet's fate (a fairy being, in Italian, a *fata*). The Fairy saves him from death, looks after him when he's ill, feeds him when hungry, sends her agents to free him from imprisonment, gives him a house to live in. She sagely guides him in his wish to study and obey, and later to save and support his father, and so become "a proper boy." Pinocchio indeed seems to need the Fairy to tell him that becoming that real boy *is* his wish. Yet in her lessons, which are the forms of her love for this child, the motherly Fairy moves in mysterious ways, she is ambiguously witch and phantasm, as Manganelli writes. Sometimes she disappears entirely from the story, only to reappear unexpectedly, close at hand, often in disguise, answering or baffling some need in Pinocchio. No Cat or Fox, there's yet much in her of the trick-ster and con artist.

The Fairy appears first when the story is already well advanced. We see this mother figure, not knowing it's her, in the shape of a blue-haired, white-faced child who refuses Pinocchio entrance to "a little white house, gleaming in the distance like snow," a house where he seeks refuge from the ruthless thieves who will shortly hang him. Her eyes closed, and speaking without moving her lips, "in a tiny voice that seemed to come from the world beyond," she tells him, "There is no one in this house. They are all dead.... I too am dead.... I am waiting for the coffin to come and carry me away." A moment of dark roman-ticism such as Hoffmann or Poe might have relished, as Italo Calvino writes, the scene aligns the Fairy with the world of ghosts, suspending her in a species of limbo, even as her ghostliness is, we will learn, a con-scious disguise.

The Fairy is indeed often ready to use lies, illusion, and the threat of violence to shape Pinocchio's choices, to extort from the puppet-child fear, regret, and obedience. Her acts of rescue have more than a touch of cruelty in them, even childish cruelty, like that of a practical joke, as when she calls birds to violently peck Pinocchio's nose down to size, or commands a school of fish to devour his donkey body. Nursing him back to health after his hanging, the Fairy gets the puppet to drink his bitter medicine by conjuring up a comic-gothic apparition of four "ink-black" rabbits carrying his coffin on their shoulders (their color, like the darkness inside the Shark, tying together death and writing). When Pinocchio, after having been forced to play the watchdog, returns to the site of the Fairy's house, he finds only a small slab of marble with this epitaph: "Here lies the girl with the sky-blue hair who died of grief after being abandoned by her little brother Pinocchio." Later, when the pup-pet is swimming madly to escape the Great Shark, she appears to him in the guise of a dazzling, blue-haired goat, standing on a small island of marble, urging him to swim to her before the monster swallows him. But her words seem aimed more to provoke his despair than to give him real hope of saving himself.

The Fairy's last trick fosters the puppet's translation into a boy.

We have watched the wooden son lead his father out of the gullet of the asthmatic Shark, first thrown back inside by the creature's sneeze, then tiptoeing again across its tongue and leaping free into the night, Pinocchio swimming to shore with Gepetto on his back, almost drowning in the process. For all the comic touches, it's a moment with epic and sacred analogues: Aeneas carrying Anchises on his back out of burning Troy, Jonah delivered from the belly of a whale, Christ harrowing hell, Dante finding his path out of the Inferno. In his memory book *The Invention of Solitude*, Paul Auster evokes a homelier, yet urgent pathos, as he describes reading this episode to his young son: "The son saves the father. This must be fully imagined from the perspective of the little boy. And this, in the mind of the father who was once a little boy, a son, that is, to his own father, must be fully imagined. *Puer aeternus*. The son saves the father." (It is this mutual imagining, Auster thinks, that frees the puppet to become a real boy.) Back on land, Pinocchio has months of unheroic labor ahead of him. He now does by choice a donkey's work, turning a wooden windlass to draw up water from a well— replacing a dead beast who was his metamorphosed crony Lampwick. This labor earns him enough for a daily glass of milk for Gepetto. Pinocchio, this made thing, now becomes himself a maker: he builds Gepetto a wheelchair to take him on walks and at night he weaves baskets of reeds to sell at the market. Having husbanded his earnings to buy a new set of clothes, the puppet meets on his way to the market the Fairy's servant-snail, who tells him that she is sick, without money, and dying in hospital. The puppet instantly sends his forty pennies to save her.

That night the Fairy comes to Pinocchio in a dream, blessing him, telling him that his selfless gift has proved his goodness of heart. The wooden puppet wakes to find himself a creature of flesh and blood, a blue-eyed child, elegantly dressed and living in a grand mansion, a house not unlike the one he'd imagined buying with the fruit of the money tree. In the boy's pocket is an embroidered purse filled with forty gold coins. And within the house, in a workshop of his own, a healed Gepetto sits carving puppets, presumably ones that will not abandon or betray him.

The wooden being Pinocchio was has not dissolved within this boy, nor is it buried whole inside the boy's body, as the puppet had earlier been buried in the donkey. Instead, there are now two Pinocchios. The newborn boy asks after "the old wooden Pinocchio," and Gepetto points it out, propped against a chair in the corner of the workshop, its legs awkwardly crossed, looking as if "it would take a miracle to make it stand upright." This wooden Pinocchio seems like something that was extracted from the boy and then abandoned. Studying the figure without nostalgia or fear, the boy speaks the last words of Collodi's book: "How funny I was, when I was a puppet! And how happy I am now that I've become a proper little boy!"—Com'ero buffo, quand'ero un burattino! e come ora son contento di esser diventato un ragazzino perbene!

This proper boy can now grow up, knowing the blessings of work, of helping others. He can live a human life and die a human death, even have children himself, make those children toys and tell them stories, watch them play. This grown-up might learn to wrestle with proverbs rather than simply repeating them. He might come to choose for himself the words he lives by. Mere puppets never grow up, the Fairy had warned Pinocchio: "They're born as puppets, they live as puppets, and they die as puppets" (however it is that we imagine puppets dying). It's hard to begrudge Pinocchio that gift of a human life. But like many readers, I'm struck by how complacent the boy's words are, how much they leave out and fail to acknowledge. This boy of flesh and blood is putting away childish things, putting away the self he was when he was a puppet. Yet in this he seems to lose all memories of his past, or simply abandons those memories, as a child might abandon a doll in the back of a closet.

"How funny (buffo) I was, when I was a puppet! And how happy I am now that I've become a proper little boy!" The words mark a blessing. They are also an epitaph. The words bury away in the boy any memory of the wild life that had shown itself in Pinocchio, a life that had been buffo indeed, but in the manner of a buffone, a buffoon or clown, if sometimes an unconscious clown. They bury, or try to bury, that creature who had seemed to animate the world around him, revealing the world to us in ever more curious and perilous forms. Pinocchio's last words look away from what it is in this puppet, now propped so awkwardly, that could provoke the world to dream.

I IMAGINE THE former puppet grown old. Fragments of a past life creep into the mind this ragazzo perbene. The memories are homeless, demanding, like hungry children, asking for food. They come back to him when he walks along the edge of the sea, watching the motion of waves and the circling of birds. They come back when he wanders through the fish market. They come in the midst of crowds in the street, when he's surrounded by a chaos of faces and noises and moving bodies. These memories come when his eye is caught by a solitary chair, when he stares at a burning log. They come to him as he falls asleep, and in his dreams, dreams from which he has for years awakened merely to his human self.

He hears the dry clacking of wooden limbs. He sees a night sky full of gold coins. He remembers how adults tried to scare him with their talk of murderers. He remembers the darkness in the gullet of the Shark. Once he knew how to bark like a dog, how to speak to a dolphin, how to listen to the whispers of a donkey. In dreams, he throws himself happily into the sea, floating for days. Someone rolls him in a blanket of flour. Fire looms around him, and the smell of burning. He's chased by shadows black as ink. He loses his feet. He searches helplessly for food. Who is that person he's killed? Always running and more running. He sees mouths monstrous and tiny, mouths that kiss and eat his body. He flies across the sea on the back of a bird. A blue ghost appears. A circle of puppets calls out to him in love. How proud he is of his breadcrumb hat!

YEAR AFTER YEAR, that kite snagged in the high branches of the tree outside my window, its cloth bleached by sun and rain, ever more ragged, moving in the wind, flapping and waving, what is it thinking?

MAISIE

THE SOUND THE fire makes that she talked about last night. Not the sharp crackling of burning logs but the low rushing breathing sound of the flames that consume the wood. It's as if the fire had lungs and a throat. We make fires each night to keep away the chill, following for hours the course of their burning, reading aloud from old books, thinking where to walk the next day.

*

Watching the motions of the fire, I run over in my head some lines from Percy Bysshe Shelley's "The Witch of Atlas":

> Men scarcely know how beautiful fire is—
>   Each flame of it is as a precious stone
> Dissolved in ever moving light, and this
>   Belongs to each and all who gaze upon.
> The Witch beheld it not, for in her hand
> She held a woof that dimmed the burning brand.

*

Henry James's Maisie is herself a fire, a fire whose beauty, like that of Shelley's Witch, "men scarcely know." It's a moving fire, for Maisie has no single home in which to keep her hearth and heart. It's the fire of her knowing, the fire of her life of feeling and consciousness, the fire of an enchantress, a witchlike child. It's a fire that she seeks to nourish and tend in others, a fire that tries to "flush and colour and animate"

others. It can be a refining fire, able to change reality, a fire that plays
and that you might play *with*, also a fire in which things are burned up
and sacrificed. James shows you this fire by glimpses, inviting you to
seek out this always changing thing, to find out its guises and disguises,
its strange currents of influence.

*

I've lit the stub of a candle I found in the study, set in a small molded
glass candleholder. I watch that flame now and then as I write.

*

I am trying to write about *What Maisie Knew* in a small cottage, a former post office, in a tiny village of seven or eight houses on a remote
peninsula in the western Scottish Highlands. A consciousness of the
place, of being in the place, keeps seeping into thoughts about the novel
and the child at its center, a child surrounded by warring and loving
adults who lay claim to her, neglect her, use her, who seek to know what
she knows of their lives. The feeling in this place is one of a great solitude, and of being surrounded in solitude by things elemental, sea and
sky and stone, things very old, or early. The sounds around me, parts of
a larger silence, are of birds, the wind, the water, the calls of scattered
sheep. It's a bare landscape, stony, stripped for centuries of its ancient
forest, the colors of its plants low gray, green, and myriad shades of
purple ("the violet range of colours can trouble the mind like music,"
writes poet Nan Shepherd), grass, mosses, heather, bracken, also knots
of twisted trees, Scots pine, silver birch, copper beech, ash, and rowan.
A lush moonscape, a place full of absences, absences shaped, I know,
by history, by human work and injustice, as much as by nature, though
of any such losses the landscape itself feels innocent. If the place reminds me of one in a book, it's not by James, it's rather the landscape
described by his friend Robert Louis Stevenson in *Kidnapped*.

*

Maisie has nothing to do with such a landscape. James's child is a creature of a populous city, the inhabitant of apartments and furnished
rooms and hotels, she moves about in streets full of carriages, fashionable and unfashionable pedestrians, a surveyor of shops and urban
parks and crowded exhibition chambers. She lives in that London "so
clumsy and so brutal," yet the place "which communicates the greatest

sense of life... the largest chapter of human accidents," as James wrote elsewhere. Maisie has nothing to do with bogs and broken trees and granite hills and gray-blue stretches of sea, peat-colored streams and midges and the sharp cries of terns. The facts of weather in all their unpredictability, one's sense of the outer air as a creature with a life of its own, one that can creep into the movements of your mind—these have little place in Maisie's story. Yet I'm reminded as I write of the human solitudes that fill the novel, and of the range of human silences, silences patient, needful, evasive, sacred, cruel, and obtuse. The cityscapes of James's book give us a desolation of houses, a gathering of ruins, of homes that have become like deserts, their loves impoverished, wasted, fearful, if not entirely lost. They are homes in which Maisie finds herself all but kidnapped; they're spaces of imperfect love that she will probe, expand, organize, and connect. These places are solitudes in which Maisie shows bursts of thought and will and voice that evoke early and old, elemental powers in this child—powers that try to overcome her isolation even as they deepen it.

*

James's novel asks readers to take the measure of Maisie's solitude, to place it alongside the solitudes of the book's other characters, many of whom communicate with Maisie through silence, or by a few uneasy or malicious words dropped into her ear. Her solitude is the harder to measure just because James so rarely shows us Maisie alone, at a moment when she has no company but herself. He does not let us hear her thoughts in solitude, or give us news of her private reveries or dreams. What he lets us know of Maisie's thoughts is almost always measured by her responses, spoken or unspoken, to those who surround her, to words and actions belonging to other creatures of this human desert—persons who in turn make their own stabs at making something of Maisie's mind, finding often only mirrors of their own thought. At best we discover the peculiar force with which, in Ruth Yeazell's words, "knowledge—half-dreaded, half-desired—thrusts itself upon the conscious mind."

*

Still she haunts me, phantomwise,
Maisie moving under skies.

Maisie, in her solitude, is a creature in motion. Yet it's a passive sort of motion. One feels this child move mainly as she's moved about by others, continually taken from one place to another, transported between different houses and rooms, borne back and forth across many thresholds. You feel her life caught by winds or currents of other lives. James gives Maisie no wild, playful, and hungry child's body, save at a few moments, as when she throws herself into someone's arms, or when she devours great numbers of buttered rolls at a hotel breakfast or, in one scene, slices of an elaborate cake, "a huge frosted cake, a wonderful delectable mountain with geological strata of jam" (a gift from her stepfather at a time when her absent mother has left Maisie and her governess scarce means to feed themselves). We do see Maisie wandering in streets, squares, and parks, yet it is mainly her eye and ear and mind that are then in motion. She keeps watch on the movements of other persons around her, the ebb and flow of a human sea, its violent waves and hidden undertows, knowing as she does their struggles, those struggles that "she appeared to have come into the world to produce."

*

This passivity shows itself in the ways that the adults around Maisie flood her with so many names, labels they use to claim and place her. Some call her "dear" and "child," "young lady." Her charming stepfather Sir Claude may call her "Miss Farange," but more often, with odd humor, "old chap" or "old man," and then at one moment of delight, "Maisie, boy!" Her actual father's coarse friends seem to enjoy, Maisie notices, calling her by anything *but* her own name, though James doesn't say what. We hear her called condescendingly "precious pet," but there's also "precious idiot," not to mention "little monster," "low sneak," "donkey," "horror," "deep little devil," "dreadful dismal deplorable little thing." How Maisie lives among these names is part of the adventure, how, say, she may embrace the role of "low sneak."

*

Maisie's passivity changes as the novel unfolds. At the start, she is a thing that her divorced parents, Ida and Beale Farange, struggle over. They use her to give form to their hatred of one another, a hatred that makes them feel, James says, almost more married than ever. At first, the parents compete to possess her, to keep her each in their own houses, however un-homelike those houses are, however unsuited to the care of a child. Later they compete even more ruthlessly to see who can leave her longest in the other's possession, making her more into burden or punishment than prize. In this novel where there are both too few and too many parents, we watch the process by which others come in time to care for Maisie—her first governess, Miss Overmore, who quickly becomes "Mrs. Beale," her stepmother; then her mother's new husband, the charming Sir Claude; and finally Mrs. Wix, her lonely, widowed, anxious, and ignorant second governess, at times as victimized as Maisie herself. Maisie and her protectors are drawn together into ever more shifting, irregular, improvised, and experimental households, each guardian fighting over who is most proper to keep this child.

*

Slowly, even in her immense apparent passivity, Maisie gathers about herself a strange power, a way of acting or trying to act despite and even *in* her passivity (something she shares with others of James's heroines, such as May Bartram in "The Beast in the Jungle," Milly Theale in *The Wings of the Dove*, and Maggie Verver in *The Golden Bowl*). Increasingly, Maisie makes herself by turns riddle, irritant, enemy, and ally, an object of uncertain love, in this drawing others to the mystery of what she knows and how she knows. The novel explores Maisie's being educated into her own power, into the eerie ways that she can turn her uncertain knowledge to a kind of choice, a kind of mastery. James suggests the dangers this poses to the adults around her, partly in facing them, against their will, with a mirror of their own failures, their own childishness, a picture of what they don't know or don't want to know about themselves. By minimal motions, blunt silences, scant words—often just by repeating the words that others speak—Maisie becomes a creature who can shape the choices of those around her. She gains in the end a power to witness, to teach, even to bless, to create new alliances, new families, a power to accomplish a marriage as well as a divorce. She tries to save what might well be lost, or to oversee its sacrifice. She comes to oversee a calculus of love as well as a calculus of hate.

*

James asks you to take note of Maisie's mysterious power of taking note. Her noting of things sends threads of thought back down into the labyrinth that lies within and outside her head. Playfully, urgently, skeptically, James asks us to keep watch over the slow, silent growth of her mind, the ever-shifting thresholds of what Maisie knows about the adults around her, what she knows of their desire, terror, cowardice, shame, treachery, falsehood, abjection, greed, coldness, and cruelty, their power and weakness, their sorrows and joys, their curious secrets, their failures of imagination, how they measure profit and loss, "her general consciousness of the way things could be both perpetrated and resented." You wonder what Maisie knows of what they know or fail to know of each other, of the harm they do to themselves and others, how they know what or whom they love, what they know of the games they play to bind or divide themselves. She is witness to the truth of marriages, marriages dissolved, broken, betrayed, marriages not yet solemnized—herself the uncertain child of all of them. She tracks their ruin and reinvention. "Oh, decidedly," says the narrator midbook, in a rare moment of first-person address, "I shall never get you to believe the number of things she saw and the number of secrets she discovered!" James pulls readers into the game as well, since so much remains unspoken between us and the author, so many embarrassments and shames and fears hover half-revealed within the story. We are aware, indeed, how much we're involved in the game of imputing knowledge to Maisie. The game makes us intimate with her and with others around her, in their passionate wish for some form of knowledge, even if our imputations are unprovable.

*

We're given to see many things that Maisie seems to know but doesn't quite understand. We see the force of her mere guesses, her often desperate surmises, and her shock at times in finding that things for adults are not quite as she thinks or needs them to be. Maisie's way of proclaiming, as she often does, "Oh, I know" is mostly the expression of a wish, a mask for her uncertainty, if not her repression of the truth. That "I know" can indeed be close to nonsense (though a more compelling nonsense than the facile "Oh, you know" and "don't you know?" that punctuate the talk of Sir Claude). So James writes, in his preface to the New York Edition, of how often those matters that Maisie understands can "darken off into others that she rather tormentedly misses." (The novelist thus, in Maisie, "officiates a connection between opacity and pain," as Sharon Cameron writes, a connection that shapes our view of other consciousnesses in this book, though the sources of Maisie's pain, like those of her fear, are hard to fix precisely.) James's narrator tells us that Maisie "held her breath with the sense of picking her steps among the tremendous things of life," this child who has "grown up among things as to which her foremost knowledge was that she was not to ask about them." She lives with the "small smug conviction that in the domestic labyrinth she always kept the clue," yet that clue of knowledge is itself a fragile, uncertain, anxious possession. One wonders if Maisie ever knows herself for what she is, at once the monster in the maze and the hero who risks entering it, also the sacrificial victim the hero must rescue. Does Maisie know that she herself is a maze, at all times mazy, amazed, and amazing?

*

Maisie, James writes in his preface, "treats her friends to the rich little spectacle of objects embalmed in her wonder." The objects of wonder include her friends themselves, those adults embalmed in their own bafflements. "She wonders... to the end, to the death—the death of her childhood, properly speaking." What Maisie knows, the substance of her knowing, belongs to her as a creature of wonder. Her wonder is part of her knowledge, even its foundation. (Is Maisie ever a wonder to herself?) James asks that one trust the expanding power of Maisie's wonder, its fearlessness. The novel makes it clear how plainly awful the adults around Maisie can be, how vain, blind, fearful, cruel, lazy, childish, weak, treacherous, self-deceiving and self-damaging. I see their flaws sharply enough as I read. But the novel also asks that I be wary about supposing that I know these adults better than this child knows them, translating them into simpler terms, even when her knowing them includes her wish to know what she cannot know, or to find out traces of a very imperfect love in them. The muddle of Maisie's knowledge is itself a part of the wonder in that knowing, part of its authority, its truth. "The muddled state too is one of the very sharpest of the realities," writes James in his preface, so it's costly to assume one can cut through that muddle instead of trying to share it.

*

The novel keeps us suspended over the question of Maisie's innocence, of how that innocence survives, how it consorts with her knowledge of the adult lives around her, with her eyes being opened, "knowing good and evil." One is asked to imagine the scope and shape of her innocence, even as one imagines its opposite. James continually suggests in Maisie "an excess of the queer something which had seemed to waver so widely between innocence and guilt." It's a wavering that undoes any certainties about either. To imagine Maisie's knowing becomes a test of our own ideas of innocence, what we imagine children know and cannot know, or what might remain innocent in the child who does know.

*

James shows his readers just how ardently, how opportunistically, the adults around Maisie make use of the idea of her being *beyond* innocence. "What the pupil already knew was indeed rather taken for granted than expressed, but it performed the useful function of transcending all text-books and supplanting all studies." Adults come to bank on her knowing the worst, knowing plainly the "horrors" of which they accuse each other. If, as happens very often, Maisie's guardians claim to be sparing *her* ears, it's mostly to spare their own. They keep silent about certain things, they declare, because Maisie already knows all. But this is a way for them to avoid facing the secrets that they themselves are half-ashamed to keep, or don't even know they keep. Thinking that she knows all, that she's already "depraved," is one way for the adults to spare themselves the need to think not just about their sexual lives but about their failures of care, their failures to know what they've done to Maisie and to themselves, how much they exile from themselves any remnant of innocence.

*

I can't keep my eyes off the sheep and lambs that wander in meadows and along the narrow paths of the village, cropping the grass. If you get close, they turn on you their animal eyes, eyes that seem curious, scared, challenging, and blank all at once. I can't keep from lending them some inquiring and mocking human intelligence, or inventing for them a voice like that of a knowing child or irreverent adult. I find myself imitating their *baas*, though this noise clearly sounds like nothing to them—it both thrills and embarrasses me to think how much more

the local shepherd and his canny dog know of the sheep, things that I
will never know.

*

We rarely see the child Maisie at play, whether alone or in company
with other children. (There are, indeed, no other children in her world,
unless we count Mrs. Wix's dead daughter, Clara Matilda, killed by a
coach when small, Maisie's "little dead sister" the governess calls her—
they will visit together the child's grave.) Maisie rather becomes the
object of play in the games of these adults who are themselves close to
children. She becomes their tennis ball, football, and billiard ball, their
pawn and shuttlecock. She's both prize and weapon in games that are
like wars, wars open and covert. Early on, she also becomes something
of a ventriloquist's dummy, a mouthpiece through which her parents
can send their half-understood words of malice back and forth between
each other. Part of Maisie's "strange office" is to allow her divorced parents to mock and insult one another at a distance. ("'He said I was to
tell you, from him,' she faithfully reported, 'that you're a nasty, hor-
rid pig!'") It's a strategy that gives the parents a hope that his or her
words will drive from Maisie's ears the awful lies that they know for certain each has been telling the child about the other. Coming to know
the cost of this, the pain and bafflement borne by such ventriloquism,
Maisie responds by falling silent, going mute. This silence leaves the
adults thinking her at first shockingly dull, "a precious idiot," while later
she seems a creature full of guile, an object of suspicion, a "low sneak"
always keeping silent watch on their lives.

*

Within Maisie herself this self-protective silence brings about a sig-
nificant change. Her silence endows a new relation to the world, produces "literally a moral revolution... accomplished in the depths of her
nature. The stiff dolls on the dusky shelves began to move their arms
and legs: old forms and phrases began to have a sense that frightened
her. She had a new feeling, the feeling of danger; on which a new rem-
edy rose to meet it, the idea of an inner self, or, in other words, of concealment." That secrecy feeds her "prodigious spirit." It becomes the basis of a stranger education as well as a stranger power, a power—or so
James lets it seem—to bring the dead to life, though in unsettling forms

("The stiff dolls on the dusky shelves began to move their arms and legs: old forms and phrases began to have a sense that frightened her"). We get glimpses of pain in this concealment—there are the pains that are concealed and the pains of concealing them. Yet this secrecy, and the inner self it breeds, gives a curious shape to Maisie's play. If Maisie remains something for the adults to play with, her secrecy feeds in her an intractable, often perverse life and will. By her secrecy, by her growing silent consciousness, by the play of her mind, Maisie "spoiled [the adults'] fun, but she practically added to her own."

*

Maisie's fun is a strange thing. We glimpse her once, in an early and rare moment of solitude, and a rare moment of actual child's play, in conversation with her French doll Lisette. She lends the doll a voice that gives us an inner echo of her own bafflement, her own demanding questions about the mysteries she sees around her. Facing this silent creature, Maisie finds herself as "convulsed" by the doll's innocence and unknowability as Maisie's mother Ida is convulsed by her daughter's. The child comes to see in "the very darkness of Lisette" the double of her own darkness and that of her mother. "She could only pass on her lessons and study to produce on Lisette the impression of having mysteries in her life, wondering the while whether she succeeded in the air of shading off, like her mother, into the unknowable." In speaking to the doll, James tells us, Maisie sometimes finds herself taking on Ida's voice. "She mimicked her mother's sharpness, but she was rather ashamed afterwards, though as to whether of the sharpness or the mimicry was not quite clear." Some fun.

*

* Maisie's attempt to impress her doll with her *own* inner mystery extends (in a less violent key) what Charles Baudelaire describes as the child's "first metaphysical stirring," its "infantile mania" to find its *toy's* soul. As he writes in "The Philosophy of Toys," "when this desire has planted itself in the child's cerebral marrow, it fills his fingers and nails with an extraordinary agility and strength. He twists and turns the toy, scratches it, shakes it, bangs it against the wall, hurls it on the ground. From time to time he forces it to continue its mechanical motions, sometimes in the opposite direction. Its marvellous life comes to a stop. The child, like the populace besieging the Tuileries, makes a last supreme effort; finally he prises it open, for he is the strongest party. But *where is its soul*? This moment marks the beginnings of stupor and melancholy."

Maisie's schooling is as strange as her play. As the book of her young life unfolds, we're continually alerted to how poor and perverse an education Maisie receives. It's an education supplied by ignorant and anxious governesses, one who comes to use her a position as a screen for her romantic relationship with Maisie's father, and another who becomes almost as struggling a student as Maisie herself. We watch the child's lessons continually interrupted or abandoned, replaced by gossip and storytelling, supplemented by random public lectures or by educational games whose rules neither Maisie nor Mrs. Wix can figure out. There's a moment when she and her stepmother "gaze in united but helpless blankness at all that Maisie was not learning." "Untutored and unclaimed" as Maisie is, such failures in her formal education yet provide the conditions for the more potent lessons she gains in watching and listening to the adults around her.

*

The riches of such a poor education lie closer to the novelist than one might think. In his late autobiographical work, *A Small Boy and Others*, James describes his own early schooling. Even in its greater scope and privilege, the company of siblings, other children, and well-trained tutors, the array of private schools in London, Geneva, Paris, and New York, what James remembers most sharply—along with the continual uprooting of the household—are his schooling's "felicities of destitution," the experience of "having seen and felt much of the whole queerness through the medium of rare inaptitudes." His truest education comes by way of things learned by accident, learned sideways, things learned at the margins of more proper subjects, matters surmised, guessed at, things known in the face of a perceived failure to know. It's a knowledge linked to a gaping hunger, open to shock. It comes through lessons oblique, inconsistent, contradictory, through witnessing matters apparently superficial, the more revelatory for what they don't show, demanding that the child Henry James imagine their meanings for himself, appealing to his "subjective passion":

> It is beyond measure odd, doubtless, that my main association with my "studies," whether of the infant or the adolescent order, should be with almost anything but the fact of learning—of learning, I mean, what I was

supposed to learn. I could only have been busy, at the same time, with other pursuits—which must have borne some superficial likeness at least to the acquisition of knowledge of a free irresponsible sort.... I recognise at the same time that it was perhaps a sorry business to be so interested in one didn't know what.

There was, he writes, "a deficiency, in the whole thing, that I fail at all consistently to deplore, however—struck as I am with the rare fashion after which, in any small victim of life, the inward perversity may work.... It works by converting to its uses things vain and unintended."

*

Herself a "small victim of life," Maisie has more literal poverty to contend with. James also lends to this child—an only child passed around among so many adults—a fiercer solitude and vulnerability, a more naked need for human love, than any which he evokes in his own childhood self. We see in Maisie a rawer sense of what's been lost or taken away. Her acquaintance with knowledge of "a free irresponsible sort," knowledge of "one didn't know what," isn't for her (or isn't *just*) the lucky schooling of a future novelist. For Maisie it's a tool of survival, teaching her to convert what she learns to more idiosyncratic uses. She makes of the adults around her less her instructors than her subjects, books to be torn, scribbled on, and blotted rather than merely copied.

*

What lessons these adults offer Maisie seem closer to those which the Mock Turtle in *Alice in Wonderland* brags of having had as a child— lessons in "Ambition, Distraction, Uglification, and Derision," lessons in "Mystery, Ancient and Modern," not to mention Classical studies in "Laughing and Grief."

*

In her silence, her opaque inwardness, her unknowable knowledge of others, her witness of unspoken things, in the fear or wonder she evokes—in all of these things Maisie can feel as uncanny, as ghostly, as any of the ghostly creatures in *The Turn of the Screw*, published in 1898, just a year after *What Maisie Knew*. She's as ghostly those dead servants with their harrowing eyes. As ghostly as those other children, Miles and Flora, with their plain secrets and eerie play. As ghostly as that un-named governess, the one who tells the tale, the one who seems to see around herself the terrible reflections of her own needs and fears, in-cluding her fear of what she imagines those children know. "The logic of the governess seems both fluid and too rigid, both subtle and too crude, both clear and yet too blurred," writes T. J. Lustig. *What Maisie Knew* gives us no *frisson* of supernatural terror like that of *The Turn of the Screw*. There's no aura of sexual violation or demonic possession, no hint of murderous madness, no actual deaths. The ghostliness of *Maisie* belongs more closely to the texture of our ordinary lives. It's a test of our ordinary selves, what we know and don't know of one an-other. It's a ghostliness sometimes in question, struggled over, the trace of a ghost whom it might be dangerous to drive away or lay to rest, a ghostliness—a deathliness—that binds us to others and to ourselves through love and doubt and fear. "The extraordinary is most extraor-dinary in that it happens to you and me," in its "looming through . . . the indispensable history of somebody's *normal* relation to some-thing"—so James wrote in the preface to the volume of the New York Edition that gathered others of his ghostly tales, including "The Altar of the Dead," "The Beast in the Jungle," and "The Jolly Corner."

*

In *The Turn of the Screw*, part of the fright lies in the governess's awful readiness to project her own assurance of corruption, her own con-taminated knowledge, onto those ordinary children, and doing so in circumstances that make them so vulnerable, so exposed to her projec-tions. ("One knows the *most* damning things about one's self," writes James in a letter to H. G. Wells, apropos of *The Turn of the Screw*.) Maisie by contrast can make you feel that you've never projected enough, that this dangerous child is always ready to absorb more and more into her thought and being, into "the excess of the queer something which had seemed to waver so widely between innocence and guilt."

*

In Maisie's speculative appetite—an appetite we ourselves speculate about—James gives us his version of that endless, often vexed theoriz-ing about adult sexual lives that Sigmund Freud saw as dominating the mental lives of children, a theorizing energy whose possibility shaped his radical challenge to narrower pictures of childhood innocence. If we can't help wondering what Maisie knows about the sexual lives of her parents and stepparents, we might recognize that it is as much about their love that she wonders, its strength and weakness, how it binds them together or divides them, how it falls away, how it fails, how it deforms or disguises itself, how it survives, how and when it turns to hatred.

*

Dozing off briefly at my writing table, I have a dream of a party of children in a meadow of grass, bracken, and wildflowers. Some of them are quite small. They're preparing a bomb in a briefcase that will be left at a house protected by other children. The sheep look on impassively, keeping their distance.

*

I think of Maisie's awkward moments of politeness, a politeness often mistaken for mockery, guile, stupidity, or malice, small gestures of kindness that try to reach across a void. It's as if she has to invent rules of civilized conversation among savages, herself "a subtle savage." She seeks to get the adults to take in some small piece of her meaning, as a way of making peace among them. You often can't tell how the adults hear her. Maisie's dilemmas in this remind me again of Carroll's Alice moving among the obstinate and insulting creatures of Wonderland, all so ready to misconstrue her attempts at courteous speech. In writing of Maisie, James asks us to develop an ear for the childish, mad, and maddening color of so many intervals in our lives, to listen to what's said for traces of buried appetites and unseen blindnesses, signs of the fear and need and guile that we bring into play within our ordinary conversations. Maisie early on gives up the game of being a mere mouthpiece for her parents' attacks on one another. Yet she does allow herself to become, at times, a kind of echo chamber for these adults, as if she is trying to interpret and shape what they say, or *might* say, conscious as she is of their always mysterious needs.˙

* Friends of Henry James left stories of his encounters with actual children. He is always earnest and courteous, never condescending. G. K. Chesterton wrote, "I saw a little boy gravely present him with a crushed and dirty dandelion. He bowed; but he did not smile." His conversations with children are not always a success. The novelist Hugh

*

Maisie's strange reticence, and her power silently to voice what's *un-said*, show themselves at a moment when she finds herself all but kidnapped by her father, and taken to the grand, bibelot-filled apartment of his current mistress, a rich American woman he calls "the Countess." James has Maisie take the measure of her father's charm, his energy, the mere beauty of his face and beard. He also lets us hear what Maisie thinks she hears behind Beale Farange's words, as he rehearses his struggles in being her father, and then announces his imminent departure for the New World. Listening to his rationalizations and self-exculpations, she sees not only that he means to abandon his role as her parent but that he wishes Maisie herself to take responsibility for this abandonment. He asks her, implicitly, to excuse and even praise him for his flight: "Then she understood as well as if he had spoken it that what he wanted, hang it, was that she should let him off with all the honours—with all the appearance of virtue and sacrifice on his side. It was exactly as if he had broken out to her: 'I say, you little donkey, help me to be irreproachable, to be noble, and yet to have none of the beastly bore of it.'" No blind puppet or ventriloquist's dummy, Maisie has at this point become skilled in imagining for herself her father's bluff and manly tones of voice. Yet hers is also a ventriloquism saturated with silence, with the sound of all he won't say, all of what she cannot say in return, and all that we as readers might *want* her to say, insofar as we feel ourselves tangled up in this ghostly conversation.

*

Walpole sees him give coins to two small children he meets walking, along with "an oration to them as to what they should do with their money, the *kind* of sweets they should buy, the best time of day for the consumption of sweets and so on." Held open-mouthed for a moment, the children throw down the coins and flee. Muriel Draper—sister-in-law of the actress Ruth Draper, whose art James admired—writes of introducing James to her three-year-old son, a child who's come to love the photograph of James himself as a child (standing beside his father) that serves as the frontispiece to *A Small Boy and Others*. James looks at the boy intently and, at a loss for words, stammers out praise for a beautiful pearl button that fastens his elegant, homemade garment. The child "fled terrified from the room," James crying out, "Would I had remained a photograph!" In the person of Maisie, James creates a child who will stay to face his words and questions, a child who questions him in turn, even as she keeps her silence.

Sitting side by side, father and daughter try for a moment to read each other's thoughts, to excavate between themselves some shared depth of knowledge and feeling. But we get only an intimate separation of minds, comical and desperate at once:

> If he had an idea at the back of his head she had also one in a recess as deep, and for a time, while they sat together, there was an extraordinary mute passage between her vision of this vision of his, his vision of her vision, and her vision of his vision of her vision. What there was no effective record of indeed was the small strange pathos on the child's part of an innocence so saturated with knowledge and so directed to diplomacy.

Where, you might ask, would the "effective record" of such a small, strange, and muddled innocence be kept? Only in our own imaginations, and only if we can imagine a mind at once so open to adult weakness and evasion, yet still driven by a young child's blind, tormented speculations about what she doesn't know.

*

Maisie's part in her mother's abandoning of her turns on a more costly sort of ventriloquism. Toward the latter part of the book, Sir Claude—long her main protector—plans for the two of them to travel to France, as a way of disentangling himself and his stepdaughter from the chaos of their lives in London. The night before their departure, waiting at Folkstone, Ida suddenly arrives, after having long been absent from the scene of the novel. She insists on speaking to her daughter alone, in the hotel garden, as twilight gathers. There she tells Maisie about her own looming departure for some warmer climate, a voyage required to repair her ruined health—health ruined, she insists, in her madly devoted, self-sacrificing care for her daughter, care shown mainly in her so grandly sparing the child all knowledge of the trials of her marriage, knowledge of the depravity of her ex-husband (who only wishes his child *dead*), also knowledge of the monstrosity of Beale Farange's second wife, not to mention her own faithless lovers. "There were things Ida said which she perhaps didn't hear, and there were things she heard that Ida perhaps didn't say." Yet listening to the harangue, Maisie grasps her mother's great theme, the idea that Ida has been not only good, but, as she declares, "crazily... criminally good." Maisie, even at the moment of being abandoned, again plays the desperate ventriloquist, rushing to second Ida's thought, her heroic sense of herself. She tells her mother that this is exactly what "the Captain" had said of her—the Captain being one of Ida's former lovers, a grave man who had, weeks earlier, briefly shepherded Maisie during a vicious encounter between Claude and his estranged wife in Kensington Gardens. This Captain, Maisie happily cries to Ida, says "what you say, mamma—that you're so good.... I think it would have given you pleasure to hear the way he spoke of you." Taking this in, Ida turns on her daughter in rage, unable to bear to be found echoing the praise of the man she now thinks of as "the biggest cad in London": "I say you're a precious idiot, and I won't have you put words into my mouth!" Ida wants to spit out any approximation of the Captain's words that Maisie had heard in her speech. Maisie herself, in a rare moment of anger, continues to insist on the truth of such love. She was, James writes, "almost capable of the violence of forcing this home," forcing on Ida her loathed echoing. But just *almost*: "For even in the midst of her surge of passion—of which in fact it was a part—there rose in her a fear, a pain, a vision ominous, precocious, of what it might mean for her mother's fate to have forfeited such a loyalty as that. There was literally an instant in which Maisie fully saw—saw madness and desolation, saw ruin and darkness and death." James does not specify whose madness it is Maisie here so prophetically knows, or whose desolation, whose ruin or death. (How does Maisie think death?) The darkness she sees is something that she shares with those around her.

*

Maisie's echoing voice comes into play again (and more plainly) at the end of this chapter, when she and Sir Claude stand on the hotel terrace in a milder darkness, and he takes in the news of Ida's flight:

> Still they didn't separate; they stood smoking together under the stars.* Then at last Sir Claude produced it. "I'm free—I'm free."

* James makes clear some pages earlier that Maisie smokes only in her imagination: "After dinner she smoked with her friend—for that was exactly what she felt she did—on a porch, a kind of terrace, where the red tips of cigars and the light dresses of ladies made, under the happy stars, a poetry that was almost intoxicating."

She looked up at him; it was the very spot on which a couple of hours before she had looked up at her mother. "You're free—you're free."

"To-morrow we go to France." He spoke as if he had not heard her; but it didn't prevent her again concurring.

"To-morrow we go to France."

Again he appeared not to have heard her; and after a moment—it was an effect evidently of the depth of his reflections and the agitation of his soul—he also spoke as if he had not spoken before. "I'm free—I'm free!"

She repeated her form of assent. "You're free—you're free."

This time he did hear her; he fixed her through the darkness with a grave face. But he said nothing more; he simply stooped a little and drew her to him.

One wonders what Maisie thinks of the cost of such freedom, what her "form of assent" keeps silent about as well as what it advances. Such a play of repetitions, a device James uses more and more in his late fiction, can only, in Yeazell's words, "blur the line between fact and desire and between the explanation of circumstances and the creation of them."

*

Taking in the landscape surrounding the cottage, I'm again aware of all that has no place in *What Maisie Knew*. There's little description of the natural world, few glimpses of sky, no changing colors on the water of a bay, no waves of sun and shadow on the meadows. There are no noises from unseen streams, no cries of animals, no mad patterns of moss and lichen on stone walls. There are no massed hills in the distance, no dark silhouettes of islands seen across the water, no mirrors of such silhouettes in the massing of clouds in the sky. There's no heath whose folds are like the waves of the sea, or like the rumpled shapes of blankets thrown over restless sleepers, forms that are like the rippling surfaces of a mind, my own or another's, in the midst of which are small isolated lakes and ruined stone houses coursed by wind. The novel's chief landscapes are drawing rooms and front stoops and hallways, city streets, a bare nursery, a lecture hall, hotel rooms, a cemetery, a railway station. Yet in reading, I often have a sense of hidden forces at work in this urban world, as if James is showing us the human and social form of vast geological, ecological, and meteorological systems, systems that give shape to the lush desert of life in *What Maisie Knew*, a life harking back to the origins of the world, even as it's also the space of the evolved, speculative mind, a space of making that always remakes and renews itself.

*

In the cottage study are shelves of books belonging to the original owner, now deceased. As I'm writing, they offer themselves as an idiosyncratic archive for research: *Island Years, The Dark Labyrinth, My Family and Other Animals, Speak, Memory, The Dark of Summer, A History of Bhutan, The Wind in the Willows, What Am I Doing Here?, A Journal of a Tour to the Hebrides with Dr. Johnson, Living in Truth, The Bhagavad Gita, Loch Fishing, The Road to Oxiana, The Wandering Scholars, The Making of Henry.*

*

The horizon of Maisie's knowledge continually shifts. As one reads, that horizon seems by turns more and less approachable, more and less visible, now covered in mist, or concealed by a line of hills, now very clear, and now mocked by a long strip of sunlight on a distant patch of water. To ask what Maisie knows is like asking what the horizon knows, as it beckons and encloses us. It's the meeting edge of what she knows and doesn't know, or only imagines, the meeting point of knowledge and ignorance both contingent and imposed. She stands at a threshold between childhood and adulthood, innocence and experience, always expanding that threshold, dwelling in that crossing place of two worlds, even inviting us in. Is it an accident that we never really know how old Maisie is? I sometimes think of this child, this wonder, as what in ancient Greek thought is called a *daemon*, a nonmortal being that crosses back and forth between natural and supernatural, material and spiritual worlds, often as a messenger that bears news of hidden or not-yet-realized things.

*

It's hard to know how many years James's novel encompasses, from the time of Maisie's life just after her parents' divorce, through the collapse of their second marriages, and the later drawing together of her stepparents. The last quarter of the novel, however, clearly spreads out over just a few weeks. The story unfolds at the edge of the sea, marked by an immense play of sadness and lightness. Sir Claude, Mrs. Wix, and Mrs. Beale come to circle around the child, this creature who is to them at once pawn and prize and magnet. Maisie at this point has been released from the claims of her warring parents, the claims of those who hate her. She now must discover or improvise her place amidst those who love her.

*

The morning after her conversation with Ida, Maisie crosses the channel with Sir Claude. They set up camp in a modest harborside hotel in Boulogne-sur-Mer, a city in which they wait and wander, as if frozen there by the uncertain future. Maisie's protectors come and go. The arrangements of this small, exiled household keep shifting. First it is Sir Claude spending time alone with Maisie, with the single addition of a servant, Susan Ash. Then Mrs. Wix arrives to join them, at Sir Claude's prescient request. Then it is Mrs. Wix alone with Maisie, as Sir Claude carries Susan back to England. Mrs. Wix at this moment clearly fears that Sir Claude has left them both for Mrs. Beale, or worse, that he and his mistress will return together, their awful alliance confirmed, requiring Mrs. Wix herself to depart. To her surprise, Mrs. Beale arrives alone, the lady seeming set, as James says, to "make love" to Mrs. Wix, to keep her within the orbit of herself and Sir Claude. With things unresolved, Sir Claude suddenly returns late one morning to the hotel. Finding Maisie alone, just awakened, he takes her out for a long walk in the city—the question of whether or not he's seen Mrs. Beale remaining unanswered. In the end, the wandering pair return to the hotel, where all four meet together for one last time.

*

Mrs. Wix—the impossible, ignorant, impoverished, anxious and comical governess—has loomed up increasingly as the novel moves toward its close, as much when she is absent as when she is present. The amazing truth about this fretful woman with her "little ugly snuff-coloured dress" and steel spectacles (her "straighteners") is that "a certain greatness had now come to Mrs. Wix." That greatness shows itself, during her time alone with Maisie in Boulogne, through a more focused aim, a more determined educational ambition: her wish to elicit in Maisie what she calls "a moral sense," to discover in this child, or impose on her, a power to judge. She seeks particularly in Maisie a power to condemn any possible relation between her stepparents—who are not divorced from their proper spouses—and any plan of their adopting Maisie and forming a shared household (Maisie being the one who, as Sir Claude and Mrs. Beale always recall, "brought us together"). Maisie, Mrs. Wix has long insisted, knows all there is to know about adult depravity. But for Maisie to find for herself a "moral sense," the governess says, would entail her crossing a line, taking upon herself the consciousness of an adult woman—something that Mrs. Wix seems to fear Maisie will *never* be. Yet if Mrs. Wix in her ambitions has grown in stature, it's something that, as James writes, Maisie herself has brought about; it's something in Maisie's silence, or opacity, or love, something in her very resistance to being taught, that has "qualified" Mrs. Wix to undertake this last program of instruction. That Maisie teaches these adults how they might teach her is a thing that Maisie may or may not know. "I am not sure," writes the narrator, "that Maisie had not even a dim discernment of the queer law of her own life that made her educate to that sort of proficiency those elders with whom she was concerned. She promoted, as it were, their development."

*

For all her new "greatness," her "development," James suggests just how limited is Mrs. Wix's obsession with finding out "a moral sense" in this child, how much she fails to recognize the force and shape of what Maisie knows, or might come know, about human love. Mrs. Wix's worries are mixed up with the governess's narrow fear of impropriety, her fear of having to acknowledge the ferocity of the bond between Sir Claude and Mrs. Beale, her fear of Maisie's own acceptance of that bond. They're mixed up with Mrs. Wix's fear simply of losing her place as governess, losing her own small freedom, losing her peculiar possession of the schoolroom, also losing this child whom she so clearly, if troublingly, loves. James shows us Maisie's fervent wish to answer Mrs. Wix's demand, even to fabricate a moral sense she doesn't have. In the end, one thing that Maisie knows most strongly is what she will *not* know of what Mrs. Wix asks for. Maisie refuses the substance and certainty of such a moral sense, its will to condemn, its narrowness as a measure of what's true. Mrs. Wix's version of a moral sense here, James says, is like a "faint flower" that she thrusts aggressively under Maisie's nose. I wonder whether that flower smells to the child of nothing, or of rot, or of a sickening perfume—of all that Mrs. Wix cannot nose out for herself.

*

Freedom has been the opening note struck on Maisie's and Sir Claude's arrival in Boulogne. Maisie is taken with her first glimpse of the Continent, her sight of a space of freer life in this shore city, everything from the crowds in the streets to the elegant play of waiters pouring coffee, from the "semi-nudity" of swimmers to the power of ancient battlements looming over the sea. She's the child incarnation of James's surprised American travelers, like Isabel Archer in *The Portrait of a Lady*. Wandering in the town, Maisie "recognized, she understood, she adored and took possession; feeling herself attuned to everything and laying her hand, right and left, on what had simply been waiting for her." The freedom of Boulogne also frees up fear. "Fear" and "free," aural anagrams, indeed hover together in this last phase of the book. The space of freedom becomes a place where fears and doubts shape themselves. The town becomes a place where love is put to the test. Love and memory.

*

Where is the fear? One feels it in Mrs. Wix's hammering on the idea of Maisie's moral sense. One also feels it hovering in Sir Claude, as he and Maisie wander through the city over the course of a morning, after he's come back from England. Together they hold off their return to the hotel, where Mrs. Wix and Mrs. Beale are waiting for them, and some final sorting out of their lives will be demanded. Sir Claude in particular stretches out the walk, his idleness and playful banter trying to conceal the urgency of a question he wants to ask, and that he does, in time, pose to her: Would Maisie be ready to give up Mrs. Wix, and to live with him and Mrs. Beale as quasi-parents in some French city remote from England (since it's clear Mrs. Wix would never be part of such a household)? As they continue to wander, what comes upon Maisie is a sense of how much Sir Claude, in asking his question, is afraid, is indeed entirely a creature of fear, a fear covered by his charm and kindness. If he fears Mrs. Wix's judging eye, his greater fear, she surmises, is of Mrs. Beale, a fear of losing her, also a fear of this woman's pitiless passion, of how much she asks him to sacrifice for her. Sir Claude also fears himself, Maisie sees, fears his own weakness in the face of Mrs. Beale's demands. He's afraid *of* his fear, afraid of how little he's ever been able to cast it out, even in love. Sir Claude fears Maisie, too, fears his love for this child, and how much he depends on her answer to his question. Knowing these fears in Sir Claude makes Maisie herself afraid, James tells us. She's afraid of something in Sir Claude, but also of something in herself. If Sir Claude fears his own weakness, what Maisie seems to fear is her strength, her strength in both keeping silent and asking questions, her strength to wait and her strength to demand, her strength to insist on her desires and her strength to sacrifice them. It's a power that takes its most startling shape in the closing pages of the book.

*

Pausing in their walk at the railway station—ostensibly to buy newspapers—Sir Claude and Maisie see a train on the verge of departing for Paris. They almost wish themselves aboard it. So preternaturally sharp is their wish, their vision of flight together, that untaught Maisie finds herself able to understand French. (A porter asks Sir Claude whether he can get their tickets: "'*Monsieur veut-il que je les prenne?*' ... [Maisie] addressed herself straight to the porter. '*Prenny, prenny. Oh prenny!*'") But they're frozen in place. The train leaves without them, as if in a dream. What it leaves behind is a suddenly crystallized knowledge in Maisie, the knowledge of how she can answer Sir Claude's proposal. The child asks of him a mirroring sacrifice: she will give up Mrs. Wix if he will give up Mrs. Beale. That new, more radical possibility haunts them as they make their way back to the hotel.

*

"If they were afraid of themselves it was themselves they would find at the inn." Their room, when Maisie and Sir Claude reenter it, becomes indeed the space of a crisis, of a terrible meeting or a battle royal, the place for a sorting out of claims and a balancing of accounts, a place of painful relinquishments and costly gains. It's like a stage space, you could say, the stage for a scene of dramatic reversal and recognition as frenzied as anything in a French farce or melodrama—though if the lat-

ter, it's a "melodrama of consciousness," in which the revelations are the
more charged for being occulted, animated by what remains unspoken,
silenced, also shared out among different minds. The hotel room also
turns into a schoolroom, the place, as James suggests, for a final examination, though who the students are and who the masters is hard to fix.
You're aware of Maisie being physically pushed and pulled at, grabbed,
held by the adults around her, thrust to the side or center of the room. If
they seize on her childish body, each also seizes on a different vision of
this dangerous child's mind, her inner life. They wrestle over the question of what manner of prodigy, monster, or miracle Maisie has been
to them, and what place she has in some future, ad hoc family—each
in their own way missing the mark. As Laurence Holland writes, such
"miracles" of knowing or love tend to appear in James, "(when they do)
in exchanges which are haunted by what is dropped unfinished or left
unsaid, bristle with nightmarish abstraction and enigma, and are subject to absurdly protracted improvisations or to sudden ruptures and
dissolutions."

*

Mrs. Beale, hearing what Maisie has proposed to Sir Claude, suddenly
sees in the child a dangerous creature ready to divide her from her
lover, the only person she truly wants to possess. And Maisie does, in a
rare act of cruelty, pose to Mrs. Beale the impossible alternative of her
willingly, as an act of sacrifice for her stepdaughter's sake, relinquish-
ing Sir Claude:

> "*Will* you give him up?" Maisie persisted to Mrs. Beale.
> "To *you*, you abominable little horror?" that lady indignantly in-
> quired, "and to this raving old demon who has filled your dreadful little
> mind with her wickedness?"

Mrs. Wix, fixated if not quite demonic, takes this moment to press the
child even more strongly about her lack of a moral sense: "Have you
lost it again?" "I feel as if I had lost everything," Maisie responds, evad-
ing the old woman's question even as she calls up starker, more absolute losses. Pressed again by Mrs. Wix, she has only "the old flat, shameful schoolroom plea. 'I don't know—I don't know.'" What Maisie *does*

know at this moment involves a different form of sense, or sensation, or sensibleness, something that is made viscerally present to her and to us. Any understanding of what Mrs. Wix might mean has left her, "and, as if she were sinking with a slip from a foothold, her arms made a short jerk. What this jerk represented was the spasm within her of something still deeper than a moral sense." James leaves it for us to imagine what kind of knowledge or recognition, what act of imagination, what rage or fear or need mingle in that bodily and spiritual spasm, what slope she's climbing when she loses her footing. It isn't Alice's free fall.

*

Sir Claude's sudden vision of Maisie startles most in this scene. Mrs. Wix has been protesting that it's he, in his charm and fear and weakness of will, who has most helped to murder the child's nascent moral sense:

> She fixed the straighteners on Sir Claude. "You've nipped it in the bud. You've killed it when it had begun to live."
>
> She was a newer Mrs. Wix than ever, a Mrs. Wix high and great; but Sir Claude was not after all to be treated as a little boy with a missed lesson. "I've not killed anything," he said; "on the contrary I think I've produced life. I don't know what to call it—I haven't even known how decently to deal with it, to approach it; but, whatever it is, it's the most beautiful thing I've ever met—it's exquisite, it's sacred."

One may have felt the revelation of some unspeakable, precious, prodigious, even sacred life in Maisie. But Sir Claude is scarcely its maker or father, or the right person to *name* it. For all its "exquisite" beauty, it's a tougher, a more pragmatic form of life than he admits. What sacredness it holds could only be profaned by the false pieties of a "moral sense" such as Mrs. Wix asks for.

*

This new life shows itself most powerfully in the way that Maisie, object of wonder, takes silent command of the scene. With stark grace, also a certain pity, Maisie's observant eye, her mastering gaze, forces open certainties of love, including the certainties of what love costs. One of these is the certainty that Sir Claude will after all never be able to leave

Mrs. Beale, even for this child of life. Maisie's gaze at this moment in-deed brings about—with the collaboration of other witnesses—a mar-riage between the two lovers, a marriage from which Maisie and Mrs. Wix know they'll be excluded. It's a marriage based on the witness of what's impossible as much as possible, a marriage based as much on impediment as freedom:

> Mrs. Beale fixed her eyes on him, and again Maisie watched them. "You should do him justice," Mrs. Wix went on to Mrs. Beale. "We've al-ways been devoted to him, Maisie and I—and he has shown how much he likes us. He would like to please her; he would like even, I think, to please me. But he hasn't given you up."
>
> They stood confronted, the step-parents, still under Maisie's observa-tion. That observation had never sunk so deep as at this particular mo-ment. "Yes, my dear, I haven't given you up," Sir Claude said to Mrs. Beale at last, "and if you'd like me to treat our friends here as solemn witnesses I don't mind giving you my word for it that I never, never will. There!" he dauntlessly exclaimed.
>
> "He can't!" Mrs. Wix tragically commented.
>
> Mrs. Beale, erect and alive in her defeat, jerked her handsome face about. "He can't!" she literally mocked.
>
> "He can't, he can't, he can't!" Sir Claude's gay emphasis wonderfully carried it off.
>
> Mrs. Beale took it all in, yet she held her ground; on which Maisie ad-dressed Mrs. Wix. "Shan't we lose the boat?"

In this curious version of a marriage rite, "he can't" takes on the force of "I will" or "I do." Mrs. Beale, "alive in her defeat," has barely time or power to see what she's won, along with what she's lost. Her final words in the novel are addressed to her stepdaughter: "'I don't know what to make of you!' she launched." To which Maisie has no response.

*

The child at this moment takes stock of other relations, again in a charged silence. As they part, Maisie holds out her hand to Sir Claude: "He took it and held it a moment, and their eyes met as the eyes of those who have done for each other what they can." What losses and gains are acknowledged in that heartbreaking exchange of looks? Is this handshake like the one James describes in *The Sacred Fount* (a book whose narrator theorizes so madly about the secret costs, the sacrifices of life and thought, revealed in relationships of love, marriage, and art), a handshake that witnesses "things unspoken and untouched, unspeakable and untouchable"? Maisie will have to forgo, as an immediate presence, the immense love of Sir Claude. Sir Claude loses the gift he's felt in caring for this astonishing child, and gains the companionship of this woman so hungry to possess him, a woman whose love makes him afraid. Maisie has secured her loving, enlarged, but still flawed Mrs. Wix. Mrs. Wix has in her hands the care of her surrogate daughter and student and sometime teacher, though any claim on Maisie's "moral sense" remains as uncertain as Mrs. Wix's claim to being the child's best guardian. You can wonder what these two will study together, where they will live, what solitudes and divisions will remain within this other curious marriage.

*

"Shan't we lose the boat?" Having lost so much else, Maisie doesn't want to lose that. James gets child and governess aboard the ferry for England almost instantly after that question is posed. They stand together, breathless and scared, finding courage to talk only when the boat arrives mid-channel. The book quickly closes:

> Mrs. Wix had the courage to revert. "I didn't look back, did you?"
> "Yes. He wasn't there," said Maisie.
> "Not on the balcony?"
> Maisie waited a moment; then, "He wasn't there," she simply said again.
> Mrs. Wix also was silent awhile. "He went to *her*," she finally observed.
> "O, I know!" the child replied.
> Mrs. Wix gave a sidelong look. She still had room for wonder at what Maisie knew.

The end of the novel circles back to the beginning—assuming that a book begins with its title. One may here feel oneself very like Mrs. Wix, trying to measure the "room for wonder" in what Maisie knows, wondering at what she says she knows, what losses or gains, what forms of life and death, her looking back at an empty balcony can witness.

*

Writing to a friend who had pressed him about Maisie's later life, James urged her to believe "how very much I don't know of what Maisie 'became.' I'm afraid I told all I *can* tell." The child's future indeed doesn't interest him at all. While her ongoing life might be part of a *story*, it's not part of his novel's *subject*. "The subject was the girl's childhood—it was the fact of that that was the whole note of the situation; and my climax, arrived at, was marked *by*, and consisted *of*, the stroke of the hour of the end of that childhood." James is blunter in his preface: "She wonders... to the end, to the death—the death of her childhood, properly speaking." Yet the novel suggests continuity as much as severance. If Maisie "wonders to the death," it's not to the death of wonder. Maisie's life in her childhood is such an uncannily expansive thing, absorbing so much, challenging so much, its motions so mysterious, so bound to wonder, comic as well as tragic wonder. Its end is thus as hard to fix as its beginning. We don't see the strange face of her childhood die in Maisie. It rather keeps its hold. In her own way, she's another dangerous child who won't grow up. The book closes on the note of our continued "room for wonder" at the unknown horizon of "what Maisie knew," including wonder at what it means simply for Maisie to declare her knowledge to another: "Oh, I know!" It's a wonder that Maisie and Mrs. Wix together carry with them into the new world, a world without mothers and fathers it seems, but not without children.

*

James places Maisie and Mrs. Wix together on shipboard at the end. They're merely returning from France to England. Yet it feels like the close of an adventure story, or the start of one—"adventure," James once wrote, is "no positive and absolute and inelastic thing," rather "a name we conveniently give, after the fact, to any passage, to any situation that has added the sharp taste of uncertainty to a quickened sense of life." The narrow space of the English Channel feels at this moment as vast as any South Sea archipelago in a novel by Joseph Conrad, as strange as the sea crossed by Prospero and his companions when they return to Italy from that mysterious island. It is a sea of time as well as a sea of space, in which they may have to improvise temporary places of rest. (James's "anchors were all sea-anchors," wrote R. P. Blackmur, "let go to windward to secure steadiness rather than position.") In my mind's eye, I always see Maisie and Mrs. Wix standing side by side, an isolated pair, patient, alert, nervous. As I look, the boat disappears, and the two are suspended in midair, far from land, the blue-green sea below their feet—not very far below—and gray clouds over their heads. Their limbs make no motion, but standing still they're moved bodily over the moving waters by a wind that blows from behind them, moved toward a place they do not know, or will have to discover anew. I think I can imagine Mrs. Wix's "sidelong look" at Maisie, the look of her wonder. The look in Maisie's eyes (looking ahead? looking back?) I can't imagine.

PETER

IT'S STRANGE TO have someone else's imaginary creature knocking about in your head, or in your heart, laying claim to spaces of reverie and longing, often with your being only half aware of it, and the creature itself not knowing what it's doing. Strange and often embarrassing. And nothing more common. What else would you have in your head? One of J. M. Barrie's gifts as a storyteller is his evocation of how things come and go in the mind, his feel for the peculiar substance and life of thoughts that invade or hide within us. He reminds us of the mind's acute susceptibility to things imagined, to things remembered, mourned, feared, and welcomed, ghosts of the future as well as ghosts of the past. He reminds us of how little we control these thoughts, how little we know what contains them, heart or head or something of both. Barrie has a sense of how our imagined worlds may seek *us* out—Peter and the Darling children only manage to find the Neverland when they first arrive there because "the island was out looking for them." His stories also know how our imagined worlds may go looking elsewhere, and seem thereby to forget us.

The grip of the novel of 1911, *Peter and Wendy*, even more than that of the 1904 stage play, *Peter Pan*—which the novel adapts—has something to do with how subtly it tracks such comings and goings of imagined things, their flights and invasions and thefts. You feel it, for instance, in how Barrie's writing can give peculiar life to rooms as well as islands, to lost shadows, stars, smiles, dreams, and kisses, to an asked, childish question. Such a life in things may emerge only for a moment, unpredictably but urgently, and then disappear from view. The effect is heightened by the shifting register of Barrie's storytelling. The book moves continually, eerily, between voices that are playful, arch, wondering, clinical, mournful, and sentimental. You're often not clear how to place things. Its maps of the mind are always in motion:

> I don't know whether you have ever seen a map of a person's mind... a child's mind... is not only confused, but keeps going round all the time... for the Neverland is always more or less an island, with astonishing splashes of colour here and there, and coral reefs and rakish-looking craft in the offing, and savages and lonely lairs, and gnomes who are mostly tailors, and caves through which a river runs, and princes with six elder brothers, and a hut fast going to decay, and one very small old lady with a hooked nose.

Along with its lightness, there's an acid, even heartless side to Barrie's writing that his contemporaries knew well—the fantastic surface can cover cold satire. Even Barrie's sentimentality, wrote his fellow Scot, the critic Sir Walter Raleigh, can seem like "satire that doesn't quite come off." A crowd of mermaids shows itself now as a pettish social clique and now as a darker threat, a vessel of archaic magic. A lost shadow is at once a mysterious prize and a shameful scrap of common cloth. An invisible fairy is both a weird, murderous imp and an "abandoned little creature," one "inclined to *embonpoint*." A crocodile with a ticking clock inside it is at one moment a fairy-tale monster, then a starker image of the malice of time, and then the picture of human beings who are "slaves to a fixed idea." One is reading at once a story for children and a story for adults, finding oneself at places where an adult's self-conscious reveries of childhood are crossed with fervent attempts to stand more immediately within the mind of a child. Barrie knew implicitly what Jacqueline Rose calls "the impossibility of children's fiction." It's an impossibility he loves to play with.

There's a moment early on in the novel when Barrie describes Wendy and her brothers listening to Peter's words as he charms them with news of the Neverland (it's always *the* Neverland): "Their faces assumed the awful craftiness of children listening for sounds from the grown-up world," sounds they may or may not comprehend. That picture calls up the mirroring image of adult readers, in craft, need, or terror, listening for sounds from the child world, which includes the child world inside themselves. (Barrie's years run closely alongside Freud's.) Neither side may know which world is which. Always placing himself at such thresholds, Barrie invites you to wonder how much each realm feeds the other, draws the other toward it, and how much each is barred from or lost to the other. In some manuscript pages dating from the time of his work on *Peter Pan*, at the head of a long list of numbered thoughts titled "Fairy," Barrie wrote: "No one has grown up ideas (not parents not any one)." You can hear in that something of a child's voice of protest against parents and other "grown ups." You can also hear an adult ironist speaking of our inevitably infantile selves. Barrie asks you to stand at once inside child and adult, to have them speak one to the other.

In such crossings of perspective, Barrie wants to draw readers to connect to more playful and volatile powers of mind. For adult readers, this may mean a *re*connecting, a bridging back to childish things too readily put away, the world of the nursery or playground. For child readers, this may mean allowing an adult to join them in a childish game ("Let us now kill a pirate"). Very often, just as he invites you to cross such gaps, Barrie also widens them, or makes the gaps more strange, more wounding, and so he makes more uneasy the work of crossing over them. Such troubled crossing points are among the things that make for the relentless, adhesive, yet vivifying sadness of the book.

The opening paragraph of chapter 8 of *Peter and Wendy*, "The Mermaid's Lagoon," begins as an address to a child reader, an invitation to that child to share in a curious game. It's a game that tests a power in the child to conjure the Neverlands inside its head, to make those places real, sensible. Barrie leads the reader into the substance of what the mind and eye can see, evoking a visionary power, a fiery seeing of an unknown landscape that turns quickly into a fiery blindness (as if in punishment for the eyes' Promethean theft of fire):

> If you shut your eyes and are a lucky one, you may see at times a shapeless pool of lovely pale colours suspended in the darkness; then if you

squeeze your eyes tighter, the pool begins to take shape, and the colours become so vivid that with another squeeze they must go on fire. But just before they go on fire you see the lagoon. This is the nearest you ever get to it on the mainland, just one heavenly moment; if there could be two moments you might see the surf and hear the mermaids singing.

Here the "you" starts as a child invited to play, to think itself "a lucky one," gifted with a seeing tied to the shutting of its eyes. By the end of the paragraph that "you" is more like a disenchanted adult (though perhaps still "lucky"?), an adult taking stock of an impossible arithmetic, or an arithmetic of impossibility. The "you" at the start and the "you" at the end might both be masks for one and the same "I." Barrie goes on after these opening words to give us a rich enough account of the mermaids of the Neverland, mingling details about their selfishness, their indifference or incivility to Wendy and the other children, their "strange wailing cries... dangerous for mortals," even taking time to tell us how the mermaids secretly steal from Wendy's brother John a way of hitting bubbles in their games, striking them "with the head instead of the hand." (It's a great sadness, one of my students felt, that John never knows of his legacy in the Neverland.) If such play brings the mermaids closer to us, partly by making them like human children, Barrie also keeps them at a distance, emblems of things we cannot see and cannot hear, though they remain for us to imagine. There's a desolation at the end of that opening paragraph that recalls some verses composed by T. S. Eliot just about the time that Barrie was writing *Peter and Wendy*, words of the wounded, nostalgic, slightly clownish brooder named J. Alfred Prufrock: "I have heard the mermaids singing, each to each. // I do not think that they will sing to me."

THE MYTHIC BOY that Barrie created in Peter Pan, with all his charmed vanity, bravado, and relentless will to play, is sadder and more unsettling than one may remember, the different facets of his personality harder to see as a whole. In published form, he first takes shape in Barrie's 1902 novel, *The Little White Bird*, where he's the center of an expansive tale-within-a-tale. Peter here is a creature who flees from his parents the day he is born. A self-made orphan, half baby and half bird, always naked, he lives alone on an island in the Serpentine, the waterway that flows through London's Kensington Gardens. It's an island from which, Barrie tells us, come all the birds that are later reborn as the human children of the city—all save house swallows, who are the ghosts of children who have died, birds to whom Peter is especially kind. Unable to fly, traveling to and from his island in a floating thrush's nest, the boy becomes the piper for the fairies who emerge in the gardens at night (his most explicitly Pan-like work). Peter is also the guide and protector for children lost in the gardens after the gates close, in particular a brave girl named Mamie, around whose sleeping form the fairies build a house. And he takes up the task of burying those children who die in the park, being a little ghostly himself, half *genius loci* and half exile. The toys that mortal children leave behind, their balls, hoops, and dolls, become Peter's property, and he plays with them, though he never quite understands *how* to play with them in the ways they're intended to be played with.

This intricately woven fable, printed separately in 1906 as *Peter Pan in Kensington Gardens*, is, in *The Little White Bird*, told by the book's narrator, Captain W——, to an ordinary boy named David. The man is himself a writer, a "confirmed spinster," a denizen of his London club, cranky, whimsical, snobbish, secretive, competitive, full of curious intrigues, as well as flights of eloquence. He's drawn to David, he tells us, and half wants draw him away from his own mother, a former governess—a woman who had, earlier in the novel, also fascinated this man, and whose marriage and even motherhood he believes are of his making. Reading his reveries, you may sense that the narrator in the end wants mainly an imaginary child, the "little white bird" of the title, and indeed he does at one point give himself a made-up son named Timothy, a child whose death he also imagines, and reports to David. Or else, as the narrator himself suspects, what he truly wants is just his own *book* about that imaginary child (like the book Barrie presents to us). It's as if, for this strange Scheherazade, the conditions of authorship are always doubled with the imagining of a child, or with the imagining of a child and its mother, their uncertain, ghostly relations: "Life and death, the child and the mother, are ever meeting as the one draws into harbour and the other sets sail.... The only ghosts, I believe, who creep into this world, are dead young mothers, returned to see how their children fare. There is no other inducement great enough to bring the departed back."

In *Peter and Wendy*, another island tale, the conditions of Peter's emergence are equally if not more haunted, and more opaque. The magical boy does not, as in the play *Peter Pan*, appear first as a face outside a window, and later leap through suddenly, preceded by the flickering light of a fairy, in search of his lost shadow. He first takes shape for readers as Barrie describes a mother's look into her children's minds.

Mrs. Darling's mothering extends, Barrie says, to "tidying up her children's minds" as they go to sleep. She puts the lovely things on top and the dark things on the bottom. It's the image of a sly, wished-for, impossible, even dangerous kind of maternal care. Despite her work, all is not so tidy or controlled. Within the children's minds, Mrs. Darling keeps stumbling across the "the most perplexing... word *Peter*. She knew of no Peter, and yet he was here and there in John and Michael's minds, while Wendy's began to be scrawled all over with him," as if Peter himself, not just his name, were a child's graffiti.

Peter's imagined presence spills briefly into Mrs. Darling's waking world in the form of skeleton leaves that she finds on the floor of the nursery, traces of his curious, fairylike clothing (he's clad in the forms of nature, but nature worn out, decayed). And then she discovers this mysterious boy as part of her own mental world, where he's associated as much with loss as with play, and with another curious image of care: "At first Mrs. Darling did not know, but after thinking back into her childhood she just remembered a Peter Pan who was said to live with the fairies. There were odd stories about him, as that when children died he went part of the way with them, so that they should not be frightened." Who told her these "odd stories" is left unclear, as is the nature of that "way" along which Peter accompanies those child-ghosts. Does he guide them because, as Pan, he is the son of Hermes, trickster-god and leader of souls to the underworld? Or because he is himself a dead child, the ghost of a dead yet always living childhood? And how much is "part of the way"?

Peter soon takes further shape inside one of Mrs. Darling's own dreams, again as an invader from an unknown world, alien yet all too close. (He's a very homebred kidnapper.) It's a dream that quickly acquires a waking substance, a mixture of the real and the hallucinated:

> While she slept she had a dream. She dreamt that the Neverland had come too near and that a strange boy had broken through from it. He did not alarm her, for she thought she had seen him before in the faces of many women who have no children. Perhaps he is to be found in the faces of some mothers also. But in her dream he had rent the film that obscures the Neverland, and she saw Wendy and John and Michael peeping through the gap...
>
> She started up with a cry, and saw the boy, and somehow she knew at once that he was Peter Pan.... He was a lovely boy, clad in skeleton leaves and the juices that ooze out of trees, but the most entrancing thing about him was that he had all his first teeth. When he saw she was a grown-up, he gnashed the little pearls at her.

Peter belongs to the dream of this particular mother, a mother who can see pearls gnashing, who finds in this child's first teeth, unlost, both menace and charm. She also knows this boy as something with a larger life, a creature found not just in the minds but in the *faces* of other women, women who have no children and also women who, like Mrs. Darling, do have them, as if this dream child were the image of something mothers miss or fear to lose in their actual children.*

This child who first acquires body and face in the dreams of a mother himself has troubled dreams, we learn later. Peter sleeps dreamlessly for the most part, even in times of danger—as on the night when Wendy and the lost boys are captured by the pirates, and he, ignorant of this,

---

* This alien boy is close to this human mother in other ways. Very early in *Peter and Wendy* Barrie writes of a kiss that Mrs. Darling has in one corner of her "sweet mocking mouth," a kiss that neither her husband nor her children can ever get, and that she may herself know nothing of. When Barrie first describes Peter, he writes that "if you or I or Wendy had been there we should have seen that he was very like Mrs. Darling's kiss." At the end of the book, after he restores the children to their mother, Peter steals from her that very kiss, as if in payment: "He took Mrs. Darling's kiss with him. The kiss that had been for no one else Peter took quite easily. Funny. But she seemed satisfied." Taking that kiss, Peter seems to be stealing himself.

peacefully dozes with "the unfinished part of his laugh... stranded on his mouth." However, "sometimes, though not often, he had dreams, and they were more painful than the dreams of other boys. For hours he could not be separated from these dreams, though he wailed piteously in them. They had to do, I think, with the riddle of his existence. At such times it had been Wendy's custom to take him out of bed and sit with him on her lap, soothing him in dear ways of her own invention, and when he grew calmer to put him back to bed before he quite woke up, so that he should not know of the indignity to which she had subjected him." Barrie tells us nothing of what Peter dreams, nor if he recalls his wailings on waking, nor what Wendy's special soothings are. We know only that he clings to dreams which cause him pain, that he is "not to be separated" from them, as a child might refuse to be separated from a toy, a wish, or a parent. Barrie surmises that Peter is dreaming of his unknown self. But how Peter feels "the riddle of his existence"— like Hamlet with his "bad dreams," his "thoughts beyond the reaches of our souls"—is left for us to guess.

BARRIE LENDS TO Peter something of the absorption and obliviousness of a child at play. He's a picture of the world-making powers of such play, its instant turns of aim, its ruthless eagerness to incorporate things and other children into itself, its strict rules and power to break the rules. (Think of those games in which a mere touch converts you instantly from chased to chaser, an isolated, infectious "it," or games in which you must seek out all those who ardently hide from you, games where you freeze yourself into a statue, in which you're made blind or lose the use of one leg, games where you imprison, terrify, kill, and resurrect your playmates, or rush in frenzy toward an arbitrary goal.) Peter is an image of the child-self seen from *within* the domain of play, an image of play pursued with a needfulness that comes barely short of kidnapping. Barrie also probes the limits of what we'd want to call play, the places where play breaks down or becomes something else, a more uncanny thing. You may feel that, as James Kincaid writes, "Peter offers his secret to all of these children and to us, but remains alone," unplumbed, ardently refusing to be touched by anyone. And there's at least one childish thing that he doesn't seem to know. As Peter tells Wendy at the opening, tempting her to come: "You see I don't know any stories. None of the lost boys know any stories."

Peter's play, the rules that guide it, can for one thing show elements of cruelty and fear that belie the charm of what it means to "not grow up." Each of the lost boys, for instance, has his own hollow tree by which to enter their underground house, but "if you are bumpy in awkward places or the only available tree is an odd shape, Peter does some things to you, and after that you fit." (The chilling "you" includes the reader as one of Peter's potential victims. What the "things" he does are is left unclear.) More darkly, if it happens that any of the lost boys "seem to be growing up, which is against the rules, Peter thins them out," like animals in a herd. Toward the end of the story, having assumed the dead Hook's command, his dress, and even his hook, Peter becomes as vain and ruthless as his enemy could have wished (whipping the lost boy Slightly, for instance, because he's failed to "take soundings," a task that Peter surely can't himself understand). There are also moments when he's all too eager to flee the consequences of his games. On his return to the Neverland at the start of the book, Peter finds Wendy, as he thinks, dead, killed with a lost boy's arrow through a trick of jealous Tinkerbell, who's told the boys that Peter wants them to shoot down "the Wendy Bird." ("Perhaps she is frightened at being dead.") The mortal girl will shortly awake to life to save that unfortunate boy, the one named Tootles, from being executed by his angry leader. But before this happens, Peter's first impulse on finding the body of the girl he's brought home to be the lost boys' mother is to hop away comically from the spot and never return.

Barrie's novel surprises us with news of more curious powers in Peter's play, sometimes powers that he can't control. One place this comes through is late in the book, during the moonlit night when he silently approaches the pirate ship to rescue Wendy, armed and murderous, also "frightfully happy," having uttered his "terrible oath": "Hook or me this time." One thing only troubles him, that he must stalk his prey on foot: "He had hoped to fly, keeping not far from the ground so that nothing unwonted should escape his eyes; but in that fitful light to have flown low would have meant trailing his shadow through the trees, thus disturbing the birds and acquainting a watchful foe that he was astir.... He regretted now that he had given the birds of the island such strange names that they are very wild and difficult of approach." That Peter himself had given names to the birds of the Neverland, and that this naming had estranged those creatures from him, had made them suspicious even of his trailed shadow—this is something we'd not known about before. It makes this boy for a moment, in his play, a double of Adam in Eden, as well as of some more idiosyncratic namer-enchanter, and perhaps of any creator of fictions.

This boy who won't grow up lives shiftingly in time and memory. That is perhaps one reason that we remember him so well. We remember him, for one thing, in his forgetting. Peter forgets things relentlessly as he moves from game to game—mirroring the forgetfulness of ordinary children but taking this much farther. Guiding the Darling children to the Neverland, he gets so caught up in the pleasure of flying that he leaves them to lose their way and, without his help, to plummet to earth, though he saves them at the last second. Peter forgets the name of his archenemy Hook almost as soon as he's killed him and, for a moment, taken his place. He forgets his companionable fairy Tinkerbell, the one who saves *him*. He forgets Wendy herself for entire years, when he fails to return to fetch her for spring cleaning. (If Peter simply *is* our childhood, as a student once wrote to me, it's partly because he offers an image of how our childhood can seem to forget or abandon *us*.) Peter even forgets, to his cost, what Barrie says actual children never forget, their first experience of being treated unjustly by adults, so that he feels each new betrayal with fresh force—as when, trying to give his enemy the chance for a fair fight on Marooner's rock, he finds the hook-hand striking him again and again, leaving him unable to swim or fly away, and so in danger of drowning when the rising tide sweeps over the rock. (Luckily, he's rescued by the Never bird, that image of fierce maternal care, who gives him her nest to float home in.)

Peter has only one unshakable memory. As he tells it to the other children, this is the picture of finding his mother, after his early flights away from home, nursing a new child, with the nursery window barred against his return. "I am not sure that this was true," writes Barrie, "but Peter thought it was true; and it scared them." That image of maternal forgetting, whether authentic or imaginary, marks the power of Peter's thought (there are some stories he *can* tell), even as it refutes all of Wendy's reassurances to the lost boys about the absolute devotion of mothers.

Barrie gives us Peter as a being, a will to play, caught ambiguously in the folds of time. Peter speaks to some idea of childhood that survives growing up. He also calls up the thought of a childishness abandoned or left behind. It's childhood as an object of fear as well as longing, partly in seeming a childishness stalled in time. So Keith Miller writes of the "dark shadows" he sees in *Peter Pan*, not so much shadows relating to "the careless violence of child's play," rather those that belong to a childishness at once frozen and lost, the twin threats of "both endless childhood and unleavened adulthood as a living death."

I think here of two actual deaths in the author's life, and of how he takes them in, makes something of them. Barrie's older brother David died just before his fourteenth birthday, after fracturing his skull in a skating accident. As he tells the story in his memoir of his mother, *Margaret Ogilvy*, published in 1896, Barrie traces his emergent ambitions as storyteller to his boyhood attempts, at age six, to take on his dead brother's manners and voice in order to console his mother for a loss she seems never to have overcome. The story fixes the thought that the boy who won't grow up is the boy who *cannot* grow up, the child who has died young, a child whose place in memory is always suffused with pain, even as his life becomes the focus of a kind of desperate, imitative play. The matter of a blocked growing up, again tied to a strange vision of survival, recurs in a notebook entry of Barrie's. It's the record of a dream the sixty-two-year-old writer had on November 7, 1922, of his much-beloved Michael Llewelyn-Davies, the brilliant boy he had watched grow up with his four brothers, boys whose play Barrie animated and organized, and drew on for the fable of Peter Pan, children whom he would come to adopt after the deaths of their parents.*

---

* Andrew Birkin's *J. M. Barrie and the Lost Boys*, first published in 1979, is still the best exploration of Barrie's complex relationship with Arthur and Sylvia Llewelyn-Davies and their five sons, George, John, Peter, Michael, and Nico, and of how this relationship shaped and came to be shaped and haunted by what Peter Llewelyn-Davies would call, as an adult, "that terrible masterpiece" *Peter Pan*. I won't try to summarize Birkin's

Michael had died a year and a half earlier, on May 19, 1921, at age twenty, drowned with a friend in a pool near Oxford—it was officially judged an accident, though some who knew him thought it might have been a suicide. In Barrie's dream, Michael has come back to him not knowing he'd drowned. Barrie, within the dream, works to keep the knowledge from him, feeling "that this so to speak was vital to his life," ghostlike yet mortal as Michael is. They go on together sadly for another year, with Michael increasingly aware of what had happened, until the time when Michael is to be drowned again the next day, the anniversary of his death. At this point "each knew the other knew but still we didn't speak of it." Barrie can't save him, and the two walk together back to the pool. In some notes he added for a possible story based on the dream, drawing out its sad strangeness, Barrie reflects, "It is as if long after writing 'P. Pan' its true meaning came to me—Desperate attempt to grow up but can't."

Peter is a victim of time as well as a creature who defeats time, who survives its losses. There's a moment late in the novel when he indeed becomes an image of time itself, of its ongoing, relentless, unknowable passage, its menace. While silently stalking through the woods of the Neverland, on his way to challenge Hook, Peter finds himself followed by the hand-devouring crocodile, Hook's other nemesis. The clock that the beast had swallowed, and whose ticking always warned the pirate of its approach, has finally run down (a possibility that had haunted Hook, as he admits to Smee, his loyal first mate). In an impulse to im-

study, with its many eerie, affecting, and tragic turns, including his careful account of how stories of Peter Pan first emerged in games of pirates and "wrecked islands" that Barrie played with the boys. ("I suppose I always knew I made Peter by rubbing the five of you violently together, as savages with two sticks produce a flame"—so Barrie wrote in "To the Five," his dedication to the 1928 published text of Peter Pan, written when two of the brothers were no longer alive.) But given her part in my chapters, I'd quote something that Elizabeth Bowen wrote of Barrie in a 1941 review of the first full biography, by De-nis Mackail: "It is apparent that Barrie existed in a hyper-personal, highly charged atmosphere of charm and pain, and that with every year of his life the temperature round him rose; that to inspire him was to become his victim, and, at the same time, to be unwilling assistant at his tortuous victimization of himself. For actors in Barrie's personal drama there was only one possible exit: death. The drama had the mysterious compulsions, the subjectivity, and, to an extent, the pathology of a dream."

itative play of which he's unconscious, Peter takes over the lost sound, ticking and ticking as he moves along in the undergrowth, clock and croc at once. He ticks relentlessly, "superbly," as he approaches the pirate ship. The sound sends Hook into shuddering, infantile, solitary terror.

JAMES MATTHEW BARRIE was studious of ghosts, their fright and charm, as he was studious of his and our sentimentalities. More skeptic than spiritualist, he knew like Henry James that our ghosts tell something about our life in time. Barrie brought together the ghost of a child and the ghost of a mother in his late play of 1920, *Mary Rose*, a work that offers kind of a coda to the fable of Peter Pan. Here a young mother returns as if from the dead, twenty years after a belated honeymoon, when she had disappeared while visiting a mysterious Scottish island with her husband and young son. It's an island full of uncanny calls and noises, also the place where, we learn, Mary Rose had been lost years earlier as a young child, for twenty *days*. (She was both times perhaps kidnapped by the island itself, whose name in Gaelic means "the island that likes to be visited.") Still the oddly naive, childish young woman that she'd been at the time of her second disappearance, Mary Rose yet finds herself haunted in her return to the present, haunted by her uncertain memories of an earlier life, by the spectacle of a world that has so changed around her, by the aged, astonished faces of her husband and parents (for whom she is herself like a ghost). She's haunted most by the thought of her lost son, whom she'd only known as an infant—we learn that, as a motherless youth, the boy ran away from home, never to be heard of again. Thus haunted, thus lonely, thus abandoned, Mary Rose comes herself to haunt the house to which she's returned, outliving parents and husband. She dwells there as an impish specter, an angry child-spirit, driving away all prospective buyers of a house now emptied of its former lives.

The only person who can lay to rest the troubled ghost is her son, a soldier and war veteran, who returns in peacetime to revisit the place where he'd spent his earliest years. Mary Rose never understands that this kindly visitor *is* her son, who is now older than his mother at the time she disappeared. But the son comes to know who she is, and something in his knowledge, in his gentle sympathy for her ("I dare say, to a timid thing, being a ghost is worse than seeing them"), frees the ghost to quit the house at the close of the play, absorbed by a music like that of the island where twice before she'd disappeared.

It's hard to catch the eerie, creepy delicacy of the play. The figure of Mary Rose bears within herself, even more closely than Peter, the loss, fright, and loneliness of not growing up. To her parents, she was and continues to be like a creature who has "never really been born," to use the phrase that so caught Samuel Beckett in C. G. Jung's description of one of his patients. Or she's like a being come into the world "before its time"—that's what the nameless speaker of Beckett's *Not I*, a mouth suspended in darkness, says of the woman whose history she recounts, in truth speaking of herself. The sense of being both in and out of time is here part of the loneliness of ghosts. "Please, I don't want to be a ghost any more" says the ghost of this childish mother to her unrecognized adult son, hoping that he has power to help her. Alfred Hitchcock, who saw Barrie's play in its original production, long wanted to make a film of *Mary Rose*, though he never got further than the draft of a screenplay.

THE GHOSTLIEST PICTURE in *Peter and Wendy* of what it might mean to look back at a lost happiness, real or imagined, is given to us filtered through Peter's gaze, rather than any adult's. It comes toward the end of the book. When the Darling children steal home from the Neverland, led by Wendy with the lost boys in tow, Peter flies ahead of them to their house in London. With Tinkerbell's help, he locks the nursery window to prevent their reentry. Yet he can't keep from watching Mrs. Darling through the glass: "'It's Wendy's mother! She is a pretty lady, but not so pretty as my mother. Her mouth is full of thimbles, but not so full as my mother's was.'... Of course, he knew nothing whatever about his mother.... He skipped about and made funny faces, but when he stopped it was just as if she were inside him, knocking.'"* At this

---

* "Her mouth is full of thimbles"—by "thimbles" Peter means "kisses." The doubling of thimbles and kisses goes back to the start of the story. Tempting her to come with him, Peter declares that "one girl is more use than twenty boys":

moment, the children's mother haunts *him*. In an impulse that mingles pity and rage, Peter unlocks the window so that the returning travelers can enter. Barrie paints for us Mrs. Darling's surprise at their impossible restoration, and then the scene of her being joyfully enveloped by her children: "There could not have been a lovelier sight; but there was none to see it except a little boy who was staring in at the window. He had ecstasies innumerable that other children can never know; but he was looking through the window at the one joy from which he must be for ever barred." There's something of terror in this, as well as sadness. There's a privilege that figures in it, in the report of Peter's myriad, unknown ecstasies, and in his being there alone to watch. But he's also a hungry, solitary ghost, a spirit caught in a kind of purgatory, suspended in time, this visitation repeating the scene of his earlier, always-recalled exclusion from his own mother's hearth. Here the gaze of the dangerous child mirrors the adult's gaze outward into other lives and backward into one's own. The barred window cuts across time as well as space.

This is not the end, however. In the novel's last chapter—based on a one-act sequel that Barrie wrote in 1908 for the play *Peter Pan*, a piece performed only once in his lifetime—Peter returns to the house many years later, after a long absence. "And then one night came the tragedy," Barrie says. The boy finds Wendy grown up and with a child of her own, a daughter named Jane, a girl who revels in her mother's stories of the Neverland. Wendy at first huddles by the fire, "not daring to move, helpless and guilty, a big woman," gazing at *un*grown Peter, who still has all his first teeth. "Something inside her was crying 'Woman, woman, let go of me.'" Facing this woman who now rises up to reveal herself, the boy is caught by a fear that he has never felt before. "What is it?" he cries. And then again "What is it?" That "it" is his unknown fear, which includes, I think, fear of time itself, now assuming the shape of Wendy's

---

[Wendy] said she would give him a kiss if he liked, but Peter did not know what she meant, and he held out his hand expectantly.

"Surely you know what a kiss is?" she asked, aghast.

"I shall know when you give it to me," he replied stiffly, and not to hurt his feelings she gave him a thimble.

grown-up body. Peter makes for a moment to strike Wendy's daughter, then breaks down into sobs. These sobs cease when, left alone with Jane, he finds that he can charm this child as he had charmed the girl Wendy, teaching her to fly about the room "in solemn ecstasy." "It was already her easiest way of moving about," Wendy sees when she returns. Her gift of love to her daughter, perhaps to Peter, is to let Jane go with him to the Neverland each year, to help with spring cleaning.

The novel ends by joining a gaze forward and a gaze backward, by joining enchantment and disenchantment:

> As you look at Wendy you may see her hair becoming white, and her figure little again, for all this happened long ago. Jane is now a common grown-up, with a daughter called Margaret; and every spring-cleaning time, except when he forgets, Peter comes for Margaret and takes her to the Neverland, where she tells him stories about himself, to which he listens eagerly. When Margaret grows up she will have a daughter, who is to be Peter's mother in turn; and so it will go on, so long as children are gay and innocent and heartless.

I always hear, at the close, an echo of Shakespeare's eighteenth sonnet, with its evocation of a secular immortality: "So long as men can breathe or eyes can see, / So long lives this, and this gives life to thee." But there's a more uncanny chill in Barrie's vision of things ongoing. The passage's sentimentality mixes, as one critic writes, with "a Beckettian flatness and abstraction," a deathly quickening. "Margaret" was the name of Barrie's dead mother, one recalls. And the closing triplet—"gay and innocent and heartless"—casts an ambivalent spell. The words are at once a promise and a gamble, a cry against time. They might be a blessing, and yet I often hear in them a curious animus, a sense of fear, even the air of a curse, if not a slander of childhood. Each word in that triplet bears its own fierce ambiguity, including those *and*s. The innocent in this book can be cruel enough, as well as alien. The careless gaiety of these children includes sorrow and fear. The last word, "heartless," is placed so as to break in surprise against the (seemingly) milder pair "gay and innocent." It has a certain bravado, but also its own kind of grown-up heartlessness. It's an adult's word for that in children which knows nothing of adult hearts, nothing of adult loves and sorrows and responsibilities and hopes, a lack that adults may regard with both affection and fear. That "heartless" also calls out to what's hidden in the child's all-too-powerful heart. It names things in the hearts of children that adults cannot or will not know, or that they needfully forget.

ODRADEK

... flat star-shaped spool... small wooden crossbar... upright as if on two legs... broken-off bits of thread, knotted and tangled together... senseless enough, but in its own way perfectly finished... extraordinarily nimble and can never be laid hold of... leaning directly beneath you against the banisters... rather like a child... "No fixed abode"... laughter that has no lungs behind it... rustling of fallen leaves... stays mute for a long time... rolling down the stairs, with ends of thread trailing after... no harm to anyone... likely to survive...

While I read Franz Kafka's "The Cares of a Family Man" (Die Sorge des Hausvaters, published in 1919), while its sentences run in my head, I simply *am* Odradek, the creature whose life the tale gives us, that small being who wanders in the house, solitary, free to leave and return— through what doors or cracks we never know—hiding and showing itself as it wishes (if it has wishes), a fragile yet indestructible thing. As I read, I share Odradek's quick energy, its carelessness, even glee, the play of its motion, purposeless as it is, an activity in which Odradek is player and plaything at once. (I sometimes call my wandering cat "Odradek.") It is a creature of strangest gravity, rolling up and down the stairs of the house, still for at most a moment, sleepless, a thing that "can never be laid hold of."

Odradek is like an orphan child, an unbegotten child, a child that does not grow up, a child that will not itself have children though it moves about at children's feet, at home in the world of children, whether they see it or not, whether they play with it or not. Odradek can seem like something *made* by a devious or clumsy child, or like a toy in a children's game whose rules have been lost. Odradek is more at home in the house than its owner. Indeed, it makes this *Hausvater*, this "head of household"—a more idiomatic translation than "family man"—feel homeless in his home, this man who tries to decipher this thing and its name, to speak to it, who tries to place its past and future history, partly to fix his own fear.

Childlike as Odradek is, it, or he (the pronouns change halfway through the story) is also an old spirit, a ghostly thing, though a ghost impossible to lay to rest. Tiny, a bit tricksterish or clown-like, Odradek suggests an entity that belongs to the order of gnomes, elves, fairies, and imps, though he's part of no nation or species, or rather he's a species of one, or the only survivor of the destruction of a species. He's neither helpful nor harmful, steals nothing, repairs nothing, does no human work. He's an object, a humanly made thing, and yet a living creature. He's a thing of fragments, embryonic or inchoate, also a strange whole—as if a small volcanic eruption had fused alien elements into a new entity. Is he the marred creation of an incompetent or vicious god? Was he once a human being, like Gregor Samsa, who discovers himself turned into an insect? Or a visitor, like the ghost of Hamlet's father, from some suspect purgatory? He's like other one-of-a-kind creatures that populate Kafka's stories—the anxious burrower, the curious lamb-kitten, the beast that haunts the synagogue—of whom Walter Benjamin writes, "There is not one that is not either rising or falling, none that is not trading qualities with its enemy or neighbor, none that has not completed its period of time and yet is unripe, none that is not deeply exhausted and yet is only at the beginning of a long existence."

What does Odradek know of the house he inhabits? He knows its hidden corners, the back shelves of closets. He knows the abysses of the house, its small labyrinths, its sacred spaces and spaces of play, spaces forgotten or never seen. Odradek knows the crevices between the floorboards where an old ring is lodged, or a coin from an unknown country, a pencil stub, the shard of a broken pot. He regards the beautiful clump of dust under the bed, and the long-searched-for shoe. He studies the crumpled note at the back of a drawer, the forgotten photograph, the useless identity card issued decades ago in a foreign city. Odradek has seen the withered apple core that lodges behind the stove, and the sprung mousetrap and the corpse of the mouse, even the corpse's shadow. He keeps company with the living mouse and spider who work in the dark. He knows the leaky pipe, the invisible crack in an outer wall, and the breath of wind that passes inside, moving from room to room. He watches the escaped marble, the dropped puzzle piece, the broken limb of a wooden soldier, the lost key for winding up the clockwork bird. (Odradek, one scholar writes, both "is and is not a *dreydl*," the four-sided top used in Hannukah games.) He keeps company with things slipped out of history, abandoned, marked as useless. "The child," says J. H. Van den Berg, "knows that the little things deserve attention; he picks up our adult shreds and scraps and hands them to us—we do not know what to do with them, we smile about it and brush them from our trousers, suspecting vaguely that this gesture compromises the ordination of things." Odradek is himself that compromising gesture, the shameful sign of a different ordination of things. He marks the shame we may feel at our forgotten tasks, our lost or unexplored gestures and powers.

If Odradek knows the hidden spaces of the housefather's abode, he may also know what lies in the back of my own head-house. He knows things lifeless and secretly alive, deathless, puzzle pieces stuck in the gray corners of my memory. He finds out old thoughts, untried ways of seeing the world, banished and buried compulsions, childish fears, or those fears I call childish, also the clichés, fixed ideas, and inert metaphors that shape my thinking. A squatter in the unoccupied apartments of my mind, he knows the things I stumble upon in the dark. He is an image of the odd life of those things, things unmapped, unnamable, things to which I can scarcely bear relation, keeping them at bay with a stranger courtesy.*

---

* I think here of something Kafka wrote in a 1904 letter to his friend Max Brod: "Whereas we are usually polite enough not to want to know anything about any insight

If I am Odradek as I read, I am as much the one who speaks the tale, the man who tries to describe this being with such urgent precision, though he is always a little behind in this work. Odradek is this man's unknown future as well as his unknown past. The narrator's voice suggests by turns the voice of a philologist, archaeologist, zoologist, rabbi, and police detective, also the voice of the insurance lawyer Franz Kafka, someone who studies the safety of bodies in factories and quarries, the risks to humans that are created by the machines that humans make. He begins with an account of fruitless debates over an unaccountable *word*: "Some say the word Odradek is of Slavonic origin, and try to account for it on that basis. Others again believe it to be of German origin, only influenced by Slavonic. The uncertainty of both interpretations allows one to assume with justice that neither is accurate, especially as neither of them provides an intelligent meaning of the word." The slightly comic voice of the baffled scholar turns more sharply strange when the unknown word turns out to be a *name*, the name of a being who is made visible by these very equivocal researches, even as they seem precisely to depend on that being: "No one, of course, would occupy himself with such studies if there were not a creature called Odradek." Some Kafka scholars think the name derives, ironically enough, from the Czech verb *odradit*, meaning to deter or discourage someone's interest or pleasure in something, even to the point of estrangement.

Part of the force of Kafka's story lies in the narrator's accepting Odradek's existence so plainly. He accepts him as one might accept that there are pine trees and clouds in the world, that the world contains doors, clocks, dogs, and teacups. Yet his attempts to explain Odradek to himself are a trial. His investigations remain inconclusive, he's self-critical, full of curious bafflements, temptations and disappointments. His arcane courtesy toward this mysterious creature is combined with a kind pettish rage. His words project a fear that becomes itself a little uncanny:

---

into ourselves, we now weaken to some extent and go seeking it, although in the same manner as when we pretend to be trying hard to catch up with little children who are toddling slowly in front of us. We burrow through ourselves like a mole and emerge blackened and velvet-haired from our sandy underground vaults, our poor little red feet stretched out for tender pity."

At first glance it looks like a flat star-shaped spool for thread, and indeed it does seem to have thread wound upon it; to be sure, they are only old, broken-off bits of thread, knotted and tangled together, of the most varied sorts and colors. But it is not only a spool, for a small wooden cross-bar sticks out of the middle of the star, and another small rod is joined to that at a right angle. By means of this latter rod on one side and one of the points of the star on the other, the whole thing can stand upright as if on two legs. One is tempted to believe that the creature once had some sort of intelligible shape and is now only a broken-down remnant. Yet this does not seem to be the case; at least there is no sign of it; nowhere is there an unfinished or broken surface to suggest anything of the kind; the whole thing looks senseless enough, but in its own way perfectly finished.

Each attempt to describe Odradek, to give him a human use or shape, comes thwarted: "at first glance it looks like... indeed... to be sure... but it is not only... one is tempted to believe... yet this does not seem to be the case... at least." The work of describing Odradek, for all its concrete detail, makes him the more hallucinatory. An anthropoid entity, he stands on two legs, even if one leg is of different shape and substance from the other. Yet these may be only imaginary limbs, since he only stands "as if" on two legs. Is Odradek all prosthesis, all crutch? His erect human posture is almost accidental, and in moving he's said to roll rather than walk, like a wheel or a top. Even if Odradek does have legs, you can't place his arms or hands, or know where to find his face, his ears and eyes, mouth.

Odradek is more like a skeleton than a body, though a skeleton that can never have had any flesh around it. With his wooden points and rods, his dangling strings, Odradek can seem like the remnant of a marionette cut free of its controls, like unstrung Pinocchio. He's also like a marionette's broken and severed control mechanism, the cross-like assemblage of wood through which, as an extension of the hand of the living puppeteer, human motion and gesture are translated into the dead figure. Such is the odd condition of Odradek's freedom. And the strings are not simply "old, broken-off," but "of the most varied sorts and colors," strings not only to move puppets but to fasten packages,

to sew on buttons, to measure out a garden bed, or to tie around a finger. The broken strings are like antennae, sensitive nerves, organs for
taking the measure of the air, of light and sound, light as dust. They
are always "trailing after him" like a mysterious tail, the interrupted or
tangled-up threads of stories, conversations, and lives. Odradek is not
a toy, tool, ornament, fetish, or sacred object, yet he mirrors aspects
of all of these. In Odradek, Kafka shows us lost *moments* in the history of such objects, what they look like when they've dropped out of
use, knowledge, play, or ownership. They remain soaked in time, but
time lost, suspended between living and dead. "Oblivion," writes Benjamin, "is the container from which the inexhaustible intermediate
world in Kafka's stories presses toward to the light.... Odradek is the
form which things assume in oblivion." It's an oblivion that is yet full
of "countless uncertain and changing compounds, yielding a constant
flow of new, strange products," an oblivion that collaborates with the
possibility of redemption, since it gives us creatures in which we may
encounter the lost forms of our own existence on earth. In his essay on
the marionette theater, the poet Dennis Silk asks, "If a cross is a witness, why not a loaf of bread, or a shoe-tree, or a sugar-tongs, or a piece
of string?"

   As Odradek assumes a shape in my mind, he often seems the dream
form of the letter K. He's Kafka's attempt to give creaturely, three-
dimensional substance to that angular, two-dimensional letter, written
or printed, not the plain K as it might appear on a child's wooden letter block or in a child's alphabet book, but a letter that has become unrecognizable, singular, uprooted, ecstatic, both more and less than a
letter, a letter with no place in the order of an alphabet, or the sole survivor of an alphabet that's been lost. It's a letter removed by some crisis from history and human use, even as it seems all-too-deeply caught
inside history's mad accidents, inscribed or scribbled on its temples.

   Kafka rejected his publisher's idea of putting an image of the insect
body of Gregor Samsa on the cover of *Metamorphosis*: "Not that, please
not that!... The insect itself cannot be depicted." He'd have hated as
much any attempt to draw Odradek, were the artist Paul Klee or Hier-
onymus Bosch. Yet if there had to be such a picture, I wonder whether
you could do better than one of Kafka's own handwritten Ks. "I find Ks

ugly, almost repugnant," Kafka wrote in his diary in 1914, "and yet I keep on writing them; they must be very characteristic of myself."*

Odradek's name makes no more sense than his shape. Yet the housefather persuades himself that this thing-letter-creature does speak a human language, even if he's no ready talker: "Often he stays mute for a long time, as wooden as his appearance." Or as Michael Hofmann renders the German, "as silent as the wood he seems to be fashioned from"—*seems* to be, as if his woodenness were more an idea or impression than a fact, something to lend substance to his silence. Perhaps to compensate for his failure to describe him, the man invites us to imagine asking Odradek to give some account of himself. "You treat him—he is so diminutive that you cannot help it—rather like a child," so the questions are simple ones: "'Well, what's your name?' you ask him. 'Odradek,' he says. 'And where do you live?' 'No fixed abode,' he says and laughs."

The first of Odradek's answers is plain enough, though I can imagine that this creature is in truth nameless, and makes up his name on the spur of the moment, a bit of nonsense speech to catch his questioner, keep him at bay. More curious is the answer to the question of where he lives: "No fixed abode," *Unbestimmter Wohnsitz*, or more literally "undefined living place." Odradek's answer evades the question even as it mocks the questioner's pretense of innocence. The narrator insists that he talks to this being as if he were a child. But his response is not in the language of a child. "No fixed abode" may speak of Odradek's

---

* The letter K is all we know of the last name of Josef K in *The Trial*, often called simply K, as is the surveyor in *The Castle*. In German, K is the first letter of *Kind* (child), *Kunst* (art), *kaputt* (broken), *Krise* (crisis), *klein* (small), *kein* (no, not), and *König* (king). The doubled letters k. k. appear often in Kafka's "office writings" for the Prague Workman's Accident Insurance Institute before 1918—they're an abbreviation for the words *Kaiserliches und koenigliches* (Imperial and Royal) in the titles of official entities in the Austro-Hungarian empire, variously objects of trust and distrust for Kafka, such as the "k. k. Ministry of the Interior," the "k. k. Administrative Court," or the "k. k. trade inspectorate." In Czech, K is the first letter of *kavka*, jackdaw or crow, a bird about which Kafka writes this parable: "The crows like to insist a single crow is enough to destroy heaven. This is incontestably true, but it says nothing about heaven, because heaven is just another way of saying: the impossibility of crows." Odradek might be what a crow looks like from the perspective of heaven.

essential, metaphysical placelessness or exile, a condition of both freedom and fear. There is no house, city, or temple that owns Odradek.
(Some readers have heard in this answer echoes of Kafka's own vexed
sense of his place in Jewish tradition.) In this he unfixes the place of the
housefather himself. The words also echo the jargon of a police report,
they're what might be said of a vagrant or a criminal. "No fixed abode"
is like a piece of official language that Odradek turns back on his questioner, as if to say, write down *that* in your report. His answer suggests
that this childish being has other words available to him, a larger and
less innocent lexicon, than his questioner imagines.

"'No fixed abode,' he says, and laughs." At what is Odradek laughing?
At the questioner's mistaking him for an innocent child? At his need to
ask such useless questions? Or is Odradek laughing at his own answers,
his childish games of evasion? As this questioner hears it, that laughter has "no lungs behind it," and thus, one supposes, no heart (though
you can't be sure of that, it may be a failure in the listener). The conversation comes to an end all too quickly, as frustrating as Alice's talks
with the difficult inhabitants of Wonderland. Are there questions that
the questioner is himself afraid to ask? Are there answers he wouldn't
want to hear, unknown histories or affiliations this creature might reveal? Is he afraid that Odradek might, in some twist of courtesy, turn
his questions back on him, and so make *him* like a child, asking What
is *your* name? Where do *you* live? In *The Castle*, when the surveyor K is
finally able to speak by telephone to the seats of power, what he hears
are sounds like "the humming of countless childlike voices," or rather
"the singing of the most distant, of the most utterly distant, voices," incomprehensible yet siren-like.

"It is only the kind of laughter that has no lungs behind it. It sounds
rather like the rustling of fallen leaves." That's not just dead sound, or
the sound of death or soullessness. It's the sound of fallen leaves with
their startling and dull colors, their curling edges, leaves that can look
like flowers or fire, that are gathered in piles, burned, scattered by playing children, or caught by the moving and living wind, leaves that are
a part of the dead and living world *outside* the house. They're leaves
that mat the ground in winter, that burn with what Robert Frost called
"the slow smokeless burning of decay," feeding the plants around them.

Or like the leaves that the naked, shipwrecked Odysseus piles around himself to stay warm in sleep, working (as Homer's simile frames it) like the ashes that a man alone in a field banks around glowing coals, saving the seed of fire. Or like the "skeleton leaves" that Peter wears, or the leaves that Alice's sister brushes from the sleeping child's face. They are also the leaves that Homer, Virgil, and Dante make metaphors for the souls of the dead, and that Percy Shelley, in his "Ode to the West Wind," makes an image of dead *words* that he asks to be scattered like sparks among mankind, leaves sibylline, prophetic. The "rattling of leaves," one scholar imagines, is among the small sounds of life that break the silence attending the grotesque execution described in Kafka's story "In the Penal Colony." As in English, the German for "leaves" in Kafka, *Blättern*, can also mean the leaves of books, the leaves of a tradition that to this questioner seems lungless, spiritless, but may only await a stranger resurrection in other mouths. In Rainer Maria Rilke's "Autumn," leaves fall "with gestures that say 'no.'" Wallace Stevens in "The Course of a Particular" hears leaves in winter sounding with "a busy cry, concerning someone else... not a cry of divine attention, / Nor the smoke-drift of puffed-out heroes, nor human cry."

"I ask myself, to no purpose, what is likely to happen to him? Can he possibly die? Anything that dies has had some kind of aim in life, some kind of activity, which has worn out." By a logic that has its own childishness, the father of the house answers his purposeless question by insisting that Odradek's very lack of a purpose guarantees his survival. This conclusion leaves Odradek with a power to resist death, a magical endowment, that has no apparent meaning. It's as if Odradek's form of survival challenged the speaker's own unvoiced desire not to die, reminding us that we don't really know what immortality looks like. Or that we cannot recognize what in ourselves is "indestructible," something that, as Kafka writes in one of his "Zürau Aphorisms," may stay forever concealed from us even though we cannot live without a steady faith in it. Odradek's existence suggests we don't even know what purposes are, he being a creature with too much as well as too little purpose, or only the remnant of a purpose. Or he has only that "more or less silent, persistent, secret" purpose that Kafka sensed in the mice who burrowed behind the walls of his room in his sister Ottla's house, in the rural Bohemian village of Zürau, where he stayed for eight months in 1917–18 after he had been diagnosed with tuberculosis. (It was there that he wrote the "Zürau Aphorisms.") Their "unexpected, uninvited, inescapable" presence terrified him—though he tried to make love to their sounds in his last story, "Josephine the Singer, or The Mouse Folk."

The energy that drives this thing-creature-child makes it the shifting, opaque form of the housefather's own fear, a fear never spoken directly in the story itself. It might be fear of life as much as fear of death, fear of the uncanniness of life, a life at once finished and unfinished. Or it's a fear of acknowledging that life, a fear of life's demand that we somehow become responsible for it. (In another of the Zürau aphorisms, Kafka describes idolatry, the human habit of lending of life and will to lifeless things, as something that takes shape from our fear of those things, and of the vast responsibility we owe them.) So Odradek would be mocking the housefather not in the guise of a *memento mori*, like Yorick's skull, but as a *memento vitae*, a form of life that can't be mourned, that makes mourning impossible. He's the substance of an ongoing life that floats free of clear purpose or design, yet is bound to an endless movement, up and down, above and below ground, inside and outside the house, an "inexorable nexus of centrifugal and centripetal motions," as Roberto Calasso writes, free of the momentum and the inertia that rule in ordinary objects, moving always "on the threshold of a hidden world that one suspects is implicit in this world." Odradek is a life and a lifelessness inside life, a form of fate that the novelist Imre Kertész called "fatelessness."

"He does no harm to anyone that one can see," the narrator says of Odradek. He is literally *innocens*, "harmless," as well as invulnerable. It is an uncanny innocence, a challenge to inherited pictures of innocence. The speaker sounds almost bitter in not being able to accuse Odradek of some harm, as if this were itself a source of harm to the speaker: "He does no harm to anyone that one can see; but the idea that he is likely to survive me I find almost painful." *Almost* painful, as if he can't quite bear to acknowledge the pain, or to know it *as* pain. Is it the pain of the writer who imagines that his work will survive, while he himself, as living person, does not? Or is it anyone's sorrow or jealousy at thinking that the world doesn't die when the self dies? Odradek's is a survival without the pathos or aura of survival, without mourning or praise to keep the dead alive, to acknowledge and consecrate their death. "Indestructible" Odradek may be, but it's a minimal, a starved, a poor immortality, hard to cling to—like the shame that threatens to survive Joseph K at the end of *The Trial*. It's as much a point of origin as an ending. A childishness not to be outlived.

"Am I to suppose, then, that he will always be rolling down the stairs... right before the feet of my children, and my children's children?" With breathtaking freedom, Kafka takes over the prophetic formula for blessing in the Hebrew Bible, the gift of continued life, the promise of a fulfilled covenant, as in Ezekiel 37:25: "And they shall dwell in the land that I have given unto Jacob My servant, wherein your fathers dwelt; and they shall dwell therein, they, and their children, and their children's children, for ever; and David My servant shall be their prince for ever." Whatever blessing of life Odradek bears, it's not something to be possessed or known, nothing that will become a place of dwelling, a literal or figurative "house," he remains rather a troubler of houses and housefathers, perpetual servant and perpetual prince, perpetual child and perpetual father, or none of these. Odradek is a troubler of blessing, hard to distinguish from a curse, a curse not uttered by God but sifted into the nature of things.

Another passage from Kafka's diary, from 1921: "It's entirely conceivable that life's splendor surrounds us all, and always in its complete fullness, accessible but veiled, beneath the surface, invisible, far away. But there it lies—not hostile, not reluctant, not deaf. If we call it by the right word, by the right name, then it comes. This is the essence of magic, which doesn't create but calls." Odradek is one among the right names for the hidden and all-too-present splendors of the world, a way of calling to what in the world is indestructible and also fragile, uncontrollable and as close as our skin.

EMILY

TEN-YEAR-OLD EMILY BAS-THORNTON stabs the bound man over and over. ("There is something much more frightening about a man who is tied up than a man who is not tied up.") No one hears her cries on the almost empty pirate schooner, its sails dropped in midocean. He doesn't die of any single wound, it's the blood he loses from many small cuts, made by the knife with which he'd hoped to cut his own ropes. The man's last words are in Dutch—"But, Gentlemen, I have a wife and children!"—to Emily a babble that only terrifies her more. She acts as if in a dream and then falls back delirious onto the captain's bed. That narrow space in a solitary cabin has been her home for weeks. She's been slowly recovering from a wound caused by a falling marlinspike (a sailor's tool for splicing rope), a dangerous object that her sister Rachel had imagined as a beloved infant and carried up into the rigging.

Soon after the death, some of the crew discover an older girl, Margaret, sitting near the cabin door, with her "small, skull-like face," staring blankly at the corpse. They decide that she and not the now unconscious Emily is the murderer. They drop her without a word into the sea, "their eyes opened to a depravity of human nature they had not dreamt of." Margaret, "swimming desperately, but in complete silence," is rescued by a boat full of other children—they're returning to the schooner after watching an impromptu entertainment staged on the deck of a captive steamer, whose captain is the dead man. The pirates had discovered a cargo of circus animals, and set a starving and seasick tiger to fight with a seasick, starving lion.

These scenes unfold about two-thirds of the way through Richard Hughes's *A High Wind in Jamaica*. The tangle of fear, violence, and vicious error takes us a great distance from an earlier glimpse of Emily in the opening pages of the novel. This is a more quietly mysterious moment, set in a place the child knows as home. We see her on a day of immense heat sitting up to her neck "for coolness" in a forest pool, shadowed by trees, thinking vaguely of her upcoming birthday party. Unseen below the water's surface, "hundreds of infant fish were tickling with their inquisitive mouths every inch of her body, a sort of expressionless light kissing," a feeling that transfixes her and that she finds almost unbearable. Death and fear also have their place in this scene, but mixed with a strange kind of play. A poor man has not long ago drowned in this pool, one of the black inhabitants of the island where the white child Emily lives with her parents. She and her siblings keep alive the story that the dead man's "duppy," or ghost, lurks there, so as to scare away the superstitious and keep possession of the pool for themselves.

We are on the island of Jamaica in the decades following "the Emancipation" in 1834, when slavery was abolished. Hughes's novel—first published in 1929 under the title *The Innocent Voyage*—makes the child's home a ruined and ruinous Eden, no pristine, paradisical place of origin but an island soaked in time, already fallen, like the nameless island in Shakespeare's *The Tempest*. It's a place where the natural world, in Hughes's lyrical, often hallucinatory descriptions, is chaotic, infectious, parasitic, and violent, full of fear as well as unsettling luxury. The island's plants seem always set to choke each other, deathly in their florid life. The ruins of a human history—a humanly inhuman history—also lie tangled within that destructive growth. The landscape is full of the traces of the abandoned slave economy: "ruined slaves' quarters, ruined sugar-grinding houses, ruined boiling houses; often ruined mansions that were too expensive to maintain. Earthquake, fire, rain, and deadlier vegetation, did their work quickly."

Hughes does not go into detail about the legalized terror and daily, entrenched violence that sustained the vastly profitable slave system in

British-ruled Jamaica. He scarcely touches on the long history of resistance and rebellion among those enslaved. It is rather the anarchic, destructive, and re-creative forces of weather and the natural world that seem unknowingly to carry through the "work" of revolution and reform, even of divine punishment—though in Hughes's descriptions, such forces can evoke the violence of masters as much as the rage against them. And then the ruinous actions of the weather also collaborate with the work of forgetting history. What we see of human wrong comes mainly through the uncertain witness of these settler children. It's there in the ruthless way the children protect their possession of that forest pool. It's there also when Emily, on a far walk, stumbles into a village of Maroons, or free blacks, descendants of those who'd escaped enslavement, living in the island's mountainous interior. The solitary white child finds a cruel fascination in becoming for the black children she first encounters an object of fear and wonder.*

Within the upended plantation economy, small groups of white and Creole planters and merchants hang on across the island, including

---

* The peripatetic Hughes worked on this novel—his first—in Wales, Venice, Morocco, and the United States, but never visited Jamaica or any part of the Caribbean until many years later. He used a range of published sources to ground his pictures of Jamaican geography, history, and culture in early chapters. As important as these, he acknowledged, were stories told him by his mother, Louisa Grace Warren Hughes (1870–1950), herself a writer, who had lived on the island as a young child from ages of three to eight, Hughes recapturing her already distant memories for his own strange purposes. It's perhaps no surprise that, as the Jamaican novelist and scholar Jean D'Costa wrote to me of the book, "so much of the detail of flora, fauna, landscape, people, cultural mood is absolutely inaccurate" (such that she could not bear to finish it). A High Wind in Jamaica is not a novel like Jean Rhys's 1966 The Wide Sargasso Sea, more devoted, more historically probing in its way of reinhabiting the social and psychic worlds of the inhabitants of Jamaica just after the end of slavery. It's possible that among the "dozens of early nineteenth-century travel books" that Hughes reported having digested (and then felt it necessary, for the sake of his writing, to forget) were writings by the slave-owning British novelist Matthew "Monk" Lewis (1775–1818) and the American naturalist William Bartram (1739–1823), and that it was from these that he borrowed the relentless feeling of some uncanny, dangerous vitality in the landscape and weather of the American tropics. Hughes may even have sensed how much, as Monique Allewaert shows, these writers' pictures of natural cycles of growth and destruction are enmeshed in evocations of the real and imagined violence of slavery, also of the rage for freedom and vengeance in those enslaved. If Hughes took in such suggestions, he also tries to transform what is unconscious in the colonial writers into something more self-aware and ironic, even in their being filtered through the sensuous perceptions and fantasies of his fictive child Emily.

recent immigrants like the Bas-Thorntons. Embedded in the island's landscape, allowed freedom to play at will, the children of the colonists, old and new, have become almost feral, bound to inhuman creatures and yet carrying something of the island's violent history inside themselves—by turns small Prosperos and small Calibans. Emily is a child Orpheus, calling tiny lizards to herself. "Her room was full of these and other pets, some alive, others probably dead." (That "probably" is a mark of the narrator's uneasy distance from his child subjects. Their world remains a mystery to him as well to us.) Other children kill jewellike hummingbirds with water shot from an air gun. They catch larger birds in snares, deciding "by 'Eena, deena, dina, do,' or some such rigmarole, whether to twist its neck or let it go free—thus the excitement and suspense, both for child and bird, can be prolonged beyond the moment of capture." (That "both" is another mark of Hughes's eerie instincts as a storyteller.) Creatures you would think they'd want dead the children leave alive—they find that when certain insects "got under their own skins, and laid their little bags of eggs there, it was not absolutely unpleasant."

Emily's strangest meeting with the elemental powers of the island comes during an excursion that she and her siblings make with the children of a wealthy Creole family named Fernandez. It's at the end of a long day the children spend, without adults, swimming in the waters of an isolated cove, lolling on the rocks that enclose it. Preparing to return at twilight, they feel warnings of something in the air. There's a low, sharp sound "as if some one were gently knocking the outside of a bath you were in. But the bath they were in had no outside, it was solid world. It was funny." Small tremors come, and then a moment when the earth seems at once to suck the sea into itself and to heave it upward, wildly transforming the landscape's already wild life. It is something that Emily has been waiting for all day without knowing it, ever since Margaret Fernandez had announced on getting out of bed, "Smells like an earthquake":

> A school of fish, terrified by some purely submarine event, thrust their heads right out of the water, squattering across the bay in an arrowy rush, dashing up sparkling ripples with the tiny heave of their shoulders....
>
> Once things vibrated slightly, like a chair in a concert-room: and again

there was that mysterious winging, though there was nothing visible beneath the swollen, iridescent stars.

Then it came. The water of the bay began to ebb away, as if some one had pulled up the plug: a foot or so of sand and coral gleamed for a moment new to the air: then back the sea rushed in miniature rollers which splashed right up to the feet of the palms. Mouthfuls of turf were torn away: and on the far side of the bay a small piece of cliff tumbled into the water: sand and twigs showered down, dew fell from the trees like diamonds: birds and beasts, their tongues at last loosed, screamed and bellowed: the ponies, though quite unalarmed, lifted up their heads and yelled.

That was all: a few moments. Then silence, with a rapid countermarch, recovered all his rebellious kingdom. Stillness again. The trees moved as little as the pillars of a ruin, each leaf laid sleekly in place.

You're both inside and outside the child's perspective here, as so often happens in the book. "It was funny." Scale and direction shift wildly. The shock of the earthquake produces a dreamlike, humanized nature in which fish have shoulders and horses yell, where some nameless creature eats "mouthfuls" of earth that fall from the shore. We also catch echoes of a more civilized world of furniture and plumbing, in that vibrating chair, in that bathtub knocked from the outside, in the image of water disappearing down a drain. There's a curious delicacy in the event, it's a delicate ruin or revolution, as witnessed by those "miniature rollers" and the silvery dew scattered on the branches, and stars on the surface of water. The apocalyptic pressure of the moment is muted. If Emily witnesses a new world, it's a revelation of something just below the surface of the old one, as if earthquake were the hidden truth of this island.

The instant the earthquake ends, Emily improvises a solitary, frenzied dance. It's a ritual by which she consecrates the mad event, claiming it with the motions of her own body. Barking like a dog, she then leaps on a horse and drives it to swim far out into the water, now restored to stillness. Her older brother John, in anxious pursuit, swims after her and then, exhausted, clings to her leg as she returns in slow triumph:

Presently John gasped:

"You shouldn't ride on your bare skin, you'll catch ringworm."

"I don't care if I do," said Emily.

"You would if you did," said John.

"I don't care!" chanted Emily.

Emily's chant of "I don't care" is childish enough—Hughes is very good at catching the rhythms of child speech—yet you feel the immediacy with which the event has seeped into her thought. That chant is part of the song of the earthquake. She is overwhelmed for days by what has happened, thinking to herself "I have been in an Earthquake," or framing in her head the story of "a girl called Emily [who] was once in an Earthquake." "Realize," Hughes writes, "that if she had suddenly found she could fly it would not have seemed more miraculous to her. Heaven had played its last, most terrible card; and small Emily had survived, where even grown men (such as Korah, Dathan, and Abiram) had succumbed.... She ate earthquake and slept earthquake: her fingers and legs were earthquake." The mysterious event is now her possession, a register of forces hidden within as well as outside herself, a fact of mind as well as nature. For Emily, the thought of the earthquake *is* the earthquake.

A larger catastrophe follows this opening episode. A hurricane arrives to devastate the island. Over many pages, Hughes makes potent the weather's violence, its almost intentional malice, its power to flatten man-made things and to leave the island's plant life "crushed, pulped, and already growing again."* This force of water and wind takes on more nightmarish shape in Emily's glimpse of the terrified family cat, illuminated by lightning, fleeing a pack of feral cats. The hurricane is indeed what convinces Emily's mother and father to send the children back "home" to the safer island of England—traveling in the company of

---

* Hughes's second novel, *In Hazard*, published in 1938, is almost wholly given over to describing the relentless progress of a Caribbean hurricane, and the trials of a ship's crew struggling to survive the storm, their cowardice and bravery, their madness and reason. As in *A High Wind in Jamaica*, the storm acquires a powerful creaturely life, even as the ship which it attacks—concretely machinelike as Hughes shows it to be—comes to feel like a living body that the creatures living within it labor to preserve.

Margaret Fernandez and her younger brother—while they, the adults, remain behind.

In Emily the memory of the earthquake outweighs any such frights. She carries it with her as a protective talisman. "I've *got* an *Earthquake*," she whispers to her mother as the children board the ship *Clorinda*, which will take them to England, though Mrs. Bas-Thornton decides that her sorrowful, "funny" daughter had meant to say, "I've got an earache."

"CHILDREN KNOW BY precognition how precariously names cling to civilization," writes poet Susan Howe. "In order to qualify for language they must stifle unrelenting internalization." That silencing begins a process which leaves children themselves banished from the world of children, freeing them to enter, at a cost, the world of adults and adult speech. But no such stifling is final, as Howe knows. In *A High Wind in Jamaica*, the exiled children find languages and games that continue to baffle the adults around them, things that witness, like Emily's earthquake, these children's still relentless powers of internalization. As a belated Romantic fable, for all its irony, Hughes's story opens up more fully the strange space of the child's imagination, always enlarging its horizons, its readiness to remake the external world, even as he renders his particular children's minds more opaque and unpredictable. The book is like *Alice in Wonderland* written by Joseph Conrad.

The novel's major turn comes when pirates capture the *Clorinda*. Emily and her companions, brought aboard the pirate schooner for what should be a brief interval, are marooned there when their own ship steals away at night—since its captain has come to believe, hearing the splash of useless booty being tossed overboard, that the pirates have thrown the children into the sea. The children show no fear in their new home. They indeed remain unsure if these *are* pirates. Left to roam almost at will, the children come to accept the ship as a space of play, and so colonize it in turn, make a home there. It's a place that's cramped, awkward, overloaded, filthy, poor, run by mysterious rules, the Neverland with flying cockroaches. Over time they become less like prisoners and more like the pirates' pets, playmates, and allies.

Later they seem invaders, monsters, awful riddles, a kind of "diabolic yeast." The children are also ghosts of a sort, since as we learn early on the news of their murder has spread throughout the larger world, and they're assumed to be dead, though neither children nor pirates are aware of this.

Hughes shows us, with endless delight, how the children in their play transform the working spaces of the ship, each game possessing its own curious power to disturb the running of things. The ropes and spars of the ship turn out to be the perfection of places to swing and climb, to play hide-and-seek and "house-on-fire." The children at times turn the deck itself into a sea, and designate only a few particular places—a bulkhead, a capstan, a barrel—as islands of safety, calling out continually to the poor sailors at work, "You're drowning! You're drowning! O-o-oh, look out!" And when the schooner heels to starboard in a strong wind, the children happily turn the tilted deck into a great slide. The filth and chaos of the boat have not fazed them, but they are collectively appalled when the pirate captain cries out at them, as they slide, "If you go and wear holes in your drawers, do you think *I* am going to mend them? . . . What do you think this ship is? What do you think we all are? To mend your drawers for you, eh? *To mend . . . your . . . drawers?*" The children "could hardly believe so unspeakable a remark had crossed human lips"—finding this adult as unfathomable as he finds them.

"What *on Earth* were children's heads made of, inside?" wonders the captain, a grumpy Dane named Jonsen. More and more, the ship is a space in which each child discovers his or her own strangeness. The space of shared play, shared childhood, becomes a place of peculiarly solitary, secret games, island games that Hughes both plumbs and keeps his distance from, always trying to come closer to the scale of things as children must know them. Such games are part of what can make children seem, Hughes writes, simply mad.

The two youngest boys play at pirates on this pirate ship, each in his fashion:

> Once, as they went into battle,
> "I am armed with a sword and a pistol!" chanted Edward:

"And I am armed with a key and half a whist-le!" chanted the more literal Harry.

Neither is quite certain whether they are fighting alongside or against the pirates.

Eight-year-old Rachel gives us a more lonely, ruthless version of a game taken up by Barrie's Wendy, as she plays at being a mother. Hughes's prose here aims to live inside the truth of Rachel's play: "She left houses and families wherever she went. She collected bits of oakum and the moltings of a worn-out mop, wrapped them in rags and put them to sleep in every nook and cranny.... To parody Hobbes, she claimed as her own whatever she had mixed her imagination with; and the greater part of her time was spent in angry or tearful assertions of her property-rights." Recalling the presence of dissenting missionaries in colonial Jamaica (viewed with suspicion by the official Anglican clergy), Rachel also gives herself to apocalyptic preaching, crying out in an incomprehensible voice and stomping angrily about the deck— "Gabble-gabble, Bretheren, gabble-gabble"—promising damnation to the pirates. It's an exhibition of her "precocious ethical genius."

Then there is four-year-old Laura, whose mind is "something vast, complicated, and nebulous that can hardly be put into language." She is at once child and baby, and babies, as Hughes says, are simply *not* human at all, "they are animals, and have a very ancient and ramified culture, as cats have, and fishes, and even snakes." Contact with a baby is like looking "a large octopus in the face," alluring yet alien, with its "cow-like tenderness of the eye... the beautiful and infinitesimal mobility of that large and toothless mouth." What then can anyone make of the inside of Laura's head, "where the child-mind lived in the midst of the familiar relics of the baby-mind, like a Fascist in Rome"? "Ninetenths of her life being spent in her own head, she seldom had time to feel at all strongly either for or against other people." At one moment, Laura "suddenly discovered what a beautiful deep cave her armpit made, and decided to keep fairies in it in future. For some time she could think of nothing else."

Emily again most claims our attention. One day walking aimlessly on shipboard, between vague thoughts "about some bees and a fairy queen... it suddenly flashed into her mind that she was *she*." That it should happen at this particular moment is almost arbitrary. She finds herself surprised by her own body, its motions, by the fact that she can be both caresser and caressed, giving and receiving the pleasure of touch. She discovers that she is "this particular one, this Emily." If her name gives her power, a self and a body to own, the sense of being a discrete person, it also bears with it a sense of being entangled in time, a tie that makes her suddenly vulnerable to "disasters running about loose." It creates a sea change in her sense of being, a small earthquake. "As a piece of Nature, she was practically invulnerable. But as *Emily*, she was absolutely naked, tender." Emily's finding of her name leads to another discovery, not that she speaks for God, like Rachel, but that she may *be* God, that she, Emily, vulnerable as she is, makes and sustains the world around her—a discovery followed by the sudden need to keep this knowledge secret. ("A child can hide the most appalling secret without the least effort, and is practically secure against detection.") Or else, if the others *do* know, she must continue to pretend that she doesn't know they know. At one moment she imagines blinding another child to show her power, and protect herself. Yet even as she knows that she is "God Himself," she knows also, "beyond all doubt, in her innermost being, that she was damned," feeling "Conscience" inside her like an unhatched harpy.

There are other children whose minds Hughes places more radically beyond our knowing, beyond any frame of play. The mind of Emily's brother John, for instance, vividly present in early chapters—we'd seen him filling his bedroom with rats and bats—has no place in the chorus of child minds on board the schooner. For John dies early on in the children's time with the pirates, during a pause at a smuggler's refuge in Cuba. Led up to the balcony of a warehouse to watch a Christmas pageant ("a nativity play, with real cattle," the cows hauled up and down on ropes), John crawls too far forward and falls and breaks his neck. The other children realize that the boy is missing when they return to the ship, but find that it is "better to pretend not to know," and do not speak of him, even forget him in time, as we may forget him over the course of reading.

Closed to us in a different way is the mind of fourteen-year-old Mar-

garet Fernandez, the child who had smelled an earthquake. This girl has
not died. But Hughes lets us know, plainly if with scant detail, that from
early on in the voyage the captain and his first mate have kept her apart
for their own pleasure. Margaret's mind at this point marks a threshold
that Hughes does not try to cross, as if it is too dangerous, or too painfully private. The other children have no idea what her sudden isolation
means. They only observe with bafflement, and sometimes contempt,
her muteness, her dull eyes, her uneasy, shrinking motions, her refusal
to play games, her "defection," as they call it. As for the pirates, there
is clearly something in Margaret's abjection and blank gaze, in the in-
sensate energy of her body—mixed with their own projected guilt—
that lets them without hesitation take her for a murderer and throw her
into the sea.

Then there are the animals that live on shipboard. Hughes makes
them as human as any of the children, even as the children themselves
are figured as animals. The animals are Aesopian, satirical creatures that
yet keep their earthly particularity. We watch the plots of a cunning,
possessive pig and the vengeful rages of a mad-eyed goat. We're alerted
to the work of those winged cockroaches below deck, insects that smell
terrible, make a frightening noise, and chew at one's feet. We see a mad
monkey who devours down to its fierce teeth a sucker-fish that's at-
tached itself to the deck. Some of these creatures become curious pets
("If I was the Queen," says Emily sitting on the pig, "I should most certainly have a pig for a throne"), others remain unclaimed, alien. The
boat becomes for them, as for the children, an ark, a floating island con-
taining refugees of a world overwhelmed by that "high wind," a wind
that also blows this ship across the water.

Hughes plays further with his wish to lend a human face to inhuman
things. The narrator's consciousness in the book, as Joyce Carol Oates
writes, "has floated deftly in and about . . . like the very sea breeze itself." This works in part because the narrator extends to the sea, and to
other elemental forces, the possession of a sensuous, conscious, and curious life: "The schooner moved just enough for the sea to divide with a
slight rustle on her stem, breaking out into a shower of sparks, which lit
up also wherever the water rubbed the ship's side, as if the ocean were
a tissue of sensitive nerves; and still twinkled behind in the mere pale-

ness of the wake." "The sun had come up like a searchlight: but it was about all there was to be seen. No land was anywhere in sight, and the sea and sky seemed very uncertain as to the most becoming place to locate their mutual firmament." We may feel that such descriptions show us broken-off or projected fragments of the thoughts, the nervous systems, of the children themselves, as well as the living, intelligent face of a world beyond them. There is, in John Ashbery's words, "the feeling that the sky might be in the back of someone's mind."

WRITING ABOUT ROBERT Louis Stevenson's *Treasure Island*, Angus Fletcher speaks of the archetypal force of pirate stories. That force lies, he thinks, in their fascination with danger, trickery, and seizure, in the idea of existence on the open sea outside the bounds of law. It shows itself in the urgency these stories find in maps of the known and unknown world, talismanic tools for finding lost islands, for recovering buried treasures—treasures that in the child's mind mark a secret life, "an unquenchable fire within," guarded by death. Fletcher knows how uncertain the category of "pirate" is in legal history; he knows that licensed privateers, merchant-adventurers, explorers, even missionaries might in the early modern period all cross over into being called pirates. Yet for him the questing, wandering pirate—cousin of Odysseus—remains "in some important sense the natural hero of romance, for he is allowed to do what no ordinary person may do." That's one reason why pirates work so well as subjects of children's games, games in which the child, pirating old stories, can imagine a "freedom from the labor and pain of basic human survival."

Hughes's pirates, however, are marked by their unheroic ordinariness. These are pirates without salty names and sea curses, without scars, crutches, cutlasses, wooden legs, or eye patches, with little interest in fighting and blood, or buried gold. Hughes goes beyond the gentle satire of the tradition we get in *Peter and Wendy*, where pirates so oddly keep company with fairies, mermaids, and the "Indians" of popular Western fiction, and are obsessed with the rituals of English boarding schools. Shabby, clumsy, by turns cunning and incompetent, the pirates in *A High Wind in Jamaica* are more like anarchic shopkeepers than romantic criminals. They've missed their century, and are the worn-out remnants of a great tradition. Captain Jonsen shuffles apishly about the deck in what look like slippers, "which he must have sliced with a knife out of some pair of dead sea-boots," often getting into pettish domestic quarrels with his first mate. Jonsen carries no cannon on board his ship, preferring to trick his prey into submission (as he'd tricked the *Clorinda* into thinking the pirate ship a pleasure vessel, sending over a boat full of his crew in gentleman's clothes, accompanied by a crowd of transvestites recruited from the smuggler's port of Santa Lucia, in Cuba). It's a mark of their odd domesticity, even sentimentality, that these pirates come to indulge the children in their games. And yet the possibility of some blunter cruelty always hovers just below the surface. You feel it in Margaret's sexual servitude, in her near murder (though they take that for just punishment). You feel it in the pirates' readiness to prod those sad captive animals to fight. It's also there in the revelation—something that comes almost offhandedly, late in the novel—that Jonsen had first learned to read the sea, to sense its moods and hidden menace, as second mate on a slave ship.

As we move through the middle chapters of the novel, the purposes of the pirates seem as disorganized as those of the children. Their schooner sails almost at random, the pirates hoping to encounter some ship vulnerable to their trickery. Hughes uses the time to give us ever more curious glimpses of the children's minds and games, to show moments of uncertain contact between children and pirates and animals and objects. Each child's mind is its own strange animal. A certain bond of mutual acceptance, even of affection and collaborative play, grows up between the pirates and their uncanny passengers. That bond is broken when, facing the children in the hold of the ship, the half-drunken Jonsen reaches out uncertainly to stroke Emily's face and she, moved by something unnamed in herself, violently bites his thumb. Though both are secretly ashamed, each regretting "the impulse of a momentary insanity," a cold war breaks out between them that bleeds into the larger world on shipboard. It's a war that ends when that marlinspike, dangerous baby, falls from its cradle in the rigging and gashes Emily's leg. Jonsen catches her up, roughly binds the wound with tar and canvas, and gives his own cabin to her. Why he later shuts her up with the captive Dutchman remains a mystery.

It's after the killing, while her reopened wound heals a second time, that we see revealed more of this child's strange powers. We glimpse Emily the artist, covering the wall of Jonsen's bunk with penciled drawings of curious creatures—walrus, rabbit, dwarf, crone—born around knots and twists in the wood grain, even around the bloodstain on the cabin floor, drawings that Jonsen will later, in a grim kind of play, enlarge with his own more explicitly erotic sketches. We also get Emily the poet, telling herself "endless stories," stories uttered in "a sort of narrative noise" or "audible rigmarole." ("No one who has private thoughts going on loudly in his own head is quite sure of their not being overheard unless he is providing something else to occupy foreign ears.") Into these she weaves tales of the trickster spider Anansi once told to her by a black servant, as well as "the creepy things he had told her about duppies," though she's now stripped of the power she once felt in absolutely disbelieving in such beings.

The death of the Dutch captain—and the more manic, uncanny, and infectious games it sparks in the children—convinces Jonsen that he must end the limbo-like state of sharing his boat with such dangerous creatures. He takes the risk of disguising the pirate schooner as a merchant vessel and sailing her into established shipping lanes. Eventually he crosses paths with a passenger steamer to which he can transfer the children. The travelers on that boat embrace them as beings returned from the dead. Jonsen sails off, believing that the steamer's captain has accepted his story about having found the children abandoned on an island, believing also that the children themselves, out of affection for the pirates, will keep secret what's happened to them.

The rescued children's return to the more civilized world of the steamer is not entirely simple. Margaret remains fearful and mute. Emily becomes fascinated with the pet of one child passenger, a baby alligator, a creature with a stony, brilliant, expressionless gaze. ("They looked each other in the eye, those two children.") Over time the group does seem to settle happily into the new, cleaner, more orderly surroundings, leaving the chaos of the pirate ship behind them. The captain's gamble appears to have paid off. But in the end, Emily, held breathlessly to the warm maternal bosom of a stewardess, whispers to her about the pirates. While Jonsen allows himself an illusion of freedom, flag signals are exchanged between the steamer and a passing British gunboat, a chase is launched, the pirates are captured and brought to London for trial.

The final phase of the novel shows us the determined efforts of adults—parents, lawyers, politicians, journalists—to find out the truth of what the children have gone through. They want to do them justice in court, to mark out who is guilty and who is innocent. The prosecutors believe that "piracy" is the wrong charge to bring against these men whom they know to be monsters. "The most eminent jurists have not even yet decided on a satisfactory definition of piracy." Furthermore, a conviction for piracy doesn't carry a death sentence, only transportation to another island. So they seek to convict the crew for the murders of the Dutch captain and of Emily's brother John. Lacking other material evidence, the lawyers need at least one of the children to stand as witness in court, though one attorney admits, "I would rather have to extract information from the devil himself than from a child."

The prosecutors have some reason to hope they will succeed. Most of the children's stories about their time with the pirates are fragmentary, incomprehensible: "There was a monkey... and a lot of turtles." "He talked about drawers." "Bing! Bang! Bong!... Bim-bam." Margaret continues in her silence. Yet the children start to accept as truth the lurid things that the adults tell them *must* have happened during their time as captives. Seized by the lawyers' stories, the children revise or cast out their own memories. "Who were they, children, to know better what had happened to them than grown-ups?" The grown-ups who manage the trial are more cold-blooded versions of the kindly Miss Dawson, a young woman passenger on the steamer with whom Emily had fallen in love, and who had continually pressed her for details of the "romantic, terrible things" she's gone through. ("Didn't you ever see a body?... A dead one?") Such melodramatic fantasies, projected into the unknown minds of the children, become the ground of legal accusation. The trial of the pirates, as Hughes takes us through it, becomes as unreal as the trial of the Knave of Hearts.

Emily is the one chosen to testify. Like a more conventional schoolchild, she devotedly memorizes a rote set of answers to the prosecuting attorney's questions about what happened on the boat, "a sort of Shorter Catechism" written out by the lawyer's clerk in his beautiful hand. Emily herself doesn't know why she's been asked to say anything, or what the trial means. She speaks her script accurately in the courtroom—a place whose drabness, Hughes writes, conceals its true ritual purpose, that of making a place for the "Real Presence" of death. The shocking thing happens when the defense attorney starts to cross-examine the child. Noticing that Emily has said nothing about the death of the Dutch captain, and hoping at least to save his clients from hanging, he takes up the thread of the prosecution's case:

> "Now a very horrible thing has been suggested. It has been said that a man was taken off the steamer, the captain of it in fact, onto the schooner, and that he was murdered there. Now what I want to ask you is this. Did you see any such thing happen?"
>
> Those who were watching the self-contained Emily saw her turn very white and begin to tremble. Suddenly she gave a shriek: then after a second's pause she began to sob. Every one listened in an icy stillness, their hearts in their mouths. Through her tears they heard, they all heard, the words: "...He was all lying in his blood... he was awful! He... he died, he said something and then he *died!*"
>
> That was all that was articulate.

Reading this, you remember the killing, its nightmarish knotting of error and fear and what it might mean to have survived it. You sense the trauma for this child of reentering the memory of what threatened her, and how much remains incommunicable, buried—you feel both the fright of what's incommunicable and the fright of being asked to communicate it, to say and repeat "all." You may even hear in Emily's words, along with a refusal or inability to speak of her own part in the killing, her rage at the dead man just for dying in so frightful a way: "He was awful! He... he died, he said something and then he *died!*" That evokes a child's demand for a different kind of justice, even revenge. But for the adults in the court, "their hearts in their mouths" (that phrase gets back its grotesque force here), it's now certain what Emily has witnessed. "They heard, they all heard, the words." Her words, confusing as they are in their unexpected, free-floating violence and witness of violence, now reveal facts, or at least legal probabilities. The pirates are condemned for murder. Emily catches sight of Jonsen and the crew only when she is leaving the court. "The terrible look on Jonsen's face as his eye met hers, what was it that it reminded her of?" Hughes never tells us what it is. Perhaps the look is something she had seen in the eyes of the Dutch captain, in Margaret's eyes, or in those of her terrified cat.

Hughes leaves so much unspoken, latent, it's often hard to know what he intends. You can imagine that the dark, unruly way that justice lands, the sense of death's presence in the court, harks back to the start of the novel, with its pictures of the ruined colonial slave system, also its vision of the ruinous "work" of wild weather and natural growth in Jamaica, inhuman processes that come to look like acts of anarchic punishment and revenge. If this is the case, no one at the trial, least of all Emily, is in a position to see it.

The court contrives to make Emily's words transparent. But the child remains a cipher at home. We've been told in an earlier chapter that Mr. and Mrs. Bas-Thornton returned to England "after the disaster," and that Mr. Bas-Thornton has found work as "London dramatic critic to various Colonial newspapers." Their children (save John) having been miraculously restored, the two grown-ups try to make for them a more proper, conventional household, despite their continuous appetite for playing in Thames mud. One night, some weeks before the trial, we see Emily's father standing "unseen in the shadows of her bedroom," watching her as she sleeps. "To his fantastic mind, the little chit seemed the stage of a great tragedy." Moved by compassion, yet still the dramatic critic, he is "delighted at the beautiful, the subtle combination of the contending forces which he read into the situation. He was like a powerless stalled audience, which pities unbearably, but would not on any account have missed the play." But as he looks, his mind moves in another direction, toward "an emotion which was not pity and was not delight: he realized, with a sudden painful shock, that he was afraid of her! ... But surely it was some trick of the candle-light, or of her indisposition, that gave her face momentarily that inhuman, stony, basilisk look?" Strange as Emily herself has been for us, the father's unfolding response to her sleeping person feels equally strange, and perhaps more dangerous, more costly, since the grounds of his pity and fear are mainly in his own head. They have no real link to what Emily has experienced, to what she herself has seen and known and done, to what she remembers or doesn't remember. (What would happen, you might ask, if grown-ups didn't find such children dangerous?)

In the last pages of the novel, Emily's parents take her to a new school, a place where, the headmistress assures the Bas-Thorntons, "our girls will have an especially kind corner in their hearts for her," and so help this child "forget the terrible things she has been through." The other children will probably learn nothing of what she truly remembers, though they may well imagine those "terrible things" for themselves. We as readers have a sense of what might be lodged in Emily's mind: those kissing fish, that maddened cat, that earthquake, knowing herself to be God, killing a bound man, an exchange of glances with a baby alligator. But we may be no better than her father or the lawyers in weighing the power of those things that are islanded within her. With a difficult-to-gauge combination of irony and charity, Hughes lets Emily vanish into anonymity at the close of the novel, placed beyond anyone's knowledge save that of an unseen, hypothetical divinity:

In another room, Emily with the other new girls was making friends with the older pupils. Looking at that gentle, happy throng of clean innocent faces and soft graceful limbs, listening to the ceaseless, artless babble of chatter rising, perhaps God could have picked out from among them which was Emily: but I am sure that I could not.

PORTIA

We can evade you, and all else but the heart:
What blame to us if the heart live on.
HART CRANE, "CHAPLINESQUE"

THERE'S A RELENTLESS and uncanny sadness about Elizabeth Bowen's *The Death of the Heart*. I keep going back over the book in my mind, trying to give shape to that sadness, to say where it lives. It's partly that the sorrow is so diffused among the characters. Their sorrows divide them yet implicate them in one another, even as their knowledge of those sorrows is left unspoken, evaded—evaded partly in how they inflict their own sorrows on each other and on themselves, at the same time as they can't imagine another's sorrows. What's uncanny lies in Bowen's will to track that sorrow, to show its myriad folds and masks, its eerie beauties, how it seeps into furniture, clothing, the very shadows of a house, animating your doubt as much as your sympathy, also calling forth a bitter laughter. It lies in how each sorrow has the shape of a life.

You can't say for sure whose heart dies in the course of the novel, or when it dies. The heart's death is not sudden, rather it's a long dying, a hardening or closing of the heart. And hearts that are already dead still keep a kind of life, a death-in-life. They come alive again in sorrow, sorrow that can kill another heart or help find it out. One loneliness hammers another. Bowen knows that talk of the "heart" is hard—thinking of the word in all its range of meaning, as a name for the seat of feeling, life, thought, spirit, and truth, a name for love, courage, or conscience, an organ sustaining and vulnerable, not always to be trusted, often "unvisited." "We hardly even know what questions to put to our own hearts," writes Bowen in an essay of 1938, the year her novel was published. The word "heart" itself indeed rarely appears in the book, though you see it floating above every left-hand page in the printed volume's running heads, paired with "Death," and flanked on the facing pages by section titles that evoke, in this very secular text, those threats to the soul arraigned in *The Book of Common Prayer*: The World, The Flesh, The Devil.

It is Portia Quayne, the orphaned sixteen-year-old girl who has come to live in a house in London, it is she who gains in the book the most preternatural presence. Portia is the book's chief picture of "the heart." We slowly come to know this creature in whom "each movement had a touch of exaggeration, as though some secret power kept springing out," who is yet like "a kitten that expects to be drowned." Portia acquires a fierce personality and mind in her own right, even as her troubling vitality emerges for us more obliquely in the bafflement, suspicion, and fear she creates in others, in how she lives in *their* minds. Portia's life takes shape from what they don't know or misjudge in her, from their curious theories about what she thinks or doesn't think. Like Henry James's Maisie and Richard Hughes's Emily, even Franz Kafka's Odradek, Portia is a dangerous child partly in being so disturbing to the adults around her, adults—all childless—from whom she seeks affection, recognition, and help.

One of these is her older half brother Thomas, to whose house she's come to live after the death of her mother—the widow of Thomas's father, a man whose first wife had insisted, against his will, that he divorce her and marry his young mistress, leading to the pair's itinerant existence outside of England, living in poor hotels on the Continent. Another is Thomas's wife, Anna, still haunted by the dead-alive memory of an early romantic betrayal, by two miscarriages and a failed career as a decorator, a woman whom Thomas loves with a passion "that nothing in their language could be allowed to express, that nothing could satisfy." Anna is fixed with Thomas in a married conversation into which a sense of desperate distance always intrudes. (Portia only gets the "clue" of their talk when she feels "the frenzy behind the clever remark.") Living in the house on Windsor Terrace is also the old housekeeper Matchett, whom Anna and Thomas seem to have inherited from Thomas's mother, along with rooms of old furniture that Matchett lovingly and inexorably cares for, sacred objects whose life as witness of a desolate past and present she cultivates, makes vivid; they become like specters, vivid and solidified shadows. Among visitors, there is St. Quentin Miller, Anna's friend and perhaps lover, a coldly satirical novelist, also Major Brutt, a veteran and ex-colonial sadly returned to London, "almost a walking entropy" (in Neil Corcoran's words), who seeks refuge at the house. And then there is twenty-six year-old Eddie, another friend of Anna's, possessed of "a proletarian, animal, quick grace," a failed writer now at work in Thomas's advertising firm, charming, treacherous, vulnerable, and self-hating, destructive of the very illusions he craves.

Like a magnet, Portia exerts on these figures both attraction and repulsion. They talk about her continually, both in her absence and to her face. It's a strange collaboration among members of a tribe who don't trust one another. They create a looking-glass world in which Portia moves, facing creatures whose games and questions she doesn't understand, who make her see "there is no ordinary life." They find her at times sweet, childish, naive, or merely ignorant, and then also a little monstrous, even ghostly, a voyeur, slanderer, and seducer. She's called at different moments "mad," "deeply hysterical," "an animal," "lunatic," "vulgar," or "potty." Portia's most ordinary words can seem to curse them, probe their guilt, their fear of another's need, or simply their deep, almost metaphysical embarrassment. Their mistakes about her would be comic if they were not so cruel. As Bowen writes of the deaf and speechless boy Jeremy in her last novel, *Eva Trout* (a very dangerous child, as it proves), Portia "imposed on others a sense ... that it was *they* who were lacking in some faculty."

To Anna, especially—the book's other central consciousness— Portia belongs to a species not quite human. It's as if she and Thomas have invited into their house an alien being, impossible to care for. "What is she, after all? The child of an aberration, the child of a panic, the child of an old chap's pitiful sexuality. Conceived among lost hairpins and snapshots of doggies in a Notting Hill Gate flatlet." The mere thought of Portia's silent, unspoken mourning for her mother makes Anna feel there's a diseased person in the house: "The *idea* of her never leaves me quiet, and by coming into this room she drives me on to the ice. Everything she does to me is unconscious; if it were conscious it would not hurt. She makes me feel like a tap that won't turn on." Simply sitting together in a firelit parlor over tea is for Anna a trial: "Had the agitation she felt throughout her body sent out an aura with a quivering edge, Portia's eyes might be said to explore this line of quiver, round and along Anna's reclining form. Anna felt bound up with her fear, with her secret, by that enwrapping look of Portia's: she felt mummified."

Portia asks these adults to "admit the unadmitted." She calls back into view heart lives that they have carefully hidden away, made irrelevant, bandaged over; she evokes pieces of memory, knowledge of loss in themselves or others and a picture of its costs, their pained conviction that something is *owed* to them. Portia offers them an echo of their concealed lunacy. She makes them quietly insane to themselves as well as to others. Unknowable as she is, even to herself ("I don't know what I was meant to be," she laments to Matchett), Portia casts back, like a mirror, the fragility of their defenses, of their visions of how to live, of what is proper and "civilized." She shows them something of their own lives as orphans, exiles, victims, and children. She marks their division, yet is like some strange glue that might hold them together. Bowen writes elsewhere that one terrible fear we have as children, along with our helplessness, is the fear "that something is being concealed from us because it is too bad to be told." In *The Death of the Heart*, the most fearful thing is what the adults conceal from themselves.

While she emerges as a screen for the projections of other characters, Portia is never just a passive thing. Her own acts and words work to sustain her presence in the book, this child with a high forehead and dark, wide-set eyes that see everything, that are full of a "homeless intentness" that makes them appear fanatical. You're very aware of the living theater of her mind, and how she takes in other minds, lays claim to them. Portia's innocence is her inheritance, her endowment, more curse than blessing—in its rawness and need, its almost unconscious power to question what it sees.*

* Portia is indeed one of an extended family of suspect and dangerous children in Bowen's work, children who speak for pieces of time, energies of life, that are invisible or lost, set adrift or fled from, children who make strange demands on the adults who love or neglect or betray them. Unquiet, often solitary spirits, Bowen's children can feel at once

"It is not only our fate but our business to lose innocence," says Bowen in "Out of a Book," an essay about how we are formed by our childhood reading. If *The Death of the Heart* promises a loss of innocence, a fall into death and adult perception, Bowen, like a suspense novelist, stretches out the crisis, the threshold moment of Portia's putative crossing from innocence to experience. Portia's innocence indeed sustains and transforms itself as we read, in a way that keeps exposing her to sharper losses, wounds, and astonishments. The book witnesses in this the terrible, even demonic *life* of the heart—especially because so often Portia's sorrows are unspoken, left for *us* to imagine in the face of others' failure to imagine them. For all her opacity, you feel Portia's sensual awareness, her "tentative, exploratory, undecided, but still intensely physical" presence. We know she is sixteen, yet her age can still seem uncertain, the child quality in her is strong, and any sexual feelings are caught up with a more elemental clumsiness and shyness, a kind of innocence. The book knows how charged the word *innocence* is, how people manipulate it to their own advantage, assume it as a mask, a ground for evasion. It also knows how compromised, how smug and bitter, is the language that people have to describe the *loss* of innocence.

Something of Portia's force of being is suggested in a passage that prefaces the early stages of her courtship with Eddie. The narrator

---

viscerally real and ghostly. I've mentioned Jeremy in *Eva Trout*. There's also nine-year-old Leopold in *The House in Paris*, grave, needful, and critical, ambitious to imagine the mother he's never met—his curious presence haunts, retrospectively, the tale we're told of the love affair that begets him. Then there are the three ardent, unpredictable children in *The Little Girls*, conspiring to bury in secret a cache of curious objects (a pistol, a book of poems, a severed toe). Coming together to *unbury* those things half a century later, they test what survives of their childhood selves and early friendship, what survives of that old magic, having lived through lives of ordinary loss and the vaster losses of two world wars. In the wartime story "Summer Night," the young child Vivie, glimpsed briefly "wanting to run the night," strips off her nightdress and covers her body with chalk drawings of stars and snakes, then wanders around an almost empty mansion—"from each room she went into the human order seemed to have lapsed"—spying at doorways and jumping madly on her mother's bed, while her father and a nervous aunt talk downstairs with "unliving voices" and her mother drives late to find her lover. In this context I also think of "cousin Nettie" in *The Heat of the Day*, Bowen's novel of the Blitz, an old woman with dementia who's possessed of an "uncanny hint of sanity." Nettie collects postcards with pictures of children "engaged innocently in some act of destruction."

stands back to reflect on the story that she's about to tell, to frame its stakes in more universal terms:

> Innocence so constantly finds itself in a false position that inwardly innocent people learn to be disingenuous. Finding no language in which to speak in their own terms, they resign themselves to being translated imperfectly. They exist alone; when they try to enter into relations they compromise falsifyingly—through anxiety, through desire to impart and to feel warmth. The system of our affections is too corrupt for them. They are bound to blunder, then to be told they cheat. In love, the sweetness and violence they have to offer involves a thousand betrayals for the less innocent. Incurable strangers to the world, they never cease to exact a heroic happiness. Their singleness, their ruthlessness, their one continuous wish makes them bound to be cruel, and to suffer cruelty. The innocent are so few that two of them seldom meet—when they do meet, their victims lie strewn all around.

Bowen's narrative voice here has its own uncanniness. Whose voice speaks, after all? It is hard to know how she takes sides, or predicts the unfolding conflict, who the heroes will be and who the victims, what the "thousand betrayals" will look like. You can hear in these sentences the voice of experience, the voice of a disenchanted realism about what the world asks. Yet the sense of the word "innocence" shifts as we read, by turns familiar and unfamiliar. The speaker is both outside and inside that innocence. It is an innocence that seems *not* likely to fall, or to be destroyed by what betrays it, it's likely rather to gain thereby a stranger force. This voice—embracing "us" as readers and reflecting on "the system of *our* affections"—also speaks about innocence as a substantial thing, a kind of demonic entity, part of a more elemental order. It invites us to think of "the innocent" as a race apart, incorrigible, ruthless, "incurable strangers to the world," surviving by "one continuous wish." If these are children, they are children who do not outgrow their innocence. Bowen speaks of their readiness to "exact" from the world not payment or revenge, but rather "a heroic happiness." To *exact* a happiness! That suggests a massacre *by* rather than *of* the innocents, or it pictures the innocent as themselves serpents in Eden. If these sentences witness Portia's power, they also echo something of that irrational, demonizing fear of Portia that we hear especially in Anna. They make you wonder whether "innocence" is a word that the innocent would ever use to describe themselves.

"YOU WERE MAD ever to touch the thing."

These are the first words spoken aloud in the novel, just a page from the start. It's the novelist St. Quentin Miller who speaks, talking with Anna as they stand together on a bridge in Kensington Park in the midst of winter, watching swans make their way through broken sheets of ice on the water below. "The thing" here given such dangerous shape, such infectious power, turns out to be Portia's diary. Anna has discovered it while clearing up a box of papers in the nicely redecorated room that Portia keeps in "a sort of savage clutter," a clutter with unsettling traces of order ("salvage clutter," you might call it)—unfinished jigsaw puzzles, for instance, or the tea party she's arranged on a table with her many wooden bears, souvenirs of years of charmed, impoverished wandering with her mother after her father's death. Anna reads the diary with pained hunger, finding in it signs of just how invasive, critical, even malicious is the young girl that she's taken into her house. The pages are more awful than she'd expected, she tells Miller, "I mean, more, completely distorted and distorting. As I read I thought, either this girl or I are mad." "In fact it was not like *writing* at all," she adds, yet can't help but admit some truth in it: "She has got us taped."

Just what there is to fear in the diary becomes plainer when we read the thing itself, in two extracts that Bowen places as the closing chapters of parts 1 and 2 of *The Death of the Heart*. We as readers are here in the position of prying Anna (though given the dates of the entries, it's clear that we never read any passages that Anna has read). Portia's writing gives the sharpest picture of the girl's mind at work, lets us hear what her innocence sounds like. The diary is the space where Portia herself most *acts*, most lays claim to reality, where she tries to inhabit the house in which she's a stranger, to name its inhabitants, to speak for *their* minds. She copies out home lessons that run alongside those other lessons—odd enough in context—which she learns at her fashionable school. The diary's odd, childlike cadences sharply contrast with the intricate, reflective prose of Bowen's narrator. Yet Portia's words have their own authority, irony, sensuality, and lyricism, their own power of witness.* There is in them something of the "howl" that Victoria Glendinning says Bowen, unlike Virginia Woolf, always suppressed in her fiction. They also have something of the stripped, desolating force of the words of Bowen's Anglo-Irish contemporary, Samuel Beckett:

When Thomas comes in he looks as though he was smelling something he thought he might not be let eat. This house makes a smell of feeling. Since I have known Eddie I ask myself what this smell is more.

She said she had a headache, and I said then didn't the concert make it worse, and she said yes, naturally it did. It was a disappointment having to take me.

Today we did Hygiene and French Composition about Racine, and were taken to look at pictures of Umbrian Art at the National Gallery.

All Thomas's looks, except ones at Anna, are at people not looking.

The whole house was just like that, it was not like night but like air being ill.

We were to have had a lecture on the Appreciation of Mozart, but because of the fog we had a Debate on Consistency being the Hobgoblin of Small Minds. We also wrote essays on Metternich's policy.

Tonight Anna and Thomas stayed at home for dinner. She said that whenever there was a fog she always felt it was something that she had

* Reading Portia's diaries, I think of something Bowen writes in a review of James Joyce's *Finnegans Wake*: "The language has two violent intimacies: the child-talk (the talk to the self in the half-dark) and the lover-jargon, a terrifyingly urgent melting, slurring, and dislocation of words. All nonsense is erotic-infantile, with a pathic source. This tactile intimacy of language disturbs the chastity of the mind." In describing the workings of such nonsense Bowen sounds a bit like Anna, so disturbed by the violent intimacy of Portia's writing, by what she feels as its madness, its "pathic" origins.

done, but she did not seem to mean this seriously.... Then we sat in the drawingroom, and they wished I was not there.

Matchett was busy with Anna's clothes. I went down to her for tea, she said, well, you're quite a ghost. But really it is this house that is like that.

He says that when you love someone all your saved-up wishes start coming out.

Last Thursday evening, when I first got to Eddie's it was not like where I imagined he lived. He does not like his room and I'm sure it knows.

IN READING THE *Death of the Heart*, Liza says to me, you keep on waiting for some catastrophe that never comes. It makes me think of the book's slow-motion sense of menace, such as you feel in a dream. (Are they trying to *kill* her? I sometimes wonder—there are, it should be said, no actual deaths in the book.) You feel an accumulation of small wounds, small betrayals, small revelations of distance, failed sympathy, also fear, small bits of death, all framed by silence, by the inability to communicate or measure these things. Portia is like an eggshell, easily crushed, you'd suppose, yet an eggshell that somehow keeps its curved shape intact, supported by the very network of fissures and hairline cracks that cross its surface.

Portia's emerging love for Eddie is one central mystery in the book. It starts from a letter he sends to thank her for simply bringing him his hat after a visit with Anna, a letter at once raw and forced, a mix of candor and flirtatiousness, speaking of shared loneliness, their cruel susceptibility to others. The letter is a prize that she hides under her pillow and that's later discovered by Matchett, who crushes it before giving it back to the girl. Portia finds in Eddie some mirror of her own innocence. He's glad that she lets him read her diary, and yet he says nothing to her about it, other than demanding that she write nothing there about *him* or about their relationship, as if that would expose him too much. ("But *swear* you won't write down what you feel.... Between you and me there must never be any thoughts.") Inviting Portia to tea at his small apartment, he can't help offering her a pantomime of the other "ladies" he has entertained there, ending with a gleeful imitation of stomping on one of the ladies' fancy hats. After this, he lays his head in Portia's lap, pretending to sleep, but the gentle moment has its own self-mocking theater: "When he woke up," Portia writes in her diary, "he said that if he was a lady's fox fur and I was him, I would certainly stroke his head. While I did, he made himself look as if he had glass eyes, like a fur."

Eddie always puts on a painful show for Portia, always looks at her with dead eyes. What he asks most of Portia, indeed, is for her to demonstrate her essential being by disappearing, by making no human claims on him. It is what allows him to disappear from himself, to be less ashamed of such disappearance: "Only Portia had this forbidding intimacy with him—she was the only person to whom he need not pretend that she had not ceased existing when, for him, she had ceased to exist.... No presence could be less insistent than hers. He treated her like an element (air, for instance) or a condition (darkness): these touch one with their equality and lightness where one could endure no human touch. He could look right through her, without a flicker of seeing, without being made shamefully conscious of the vacuum there must be in his eyes."

The plainest crisis comes in part 2 of the novel ("The Flesh"). While Anna and Thomas take a holiday in Italy and Matchett oversees a ruthless spring cleaning in London, Portia is sent to stay on the southern coast of England, at a house in the invented town of Seale-on-Sea. The house belongs to an abjectly devoted former governess of Anna, Mrs. Heccomb, a widow who lives there with her two stepchildren, loutish Dicky and eager, vulgar Daphne ("she made up her mouth with the gesture of someone cutting their throat"). Named "Waikiki," the house's thin walls, loud radio, garish lights, visceral smells, and audible plumbing make it the opposite of a Gothic country house, something more readily suggested by the interior distances and haunted furniture of Windsor Terrace. With surprising force of will, Portia arranges for Eddie to make a visit to Seale and to stay at Waikiki. While there, Eddie throws himself into the young people's restless socializing with a kind insinuating, oily glee. Along with Dicky, Daphne, and some

of their friends, Portia and Eddie go to a movie. In the midst of it, lit
by the flame of a cigarette lighter held for a few cruel seconds, Portia
sees something: "The light, with malicious accuracy, ran round a rim
of cuff, a steel bangle, and made a thumb nail flash. Not deep enough
in the cleft between their *fauteuils* Eddie and Daphne were, with emphasis, holding hands. Eddie's fingers kept up a kneading movement:
her thumb alertly twitched at the joint." It is the most bluntly physical,
sexual moment in the book, yet also a frozen, displaced, dismembered
thing, as if that awful "emphasis" is alien even to the two who are holding hands.

Bowen places this sudden picture at the end of a chapter, leaving
Portia's response unspoken, hovering in the white space. It is not until the next day, while Portia and Eddie explore an empty, decaying
house along the shore, that she asks for an explanation. He tells her,
half-accusingly, that the hand-holding meant nothing, that he was just
being "matey," that he needs to "get off" with people because he can't
"get on." How fully she believes this we don't really know, that is another mystery of her innocent knowledge. But we know that this avert-
ing of one catastrophe only begets others, extends Portia's suffering.

There's first the shock when Portia shares Eddie's excuse with
Daphne, who calls her "bats" and "common," someone with "the mind
of a baby—and an awful baby." ("The civilisation of Waikiki seemed to
rock on its base.") The misery that Bowen brings out in a later conversation between Portia and Eddie, as they wander in a tangle of some
nearby woods, is almost unbearable. Portia's love is at all times a baffling, if not a blank thing; there is again a physical urgency, an attention of sense, mute, clumsy at times. She makes a despairing attempt
to kiss him, registering his hand like that of a "solicitous ghost whose
touch cannot be felt." When she talks, Eddie can hardly stand to listen,
though he finds his way to his own kind of lyric revelation (you can
think his language too good for him):

> "I can't bear it when you talk." When she got her wrists free, she once
> more locked her arms round him, she started rocking her body with such
> passionless violence that, as they both knelt, he rocked in her arms. "You
> stay alone in yourself, you stay alone in yourself!"

Eddie, white as a stone, said: "*You must let go of me....* You and I are enough to break anyone's heart—how can we not break our own? We are as drowned in this wood as though we were in the sea."

Portia's devotion shocks him, it becomes a fright more than a refuge. If Eddie frees her from any imputation of malice—as Anna can scarcely do—he yet feels Portia, in her innocent love, turn into a dangerous blocking agent. He cries at her: "You're damned lucky to have someone even as innocent as I am. I've never fooled you, have I? ... If I weren't innocent to the point of deformity, would you get me worked up into such a state? ... You've got a completely lunatic set of values, and a sort of unfailing lunatic instinct that makes you pick on another lunatic— another person who doesn't know where he is. You know I'm not a cad, and I know you're not batty. But, my God, we've got to live in the world." He claims innocence here as both mask and weapon. His appeal to conventional existence—"we've got to live in the world," supported by that banal cry of "my God"—this is exactly what Portia *doesn't* know, or doesn't know so simply as Eddie claims to know it. Whatever God or Devil Portia recognizes is of a different sort.

Portia does find at Waikiki a thing that calls out to her unknown knowledge, even another a kind of ghost. Mrs. Heccomb has placed on the mantlepiece in Portia's room an amateurish drawing of the nine-year-old Anna holding a kitten, a picture that Mrs. Heccomb herself made when she was Anna's governess. It is an act of kindness, her mistaken attempt to give Portia something that links her to her beloved home in London, to what she believes is Anna's motherly affection for the girl. The drawing is, Bowen writes, proof of the peculiar truth even of bad attempts at portraiture. For what Portia sees, what Portia *knows* in the sketch of Anna, is no image of innocent love. What the drawing records is instead the "misguided authority" of sadness, a ghost sadness that "stays behind the knowing and living look." (Everyone in the book is, at some moment, a novelist *manqué*, a witness of hidden truths.) "That urgent soul astray in the bad portrait, only came alive by electric light.... She saw the kitten hugged to the breast in a contraction of unknowing sorrow." She wonders whether the picture offers "confirmation that the most unlikely people suffer, or that everybody

who suffers is the same age?" You could say that it's Portia's unconscious projection, her inner electric light, that is at work. It is also as if,
far from Windsor Terrace, Portia has stumbled upon a memory of Anna's childhood that Anna herself has lost, a memory in which she is a
double of Portia. This might be an image to guide Portia more sympathetically back to that house, and help Anna open up to her in turn. Yet
when Portia speaks of the drawing later, back in London, Anna does
not remember it at all. She says that she only *just* remembers the kitten,
who died before growing up, quickly changing the subject to something else.

IN PART 3, "The Devil," Portia becomes a more knowing, demanding
and sharply critical being, more like what Anna has said she is. She's
now returned from Seale to the house in London. Windsor Terrace
has been made pure by Matchett's relentless work of cleaning, so that
Portia is even more bluntly like some polluting force, like the urban
dust that Matchett fears will drift into the pristine house through the
upper-floor windows. The memory of the seaside visit, in all its pain,
stays with her. Early in this section, in an echo of the book's opening,
Portia meets St. Quentin Miller by chance in the park behind Windsor Terrace (it's now summer instead of winter). In his embarrassed
attempts at polite banter, he unthinkingly asks, "How is your diary?"
After further embarrassment and clumsy evasion, he must spill the
truth of Anna's having read the diary and told him about it. What Portia
had thought safely enclosed in her room is suddenly scattered among
the trees.

Put on the defensive, the novelist murmurs fragments of a sermon
against diaries such as hers. Their fault is that they violate the polite
masks and avoidances that help adults survive. "I should never write
what had happened down. One's nature is to forget, and one ought to
go by that.... You do a most dangerous thing. All the time, you go making connections.... You put constructions on things. You are a most
dangerous girl.... It's not just that we are incurious; we completely lack
any sense of each other's existences.... The fact is, we have no great
wish for each other." You imagine what Portia feels listening to Mill-

er's opportunistic, cynical speech, the chill running through her blood, the inaudible howl that sounds in her head, the astonishment, the disgust, the sense of having her worst fears about adults confirmed. (And Miller echoes things that Bowen's own narrator has said, though his advice flatly contradicts her actual practice as a novelist.) Portia's silence makes Miller justify himself more coldly:

> "I should never talk like this if you weren't such a little stone."
>
> "It is what you've told me."
>
> "Naturally, naturally. Do you like to walk through the graveyard? And why has it got a bandstand in the middle? As you're quite near home, do something about your face."

"The idea of Portia as the childbride of Death, doomed for early sacrifice, is every so often suggested by her physical demeanour," writes Hermione Lee.

Portia flees her unhomely home right after this conversation, not saying anything to anyone, and disappearing from view for the whole of the book's long last chapter. Our last direct glimpse of Portia is when she's angrily weeping in Major Brutt's tiny attic room in the old-fashioned Karachi Hotel, where she has gone, in despair, to seek refuge from the adults who've betrayed her. The Major here learns from Portia what he should have known all along: that Anna and Thomas, who he thinks care for him, are always laughing at him, that they think him a pathetic child. She may not know the cruelty of her whispered cry: "You and I are the same." And indeed Major Brutt "felt her knocking through him like another heart outside his own ribs." But this knowledge doesn't change things. The lonely man knows he can't take care of her, much less, as Portia suggests, marry her, though he can't suppress a sensual shudder as Portia sits on his bed, the covers pulled around her.

Major Brutt calls Windsor Terrace—this is a novel alive to the strange work of phone calls, their delivery of news from an alien world, news of alien intimacies—where Anna, Thomas, and Miller sit in increasing bafflement over Portia's absence. ("We either have dinner or telephone the police," says exasperated Anna.) Thomas takes the call and reports: "She is waiting to see whether we do the right thing." That demand troubles their consciences. It asks them to imagine Portia herself, to weigh what sympathy they might have for her, to think what they themselves have done to her. They feel "the air of a court," "an individual deep guilty knowledge" that isolates them from one another. (Absent as she is, Bowen's Portia here claims her likeness to Shakespeare's Portia in *The Merchant of Venice*, who invades the final trial disguised as a lawyer, trading in ruthless and unregarded ideas of mercy.) Miller speaks of the "fun" that Portia is having, knowing that "this evening the pure in heart have simply got us on toast." He adds: "I swear that each of us keeps, battened down inside himself, a sort of lunatic giant—impossible socially, but full-scale—and that it's the knockings and batterings we sometimes hear in each other that keeps our intercourse from utter banality. Portia hears these the whole time; in fact she hears nothing else. Can you wonder she looks goofy most of the time?" Miller decides that Portia's "right thing" must be "an absolute of some sort, and absolutes only exist in feeling," and so it is only feeling that they have to go on.

Their solution is to send Matchett to fetch Portia home. The final pages of the book are given over to the servant's angry interior brooding in her taxi as it passes on a wandering journey through London— Bowen's version, as critics have noted, of a Joycean stream of consciousness. We take in her vexed sense of being, in her errand, both a trusted agent and a mere tool. We catch her rage at never being told *where* the taxi is taking her, her unwillingness to let this be known by the lower-class driver, her fear that she might be dropped off not knowing where she is. "It puts me wrong," she cries to herself. In time, she begins a conversation with the absent Portia. It starts in anger, with reproaches to the child for keeping secrets, for questioning things, for leaving what should be her home. "You're not like what you were.... You did ought to know better, after all what I told you. No good ever came of secrets— you look at your father." In time it turns more kindly, as she imagines urging Portia to her bed, to her tea, to her care, to Matchett's care. "You stay quiet, now, and remember what I said. I've got your fire on; it looks nice in your room now; and I've got those biscuits you like. You'd be all right if you'd only be like you were."

After a long interval, the keeper of ancient furniture arrives. "The sad gimcrack cliff of the hotel towered above her." In the book's last sentence, she enters: "Ignoring the bell, because this place was public, she pushed on the brass knob with an air of authority." It is as if some troubled spirit from the house on Windsor Terrace has come to claim the child. The blank space that follows that final sentence may remind you that Matchett's authority, like that of the other adults, is itself a blank, a thing of air, an imagined thing, one whose relation to Portia's world is uncertain.

The distance Matchett must cross from the hotel's front door to the cramped attic room where Portia waits seems unbridgeable. Whether she will find Portia, whether Portia will speak to her, or take her having come as "the right thing"—all is unknown. The "stretched mauve dusk" of early summer outside, the sound of an unseen piano, these hold a promise of life, a second chance. It's a season when, Bowen observes, "light struck into the... unvisited hearts" of forested islands in the waters of the park. But this also seems a world without escape. There's no lighting out for the territories for Portia, no possibility of a return to her childhood wanderings with her mother. There are no new parents to adopt her, no promise of a better lover. Yet Bowen gives a curious power to this blank space, this stopped, impossible space of waiting, of final judgment and final doubt. It crystallizes the force of Portia's joined innocence, knowledge, risk, and claims of power, of a life not quite born in her, the curious weight put upon what is after all so commonplace. There is something hallucinatory in the ending, cruel, dire, delicate. It trusts in an inward rather than an outward reality. Yet the theater of Portia's state of mind is a volatile thing, you're excluded from living in it even as you can't stop imagining it.

Bowen gives us no excerpt from Portia's diary at the end of part 3. It's a voice we may miss. In lieu of that, we have Matchett's interior monologue. We also hear the conversation of Anna, Thomas, and Miller that expands in the space of Portia's absence, including their response to her demand to "do the right thing." How much they get at any truth that Portia could share is an open question. But something that Anna says at this moment is striking.

She's been rehearsing her fears. The very *idea* of Portia is, again, like a demon that never leaves her quiet. "She drives me on to the ice.... She crowds me into an unreal position." Anna had said earlier that she deplores the demand that she try to enter into another's mind: "If one thought what everyone felt, one would go mad. It does not do to think of what people feel." Yet she has in this scene a burst of imaginative sympathy. Thomas, trying to reason out a solution to Portia's flight, asks Anna, simply, "How would you feel?" She responds with quick, deliberate force:

> "If I were Portia? Contempt for the pack of us, who muddled our own lives then stopped me from living mine. Boredom, oh such boredom, with a sort of secret society about nothing, keeping on making little signs to each other. Utter lack of desire to know what it was about. Wish that someone outside would blow a whistle and make the whole thing stop. Wish to have my own innings. Contempt for married people, keeping on playing up. Contempt for unmarried people, looking cautious and touchy. Frantic, frantic desire to be handled with feeling, and, at the same time, to be let alone. Wish to be asked how I felt, great wish to be taken for granted—"

Perhaps this is what Anna actually thinks Portia's diary is saying, or what she reads in its silences. She seems for a moment to catch at Portia's knot of misery, her rage, her weariness at adult games, her wish to escape, her need to be loved and also left alone. That Anna can imagine these things might lead you to think that these two women could learn to share a house, a world. But the moment breaks quickly. Anna's ventriloquism of Portia is so blindly full of her own despair, her own rage at others and at herself. "Contempt" is not Portia's mode. Anna's words also have an absoluteness alien to Portia's, an unhesitating universality about the tribe of "others" to which Anna belongs ("the pack of us"). And for all their urgent force, her words can't or won't mark the plainer sorrow for the loss of things that emanates from Bowen's dangerous child. Nor does she speak to Portia's strange freedom at this moment, her discovery of her power over those she's fled from.

Surprised at his wife's sudden passion, Thomas says, "This is all quite new, Anna. How much is the diary, how much is you?" To which Anna can only respond, finding herself again in a region of unlikeness: "You said, if I were Portia. Naturally that's impossible: she and I are hardly the same sex. Though she and I may wish to make a new start, we hardly shall, I'm afraid. I shall always insult her; she will always persecute me." It's a purgatory, one of her own making, shaped in her mind, but no less a purgatory for that.

LOLITA

THAT WE ARE reading the testament of a dead man. That we read his words after the death of the dangerous child, that child whose disappearance from his life the dead man keeps on mourning. He mourns her absence even as he tries to evoke her life and what he has cruelly made of it, what he took away from her, what he killed. He gives us the shapes of his loss and the shapes of hers. His memories emerge with unresting, grotesque, hallucinatory, luminous, and parodic force, memories that are at once scars and jewels (like the string of "rubies" of coagulated blood that he sees in a scratch on Lolita's arm). We're caught up in a terrible work of mourning, mourning driven by rapture, by the wish to reanimate the dead, the wish to explain, accuse, confess, and justify, to offer a mad analysis of his own desire, to fix precisely "the perilous magic of nymphets," "to fix... that borderline" where "the beastly and beautiful merged at one point." That borderline, always changing, impossible to fix, for him becomes an image of immortality, a desperate pitch against death.

*

That we learn to mourn as we read, caught by memorials the dead man may not see, hints of ghosts and losses he does not recognize, for all his restless work of writing and rewriting the past. A perverse student of his own nostalgias, Humbert Humbert appeals to his readers throughout, he speaks to us as judges, rational jurors, angels and demons of pity, priests at a confession—and then as psychologists, scholars of lying, adepts of play. He wants us to become complicit in his telling, even if we turn our eyes and ears away from what he says. His telling imprints itself on the inside of the eye, on the coils of the inner ear.

*

That this book tugs so terribly at the heart, even though Lolita's heart is all but invisible and Humbert's heart a monstrous riddle, at times a void, a parody of a heart, hardened beyond knowing, the object of a kind of sickened, mad bafflement, love, and also strange laughter, a *test* of laughter. One alternative title for *Lolita* would be *The Death of the Heart.*

*

We know from the book's opening pages that the writer of what we're reading has died of a heart attack while in prison. We may not realize until we finish the book, going back to look at the names in the foreword, that the child who has disappeared from his life is also dead, that she died in childbirth along with her baby, and far away. That death is something Humbert never learns of, he having died a month earlier. Yet in line with his last wishes, the book is free to come into the world—with fears of being stillborn?—just *because* both he and Lolita are dead.

*

Part of the fascination of reading *Lolita* is that it's almost impossible to say, for all his endless self-description and self-analysis, what Humbert feels or thinks about himself. That makes it harder to know what pity, if any, to have for him. You're borne along by a relentless, shifting linguistic energy in this narrator who brings us news of the child he's adored, captured, destroyed, lost—lost through what he says and through what he keeps silent about. (Here "the word-play leads back to the love-play always," as John Hollander wrote in one of the first American reviews of *Lolita*.) Wherever you open the book, the compulsive and compulsively playful, gloating and self-mocking voice hits you, takes you in, closes around you like a fog by turns translucent and opaque, keeping other realities at a distance, setting them in motion, following an odd tangent, interrupting itself, switching registers abruptly. In these notes from the underground, this diary of a madman, you can't say how much that voice is in control of its own motions, even if we assume that the novelist is in control. What does this put to the test? I write about *Lolita* to catch the book's own "perilous magic," the kind of grim fairy tale it is, to give shape to this last instance of the dream of the dangerous child.

*

A bit more than one hundred pages into the book—after stories of his lost first love, his abortive first marriage, his periods of insanity, after the awful death of the girl's mother, Charlotte Haze—Humbert takes pains to describe his first night lying beside the imperfectly drugged child in the room of a hotel named The Enchanted Hunters. He dilates on his slow, hallucinatory, and always thwarted approaches to her: "A breeze from wonderland had begun to affect my thoughts, and now they seemed couched in italics, as if the surface reflecting them were wrinkled by the phantasm of that breeze." The very unreality of the scene makes the more outrageous Humbert's appeal to us: "Please, reader: no matter your exasperation with the tenderhearted, morbidly sensitive, infinitely circumspect hero of my book, do not skip these essential pages! Imagine me; I shall not exist if you do not imagine me; try to discern the doe in me, trembling in the forest of my own iniquity." If we let Humbert's demand work on us, it should also call us to imagine the child who is burning or dreaming in the forest of this night, to imagine the child whose dangerousness may lie just in what Humbert can't know of her, what of her can't be absorbed by *his* imagining of this child, his pictures of a creature "not human, but nymphic (that is, demoniac)," "the little deadly demon among the wholesome children... unconscious herself of her fantastic power," "the body of some immortal daemon disguised as a female child." To imagine this child would mean imagining what Humbert himself fails to imagine, even if he often knows her plainly enough to be a thing of his own making, a desperate consolation, an "ineffable life which, ably assisted by fate, I had finally willed into being." It may be quixotic to try to imagine the living girl behind Humbert's mad screen of words. There's nothing to suggest that the child herself would ask this. The effort also risks its own sentimentality. Yet like many readers I can't help asking what in her energies of life fuel this book, or trying to catch glimpses of her capacity for wonder, pleasure, fear, cruelty, rage, desire, pity, knowledge, and love.

*

I sometimes don't know what name to use for this child. To call her "Lolita," as a student once reminded me, yields authority to Humbert's inventions, his relentless sentimentalizing and miniaturizing of her, his capturing of the girl—as in the novel's opening lines—within the self-delighting motions of his mouth, "Lo. Lee. Ta." "Lolita" is a name for the shadow that Humbert Humbert imposes on her substance, he being someone whose own name, an acknowledged fabrication, echoes that of another authoritarian namer—the pompous egg Humpty Dumpty. "Lolita" is not a name that the child ever calls herself. It's also hard—for all her sorrows—to call her Dolores, her Spanish-derived legal name, evoking the weeping Virgin Mary (*Nuestra Señora de los Dolores*), or Dolly, evoking childish play, or Lo, the announcement of a wonder or a word for her struck condition of life. (Humbert himself uses all of these names at one time or another.) The very volatility of the child's name says something, the way it lends her life and deprives her of it at the same time. You need to imagine a form of life for this orphaned child that is half capture, half escape.

*

You sit inside this fiction that keeps on asking you to enter defiled temples, defiled and defiling games, a kind of lucid nightmare that spills outward into life and then gets taken back inside itself. You grow to be at home in that nightmare, to be charmed, even to laugh there, and then are suddenly pulled out of it, never knowing quite where to step, how to claim your own place in that eerie, compulsive travel-through, moving about with all of its phantom limbs.

*

For every name Humbert gives to his own evil—as when he speaks of the "cesspoolful of rotting monsters" behind his smile, the "hidden tumor" of his lust, or his place as "one of those inflated pale spiders" in Charlotte Haze's house—there's some bland cruelty that he scarcely notices, some witness of suffering he marks without comment, or with curiously aesthetic delight, as when he speaks of the girl's eyes "bright with tears." At other times, Humbert knowingly names his cruelty, but does so through some turn of wit that mocks or questions the weight of his acknowledgment. You see this in the list of things he buys for Lolita before he finds her at Camp Q: "pumps of crushed kid for crushed kids... some prim cotton pajamas in popular butcher-boy style. Humbert, the popular butcher." Then there's the image that closes his dreamlike description of the elaborate mural he wants to paint on the wall of The Enchanted Hunters, to memorialize his first night with her: "There would have been a fire opal dissolving within a ripple-ringed pool, a last throb, a last dab of color, stinging red, smarting pink, a sigh, a wincing child."

*

Nabokov shows Humbert's desire keeping close to a sense of our sensitive, uncanny, and vulnerable bodies, yet with scale and relation transformed, often imagined in ways strangely obscene, through obscene play. I think of the moment when Humbert happily metamorphoses himself into a vampirish insect-aesthete, finding "on her brown shoulder, a raised purple-pink swelling (the work of some gnat) which I eased of its beautiful transparent poison between my long thumbnails and then sucked till I was gorged on her spicy blood." Or when he remembers "feeling... her warm weight in my lap (so that, in a sense, I was always 'with Lolita' as a woman is 'with child')."

*

Such motions of thought in Humbert's language are doubled by the movement of Humbert and Lolita's travels together in the second half of the novel. They're matched to the hallucinatory motion of Humbert's car as it slides and wanders and pauses in its journey across the ordinary American landscape, a wandering that's at best a parody of freedom, a freedom that sustains entrapment, an "exilic velocity" through which we follow the travels of a child exiled from childhood, an orphaned child obscenely parented. Traveling with this child, Humbert at one moment feels "as if I were sitting with the small ghost of somebody I had just killed." Space and vision expand and then suddenly contract. In the midst of accounts of stark beauty—"heart and sky-piercing snow-veined gray colossi of stone, relentless peaks appearing from nowhere at a turn of the highway"—you feel a relentless play of the pathetic fallacy, as Humbert gathers up from their travel mirrors of his own desire, cruelty, and guilt, so many lyric screams. Scattered in the expanding catalog of the sights they've seen—sights of things that, we're told, Lolita herself wanted to see, sops for the captive child—we glimpse strange shadows of their history together. These reclaim, re-map, translate the landscape:

> ... a collection of guns and violins somewhere in Oklahoma... rustici-ties became stranger and stranger to the eye... tall trucks studded with colored lights, like dreadful giant Christmas trees... hideous bits of tis-sue paper mimicking pale flowers among the prickles of wind-tortured withered stalks all along the highway... Skeletons of burned aspens, patches of spired blue flowers... Mission Dolores: good title for book... simple cows... cutting across all human rules of traffic... an atrociously crippled tour book in three volumes... impaled guest checks, life sav-ers... A patch of beautifully eroded clay; and yucca blossoms, so pure, so waxy, but lousy with creeping white flies... Crystal Chamber in the longest cave in the world, children 12 free, Lo a young captive... The mummy of a child (Florentine Bea's Indian contemporary). Our twenti-eth Hell's Canyon...

*

That the most dangerous child is the ordinary child in Lolita, the child whose thoughts and feelings are often unknown, unimaginable, or known too plainly. (Humbert remembers, as he heartlessly, creepily describes it, hearing her sobbing "every night, every night—the mo-ment I feigned sleep.") It's the child who refuses Humbert's enchant-ments even if she submits to his coercions and bribery. Are there places where she slips the boundaries of his fantasy? Is there a magic in her dif-ferent from the one that he awfully projects onto her? How do you trust this most untrustworthy of speakers to let you know what he doesn't know, what he can't imagine, "a Lolita whom Humbert can record but hardly see," as Michael Wood says, this writer who always finds his own "slippery self" eluding him, "gliding into deeper and darker waters than I care to probe"?

*

I think here of something that Humbert sees when Lolita doesn't know he's looking at her, a glimpse he catches through the open door of a motel bathroom, by means of an artful accident of angled mirrors—the kind of shunting or deflection of ordinary perception that Nabokov elsewhere associates with the peculiar powers of artistic vision. Humbert sees "a look on her face..., an expression of helplessness so perfect that it seemed to grade into one of rather comfortable inanity just because this was the very limit of injustice and frustration." At another moment he finds her half-asleep on a rented bed, "mouth open, in a kind of dull amazement at the curiously inane life we all had rigged up for her." (The "we all" is as chilling as the "rigged up," or the sense of a "curious" state of inanity.) Then there are some words Humbert overhears Lolita saying to a friend, when she thinks he isn't listening: "You know, what's so dreadful about dying is that you are completely on your own." Those words make him think that "I simply did not know a thing about my darling's mind and that quite possibly, behind the awful juvenile clichés, there was in her a garden and a twilight, and a palace gate—dim and adorable regions which happened to be lucidly and absolutely forbidden to me, in my polluted rags and miserable convulsions." The shiver of wonder in Lolita's words is the more startling because Humbert, in evoking "dim and adorable regions" he may not know—his "quite possibly" is astonishing—never acknowledges the plain fact of her loneliness, the dead space of her present life. He writes elsewhere that his "only grudge against nature" was that he could not turn this child inside out, so that he could kiss—along the "the seagrapes of lungs, her comely twin kidneys"—"her unknown heart." Do I imagine him wishing to *know* that heart, for all the romance of his language, or to treasure what in it remains unknown?

*

You might want to trust, more than anything Humbert says about her, the bare adjectives Lolita's mother chooses from a questionnaire in *A Guide to Your Child's Development*: "aggressive, boisterous, critical, distrustful, impatient, irritable, inquisitive, listless, negativistic (underlined twice) and obstinate."

*

That the most dangerous child is not the fey and demonic "nymphet," but whatever it is in Lolita that ties her to those "dirty and dangerous children in an outside world that was real to her," children whom Humbert keeps Lolita from playing with, keeping her from games that are real, or that claim the real, binding her instead to games that make her unreal to herself.

*

That the most dangerous child is Humbert Humbert. Of his Neverland of nymphets he says, "Let them play around me forever. Never grow up." *Never grow up*—Peter Pan's cry. Humbert speaks that to himself as much as to those playing children.

*

At moments, Nabokov shows us pieces of an uncontrollable reality or knowledge breaking through from a world outside Humbert, beyond his control. At one point something breaks through from within the very house he inhabits with Lolita, during the interval when he interrupts their travels to live in the eastern city of Beardsley. Humbert finds himself talking with Mona, a precocious friend of Lolita who's come early for a visit, before Lolita has gotten back from school. Then "Dolly arrived—and slit her pale eyes at us. I left the two friends to their own devices." Then follows this, without transition, to close the chapter:

> One of the latticed squares in a small cobwebby casement window at the turn of the staircase was glazed with ruby, and that raw wound among the unstained rectangles and its asymmetrical position—a knight's move from the top—always strangely disturbed me.

The red square is a bit of lawlessness that suggests the rule-bound power of the chess knight to leap over files and boundaries. Humbert leaves it uncertain to whose side the knight belongs and to what end it moves, attack or flight. A glazer's whim perhaps, the square has the look of a wound, the memory of a wound, whether his own or Lolita's you couldn't say. A stain in a space of things unstained, it's the red of desire, also the trace of a sin or shame, a blush in a field of white transparency.

*

Such outward glimpses of inward mystery, marks of an unknown wound, an unknown pattern or game, always call up for me what Nabokov describes in his afterword to *Lolita* as the "first little throb" of the novel, felt years before he began writing. It came from reading "a newspaper story about an ape in the Jardin des Plantes, who, after months of coaxing by a scientist, produced the first drawing ever charcoaled by an animal: this sketch showed the bars of the poor creature's cage." Nabokov leaves it for us to imagine the nature of that coaxing. And he makes no further comment on the drawing itself, a drawing that can seem both rebuke and self-recognition, a mirror of loss and a bitter attempt at mastery, even the ape's mute appeal to his captors. The story—mused over by many critics—offers a picture of the whole work in which Humbert draws and redraws the bars of his own cage, traces the bondage of his fantasy and his bondage to that fantasy, his own wounded and wounding desire and memory of loss. ("My fancy was both Proustianized and Procrusteanized.") It's an image of the delights and dangers of self-entrapment, the claims of an "umber and black Humberland," its strange namings and misnamings of the world. The ape's drawing also evokes the cage that Humbert creates around the girl he calls Lolita, around the thought of her, around her person, he being himself an artist of seductive, enchanting cages, working with bars and the shadows of bars, working through a shifting combination of coercion, temptation, and habit. It is the cage that Humbert seeks to draw around us as we read, a cage made up as he sits writing within his own jail cell, "under observation," held within the cage of his memory, trying to puzzle out how things work "in this wrought-iron world of criss-cross cause and effect." The bars of the cage are the long horizontal bars of his writing, the printed text of the book, through which we are to glimpse his face, or what becomes of it, and what we can't see of his face.

*

"We are most artistically caged," writes Nabokov's invented poet John Shade in the poem entitled "Pale Fire." Shade is referring the lovely accidents of shadow and light, sun and cloud, that animate the world of visible things enclosing us. Yet his words point to less beautiful cages, their wounds and wonders, prisons and prisms combined. Nabokov is a great scholar, artist, and comedian of cages. Many of his stories take us inside veritable jails and prison camps, locked wards for the insane or those said to be insane. He lets us see their terror and piteousness, their frightening *uses* for those in power. He likes to imagine the strange vanity of those who oversee such prisons, as in *Invitation to a Beheading*, where Cincinnatus C, condemned to death for the crime of being opaque in a world of assumed transparency, finds himself courted by a repulsive, cheery, insinuating fellow inmate, a man who turns out to be

Cincinnatus's executioner—this game serving the state's "noble" idea
that a condemned man should only be killed by someone who knows
him intimately, even better than he knows himself. Nabokov also studies forms of entrapment disguised as love or freedom, cages self-made
as well as imposed from without. He explores how our real and imagined cages collaborate, how our cages come to know and desire us, seek
us out. Thought can be both a prison and a dark form of transcendence.
So the philosopher Adam Krug in *Bend Sinister*, living in a state that's
ordered by mad and tyrannous laws, is invited to imagine an Ophelia
whose mind frees itself in madness, an eroticized mermaid teasing out
secrets, studious of death. Time can be a prison ("spherical and without
exits") and memory a cage, a self-made purgatory—yet also a source
of blessing, as when you find "a face, a phrase, a landscape, an air bubble from the past suddenly floating up as if released by the head war-
den's child from a cell in the brain while the mind is at work on some
totally different matter." Nabokov writes in *Speak, Memory* of "a sea-
shell in which I found the imprisoned hum of one of my own seaside
summers." *Lolita* asks you to find a home in such constantly changing,
equivocal cages.

*

The cages of *Lolita* often take the form of games. You are always caught
up in shifting, conflicting games, including the games the mind plays
on itself, also games by which one mind draws in another, or in which
they're bound together through disguise, bribery, menace, violence,
and accident, through secrets kept and exposed, secrets stolen and profaned. It's within such cage-like games that you can seek for traces of
the unknown child.

*

In *Vladimir Nabokov and the Art of Play*, Thomas Karshan wonderfully
traces scattered moments in which the novelist gives us a child Lolita
full of the energy of play, even if only seen in the net of Humbert's
memory. This energy surfaces in her mocking repartee and slangy wit,
in her attachment to stray dogs, in her skill at tennis ("teetering on the
very brink of unearthly order and splendor"). It's there in her early flir-
tations with Humbert—Nabokov never slanders children by making
them innocent of erotic impulses, however hard to fix or name, refus-

ing established categories, one thing he shares with Freud, whom he so vocally despised. Lolita shows an appetite for play that can both seduce and thwart Humbert—"very infantile, infinitely meretricious," he calls it—an appetite that he often tries to bury, distract, or block, or absorb to other games.

*

Humbert Humbert knows that he himself is drawn to "the magic of games." There's a moment when he plays chess with a friend in Beardsley, Gaston Godin, a man with his own concealed pederastic inclinations. Humbert brags that, as a master of play, "I saw the board as a square pool of limpid water with rare shells and stratagems rosily visible upon the smooth tessellated bottom, which to my confused adversary was all ooze and squid-cloud." In the elaborate, often desperate games by which Humbert tries to bind Lolita, you feel the cruelty, corrosiveness, and vanity that can become a part of the "magic" of human play. You can also feel increasing gaps in Humbert's mastery, traces of intelligences that surprise him, stratagems that he can't control. They're like what's marked by that red square of glass in the "cobwebby" tessellated window in the Beardsley house, a piece of orderly disorder, the mark of an unknown wound, lit from a place beyond him, recalling a leaping knight's move in a game that he does not know his part in.

*

I think here of the games devised by Clare Quilty, Humbert's nemesis, that dog him during his travels with Lolita. These games leave Humbert confused as to whether his pursuer is "secret agent, or secret lover, or prankster, or hallucination." Lolita herself abets these games, since they're her best chance to free herself, even though they only lead her to another jailer. The unknown follower—Humbert nicknames him "Trapp," after a Swiss uncle—"succeeded in thoroughly enmeshing me and my thrashing anguish in his demoniacal game. With infinite skill, he swayed and staggered, and regained an impossible balance, always leaving me with the sportive hope—if I may use such a term in speaking of betrayal, fury, desolation, horror and hate—that he might give himself away next time. He never did."

*

Quilty's games keep Humbert tied to him even after Lolita has fled, as when he retraces their travels, returning to inns and motels where he and his captive had stayed. Peeking into guestbooks, he discovers, or thinks he discovers, the mocking names his pursuer has inscribed and trusted him to find, names that mirror Humbert's anxious memory and fantasy. They include "Harold Haze, Tombstone, Arizona" (evoking Lolita's dead father, another H. H.), "Ted Hunter, Cane, NH" (an "anagramtailed" reminder of The Enchanted Hunters), and "A. Person, Porlock, England" (recalling that "person on business from Porlock" who interrupted Samuel Taylor Coleridge while he wrote down his dream poem "Kubla Khan," a dream with its own demon lovers and enchanted maidens). "What a shiver of triumph and loathing shook my frail frame when, among the plain innocent names in the hotel recorder, his fiendish conundrum would ejaculate in my face!"

*

Play, like childhood and memory, keeps slipping its moorings in *Lolita*. Memory itself is the game-cage Humbert builds around himself, memory wrought up with the life of what charms it and what wounds it, things he cannot see even as he gives them shape—a counterartifice, a counterlove. It's not clear at any moment what is a further turn of the labyrinth and what a twist of the thread that solves the maze. Humbert is at once a questing Theseus and the maiden-devouring Minotaur, and then also Daedalus himself, the maker of the maze through which he moves. How would you free an idea of Lolita from such a cage as Humbert has built around her?

*

We learn late in the novel of a less coercive game that Lolita has played during her time with Humbert. This game evokes something in the child that might surprise him. It asks us to imagine what Humbert has not imagined. His mind wanders back to Lolita's drama classes at the Beardsley School, recalling how she threw herself into rehearsing the part of a witch in Quilty and Vivian Darkbloom's *The Enchanted Hunters*—a play in which six ordinary men remember their real lives "only as dreams or nightmares," while a seventh, a poet, insists he'd invented those dreams. Humbert gives us the text of a mimeographed sheet that he's kept from that time, the description of a series of dramatic exercises, improvisatory games. They suggest to jealous Humbert Lolita's training in deception, even as they evoke "a mystic rite," or "sophisticated versions of infantile make-believe":

Tactile drill. Imagine yourself picking up and holding: a pingpong ball, an apple, a sticky date, a new flannel-fluffed tennis ball, a hot potato, an ice cube, a kitten, a puppy, a horseshoe, a feather, a torchlight.

Knead with your fingers the following imaginary things: a piece of bread, india rubber, a friend's aching temple, a sample of velvet, a rose petal.

You are a blind girl. Palpate the face of: a Greek youth, Cyrano, Santa Claus, a baby, a laughing faun, a sleeping stranger, your father.

The game composes a kind of animated collage. It's a redemptive rather than a cursed list, as so many of Humbert's lists are. The exercise invites us to imagine the otherwise unseen play of Lolita's hand and mind, to imagine her imagination of touch, picking up objects ordinary and fantastical, things animate and inanimate, parts of a child's world and parts of an adult's. Some are things that she must know, others she's asked to conjure out of nothing (including not being able to see). You feel the work and pressure of the game, the loss and danger there— you might think, for instance, of just how little kneading a rose petal might bear, as a student once said to me. You're invited to think of Lolita's living, groping, playful, and sensitive body, her imagining body. You can also think of how the game would conjure for Lolita memories of being herself an object of touch, touch hot and cold, dead and alive. You could suppose that some items on the list have been put there by Humbert, retrospectively toying with himself and her, as in that final, uneasy pairing of "a sleeping stranger" and "your father." There is also much among those games that slips the reins of Humbert's mastery, tracks into an unknown wilderness where he himself might be afraid to follow. They suggest forms of possibility in which Lolita leaves traces of her conscious life, forms in which she survives. The game points to Nabokov's obsession with, in Wood's words, "the precarious but possibly continuing life of whatever has been thoroughly, painfully or ecstatically imagined."

*

Another slight and eerie memory of Lolita's play breaks through late in the book. It's during that space of time when Humbert is vengefully making his way toward Quilty. He pauses after midnight in the

empty street of a small town "to enjoy the innocent night and my terrible thoughts."

Let me dally a little, he is as good as destroyed. Some way further across
the street, neon lights flickered twice slower than my heart: the outline
of a restaurant sign, a large coffee-pot, kept bursting, every full second or
so, into emerald life, and every time it went out, pink letters saying Fine
Foods relayed it, but the pot could still be made out as a latent shadow
teasing the eye before its next emerald resurrection. We made shadowgraphs. This furtive burg was not far from The Enchanted Hunters. I was
weeping again, drunk on the impossible past.

Here the thoughtless, mechanical signage of an American street becomes the material of a dream romance, a self-delighting and self-
mocking "dallying." For me, the starkest shiver comes in one brief sentence: "We made shadowgraphs." It's the mark of a wonder-wound in
memory, touched by loss and self-pity, furtive itself, blinded by these
shifting lights. The words that break into Humbert's mind are Lolita's.
She said them to him when he found her at Camp Q, just before carrying her off to The Enchanted Hunters. Listing the games that she's
played, Lolita adds archly, "We made shadowgraphs. Gee, what fun."
Nabokov, dark scholar of nostalgia, invites you to measure the distance
between the two occasions. As remembered in that late-night pause,
the child's mocking exclamation calls up crueler acts of making, darker
shapes of "fun," darkenings of life and love. Between the shadowgraphs
Lolita made at camp and those that Humbert makes, what is the relation? (And how do these sit together in a novel that is itself a shad-
owgraph, a writing of and with darkness?) The simple word "we" in
that remembered sentence now evokes a different, more unsettling intimacy, even as it marks the wound of an absence, like that ruby square.

*

Humbert's own nightmares during this time call up forms of violence
that have no place in his waking narrative. They are dreams both fantastic and all too concrete, the more frightening for his describing them in
a slightly mocking, throwaway fashion: "I would be entertained at te-
dious vivisecting parties that generally ended with Charlotte or Valeria

weeping in my bleeding arms and being tenderly kissed by my brotherly lips in a dream disorder of auctioneered Viennese bric-à-brac, pity, impotence, and the brown wigs of tragic old women who had just been gassed."

*

Lolita keeps no diary, as does Bowen's Portia, noting other people's words, gestures, and hidden thoughts. (It's rather Humbert whose diary figures prominently in an early chapter, its dire honesty stripping Lolita's mother of her illusions about the man she's married, a spur to her death.) Nor does Nabokov shape his novel, as James does his, around mysterious hints of "What Lolita Knew," inviting us continually to note the child's unspoken thoughts about the adults around her, their love, possessiveness, fear, and regret. But the games proposed on that mimeographed sheet, or such a cry as "we made shadowgraphs," these are among myriad small moments that evoke the mind and history of this child in ways that break free of Humbert's control, even if he also translates them into a new key.

*

We hear Lolita's words more starkly in another remembered piece of paper, a letter that Humbert finds in his mailbox three years after the girl's disappearance. He first takes it for a letter from his current lover's mad mother, but then finds that the page "began talking to me in a small matter-of-fact voice":

DEAR DAD:

How's everything? I'm married. I'm going to have a baby. I guess he's going to be a big one. I guess he'll come right for Christmas. This is a hard letter to write. I'm going nuts because we don't have enough to pay our debts and get out of here. Dick is promised a big job in Alaska in his very specialized corner of the mechanical field, that's all I know about it but it's really grand. Pardon me for withholding our home address but you may still be mad at me, and Dick must not know. This town is something. You can't see the morons for the smog. Please do send us a check, Dad. We could manage with three or four hundred or even less, anything is welcome, you might sell my old things, because once we get there the dough will just start rolling in. Write, please. I have gone through much sadness and hardship.

Yours expecting,

DOLLY (MRS. RICHARD F. SCHILLER)

The letter's voice cuts sharply through the dense, infected texture of Humbert's language. It's a voice we have not heard before. Has Humbert himself ever heard it? The past child speaks in the naked present, an adult now free of her captor, self-possessed, full of candor, even when in need and afraid. The "Dear Dad" is astonishing. She asks for a simple generosity Humbert has never before shown. If the letter gambles on his love, contrives to draw him in, you may also hear unspoken forms of need and pain hiding within the flat, formulaic phrases, "How's everything?" "I'm going nuts," "Dick is promised a big job," "the dough will just start rolling in." There's something desperate in the strained politeness of "Pardon me," and "Yours expecting." ("Yours"!) What would it mean for this exiled girl to speak of "our home address"? Or of "expecting" help as she expects a child? "This is a hard letter to write" (just after "I guess he'll come *right* for Christmas"). You can wonder how much it cost Lolita to write that letter, or to say to Humbert, whose words had so entangled her, "Write, please." (*Lolita*, Nabokov tells us, was a hard book to write, "a painful birth, a difficult baby.") You may wonder what, even in breaking silence, the letter will not speak about ("I have gone through much sadness and hardship"), and what it seeks to silence for the sake of others ("Dick must not know"). At its close, we're left to imagine the unknown interval of time between the life of the girl who signs herself "Dolly" and that of "Mrs. Richard F. Schiller," a name enclosed in protective parentheses.*

*

* Karshan suggests that Lolita's married name aims to remind us of Friedrich Schiller, the German Romantic poet, playwright, and essayist who, in his *Letters on the Aesthetic Education of Man*, wrote about play as a special mark of the human in its fullness, as an essentially free activity that balances the conflicting demands of nature and reason, matter and spirit, sensation and reflection. The allusion mainly marks how far Lolita is at this moment from the world of play, play whose potential for unfreedom she knows very well.

Most startling is the "I" that pulses urgently in the letter's opening sentences, and then returns at the end: "I'm married. I'm going to have a baby. I guess... I guess... that's all I know... I have gone through..." You have to guess at the hopeful, pained, troubled force of her mind in those repetitions of "I guess." In his afterword to *Lolita*, Nabokov makes fun of an editor (perhaps invented) who wanted him to change his dangerous book into an American story about a boy and a farmer, a story composed in short, blunt sentences: "'He acts crazy. We all act crazy, I guess. I guess God acts crazy.' Etc." Lolita's letter, itself marked by that very American "I guess," marks the ironic triumph of such a voice.

*

You could take the letter as a fabrication of Humbert's. That might be just as startling. It would mean that he can for a moment break through the bars of his solipsism and narcissism, that he's capable of torturing and amazing himself with a Lolita independent of him, if also in need of him, a Lolita so bluntly able to describe the shapes of her new cage and her new freedom.

*

And then there is the voice we hear in Humbert's last meeting with Lolita. Fully prepared to assassinate the girl's supposed kidnapper, he's found her poor, married, shabby, "frankly and hugely pregnant," living in shack in a grim corner of an industrial city. He finds her in the company of needful men, her half-deaf husband ("instantaneously reprieved") and an older, one-armed friend, a veteran. This is a place beyond Humbert's and Quilty's games, even if it shows what these games have cost Lolita. We catch more intensely here the voice of a grown, self-possessed woman, refusing seduction, refusing to return to the past, however willing she is to mine the past for money. She bluntly, with a curious smile, turns back Humbert's frenzied requests that she go away to him ("I will create a brand new God and thank him with piercing cries, if you give me that microscopic hope"). She is eerily gentle to him as he weeps ("No, honey, no"), even blaming herself ("I'm so sorry I cheated so much"). And she claims her silence. Asked to recall the "weird, filthy, fancy things" Quilty had asked of her, she replies "'Oh, things... Oh, I—really I'—she uttered the 'I' as a subdued cry while she listened to the source of the ache, and for lack of words spread the five fingers of her angularly up-and-down-moving hand. No, she gave it up, she refused to go into particulars with that baby inside her."

*

The sadness of the scene feels starker when I think that Nabokov here restages a moment from the end of *Peter and Wendy*, the saddest moment in that saddest of books. "Then one night came the tragedy." It's when Peter returns unexpectedly to the house in London to fetch Wendy back to the Neverland for spring cleaning, unaware that, over the many years of his absence, she's become a mother with a child of her own. Crouching down at first, ashamed, "a big woman," Wendy finally rises up, stirring in Peter a fear he's never felt, at once a fear of this unknown creature and a fear *of* his fear. "'What is it?,' he cried, shrinking. . . . What is it?" After a momentary impulse to strike the child, Peter sits on the floor and sobs. Wendy holds him, yet cannot comfort him as she had in the past, cannot answer his unreadable love and need and terror. "She was not a little girl heartbroken about him; she was a grown woman smiling at it all, but they were wet smiles."

*

Arriving unexpectedly at Lolita's house, Humbert-Peter has *not* forgotten the years when he has not seen her. It's hard to be sentimental about Humbert's tears (at least not without being ashamed), or about his knowingly mad prayer that she come back to him. "'No,' she said smiling, 'no.'" Lolita's smile of refusal is not a "wet smile." There's exhaustion and more bitter knowledge behind that smile, and perhaps a greater shock at seeing that Humbert has still "not grown up." Lolita insists, like Wendy, on how much time has passed, the fact of her pregnant body facing Humbert more bluntly than Wendy's adult height and sleeping daughter. Nabokov also fixes a more absolute bar between past and present. There's no second chance for Humbert, a chance such as Peter gets when Wendy's daughter Jane returns with him to the Neverland—as Jane's daughter and her daughter's daughter will also do, each "gay and innocent and heartless." Dolly Schiller's child is as yet unborn, and she will herself die "in childbed, giving birth to a stillborn girl, on Christmas Day 1952, in Gray Star, a settlement in the remotest Northwest," a very different Neverland. Humbert flees, like Peter forgoing present violence, but unlike him turning his weapon on another.

*

It's hard to imagine how this woman might take in the killing of Clare Quilty, the former idol, seducer, and abuser whose identity she's revealed to Humbert. (We never learn if she hears of the murder.) Lolita knows Humbert's deviousness, his susceptibility to "the magic of games." She knows a real violence in him. And she knows Quilty's penchant for intricate, ugly play. Still, standing in the stripped shack in that desolate town, it might be hard for her to imagine, and then only with horror and disgust, the baroque farce of the murder that slowly unfolds in the labyrinthine Pavor Manor (*pavor* is the Latin word for fear or dread). The killing of Quilty is Humbert's last attempt to banish his despair and rage at his loss, to redeem his past. It only makes his despair reveal itself more sharply, along with the grim shape of his fantasy.

*

Humbert walks through Quilty's house like his own ghost. He wants to become a form of fate, a bringer of ironic justice—justice to be accomplished, in part, by Humbert's new cherished companion, the pistol he's nicknamed "Chum." Each game Humbert tries out is undone, its rules get shifted, stolen, and deformed. Quilty himself works a little like the creatures Alice meets in Wonderland, turning Humbert's games into their own species of nonsense, revising his carefully scripted revenge tragedy into sharp, panicked comedy. At one point, Humbert insists that Quilty recite a formal poem of accusation, a strange pastiche of T. S. Eliot's "Ash Wednesday":

> Because you took advantage of a sinner
> because you took advantage
> because you took
> because you took advantage of my disadvantage...

The effect of Quilty's reading these lines is that the "you" intended to accuse Quilty of betrayal and abuse is turned back on Humbert himself. Even more clearly than during his earlier quest, tracking a kidnapper through motel registers, Humbert faces in Quilty his own comic, infantile double, a more murderous and heartless Tweedledee entangled with Tweedledum. This is plainest when the two men struggle to get hold of the dropped pistol: "We fell to wrestling again. We rolled all over the floor, in each other's arms, like two huge helpless children. He was naked and goatish under his robe, and I felt suffocated as he rolled over me. I rolled over him. We rolled over me. They rolled over him. We rolled over us."

*

When Humbert finally grapples the gun and fires at his enemy, the bullets seem mainly to feed Quilty's clownish posturing. At a first missed shot, Quilty rushes to the piano to play "several atrociously vigorous, fundamentally hysterical, plangent chords," and then, when a shot catches him, "he rose from his chair higher and higher, like old, gray, mad Nijinski, like Old Faithful, like some old nightmare of mine." Humbert watches his victim "dreadfully twitching, shivering, smirking," responding to each bullet that enters him with faux-polite protests in a fake British accent ("Ah, that hurts, sir, enough! Ah—very painful, very painful, indeed"). "In distress, in dismay, I understood that far from killing him I was injecting spurts of energy into the poor fellow, as if the bullets had been capsules in which a heady elixir danced." That energy ironically reflects the logic of murder in Nabokov's thought, his sense that, as Ellen Pifer writes, "by depriving his victim of life, the murderer paradoxically forfeits his own powers of vital existence.... The victim's corpse is the murderer's true twin, a palpable reflection of his deathly condition."

*

Humbert wants by his murder to bury the memories of his crimes against Lolita. They come back nonetheless. You catch echoes of Humbert's long possession of Lolita in his victim's continued life (that "nightmare of wonder"), in the sexual feel of the wrestling match, in the shadowy allusion to those "magic capsules" with which Humbert drugs Lolita during their long night at The Enchanted Hunters. At the final moment of Quilty's life, which turns out not to be final, the bloodied man flees back to his bedroom and wraps himself in the bedclothes: "I hit him at very close range through the blankets, and then he lay back, and a big pink bubble with juvenile connotations formed on his lips, grew to the size of a toy balloon, and vanished." Nowhere in the novel does Humbert describe Lolita blowing bubbles of bubble-gum (though the image is sharply caught in Adrian Lyne's 1997 film). But the memory of such a game creeps into his account of Quilty's murder. That blood bubble adds a final note of clownishness and mockery to his dying. It also suggests that, at this moment, Humbert is not just killing Quilty, and his own double in Quilty, but killing Lolita. He takes revenge on the child who so ruthlessly pops the toy balloon of his desire, killing her in the image of a child at play. He takes revenge on his own play world, and on his desire itself.

*

After Quilty's murder, Humbert reports "a last mirage of wonder and hopelessness." Sitting in his stalled car, waiting for the police to arrest him, Humbert remembers a moment from his earlier cross-country chase after Lolita and Quilty. "An attack of abominable nausea forced me to pull up on the ghost of an old mountain road." After "coughing myself inside out," he walks up to a stone parapet that looks over a mist-shrouded valley. He sees from this spot, as the mist clears, a distant, glittering mill town, and hears rising up from its invisible streets sounds that he suddenly knows to be the sounds of children at play. He can't see anyone at all, he only takes in that relentless, shifting, noise-like music, "majestic and minute, remote and magically near, frank and divinely enigmatic." There's a "spurt of vivid laughter... the crack of a bat... the clatter of a toy wagon." Listening to those sounds, Humbert knows that "the hopelessly poignant thing was not Lolita's absence from my side, but the absence of her voice from that concord." This can feel, as it has to many readers, like another of Humbert's ghoulish evasions, "mawkish and self-regarding," and just skirting "the edge of kitsch." You've learned not to trust his aestheticized laments, his secret, vicarious pleasure in the losses he claims to mourn. And you know how far Lolita's absence is at this moment from mere poignancy, even hopeless poignancy. (What kind of hope does Humbert understand?) But this moment of listening never fails to move me, to cause shivers. It's partly because such sounds are real enough, and familiar. I've heard them many times, outside of windows, around a street corner, on the other side of a green-gray hill. It's also because the novel has made me so aware of the dissonances that would have been part of that wished-for concord. The book knows the discord and nonsense and tremor of strangeness, the uncanny knowledge, the desperate fear, the rage as well as freedom, that can live in the play of a child, real and imagined.

*

In the novel's afterword, Nabokov writes that he himself had heard those "tinkling sounds" of children at play during one of his own western journeys in search of unknown butterflies—it was on the mountain trail where he caught the "first known female of *Lycaeides sublivens* Nabokov." He recaptures this past moment of capture within the mythmaking of *Lolita*, reclaims the clutch of time and timelessness, the marriage of accident and recognition that, for this wandering lepidopterist, would have given the moment its magic ("a momentary vacuum into which rushes all that I love"), a magic that had been central to his own childhood. The novelist Nabokov nets stranger butterfly hunters as well as stranger butterflies. He imagines creepier namers of unknown species of being, pseudolepidopterists who ask us to study flitting creatures that they know little of, cannot truly name, and threaten with death. You catch an image of such strange hunting in Humbert's account of his first visit to Pavor Manor, his mind on killing Quilty. The scene takes place at night, as he drives along a winding rural road marked by ghostly reflectors, their light borrowed from that of his car. Humbert himself moves through the darkness like a ghost, his headlights picking out winged creatures: "In front of me, like derelict snowflakes, moths drifted out of the blackness into my probing aura." Finding the house full of guests and a loud party in progress, he decides to return in the morning to finish his work. He makes his way back to his motel in the "moonless and massive night." He drives again on winding country roads, past gesticulating silhouettes of trees, past the huge, suddenly vanishing phantom of a gunman on the screen of a drive-in movie, and then onward into the dark. "There was still that stream of pale moths siphoned out of the night by my headlights." Within the lives of those unnamed moths, there's a lot going on in the dark and under other lights, heartlights instead of headlights, that Humbert cannot know. Nabokov might have liked these lines from Wallace Stevens's "Le Monocle de Mon Oncle":

> Like a rose rabbi, later, I pursued,
> And still pursue, the origin and course
> Of love, but until now I never knew
> That fluttering things have so distinct a shade.

We make shadowgraphs.

CODA

NONE OF MY dangerous children get any final say in their stories. The strange life energies revealed in these children are usually, when things come to a close, set at a distance, silenced or veiled, often by the consciousness of the narrator or by our attention to another character. Some of the children disappear entirely from view. It's a future Alice who concerns Alice's sister when, left alone at the close of *Wonderland*, she wonders whether the child's heart will survive into adulthood. The "proper boy" Pinocchio looks at the now lifeless puppet he was and sees something he cannot recognize. Henry James closes his novel by marking Maisie's continuing mystery to Mrs. Wix, and it's Matchett's angry thoughts as she carries an unknown message to Portia that Elizabeth Bowen gives us at the end of *The Death of the Heart*, not the thoughts of Portia herself, hidden away in a high hotel room. It's the future of all *other* children, "gay and innocent and heartless," that occupies J. M. Barrie's mind at the close of *Peter and Wendy*. At the end of *A High Wind in Jamaica*, Richard Hughes lets his Emily's face and person dissolve among the "innocent faces" of the other girls at her new school; he could not pick her out of that crowd, he thinks, though perhaps God might do so. Franz Kafka's housefather stops his brief tale with the blank, incomprehensible thought of Odradek's continuing life, a thing that is to him "almost painful." Humbert Humbert's closing ode to a shared immortality makes clear just how far he is from the child he calls "my Lolita."

Such endings pay homage to the solitude that shapes the being of these imagined children. They remind one that, from the start of their stories, the children's claims on us grow from some quantity of unknown life in them. You feel that life's elusiveness, its vulnerability, the dangers that surround it. You feel also its power, its strange capacity to defend its freedom and separateness, and then to claim others, to open up stranger threads of connection. It's a life that may be unknown to the children themselves. It's even more likely to be unknown to the adults around them, however much those adults may struggle to interpret that life, or shape it in ways that serve their own needs and fears. Simply the children's names can become a mystery or a stumbling block. ("Why is she called Portia?" asks the novelist St. Quentin Miller in *The Death of the Heart*, never receiving an answer.) How close is the child's life to an adult's life, after all? The books ask that we keep watch on these children's solitude, on what it makes visible, even as that solitude continues to change.

Stories of the dangerous child give shape to things otherwise difficult to speak about. They face us with forms of appetite and feeling, forms of play and wonder, histories of pain, that are by turns more alien and more ordinary than we might expect. Odd secrets loom up in them. Or they start to have the look of madness. A small gesture, a sudden leap or fall, a way of running, will link these children to elemental forces in nature, link their life to motions of fire and air. It will tie them to the lives of animals, real and imagined—hedgehog, serpent, mouse, jackdaw, and lordly pig. It will bind them uncommonly to the world of common objects. The games of these children touch the roots of making, even as the children evoke corrosive and self-destructive energies in themselves and others. Their words may seem both ancient and newly hatched, words bound to silence, to a muteness that weaves itself within speech, asking more acute forms of listening. They at once mark and cross the threshold between adult and child, they're like double agents who move between one world and the other. We may scarcely know what these children look like. They show us different faces of loss, of life and death, or forms of death-in-life and life-in-death. There are in them losses to be buried and losses to be reclaimed, to be made the ground for a different happiness. The traces of their wounded and wounding life call out to an unfathomable healing.

Within these stories, the pressure of time, of living in time, shows itself in more mysterious ways. Time and growth can seem suspended in these fictive children. Or time moves brokenly, stopping and starting, abruptly jumping forward and back. It claims us with odd moments of mourning and sentimentality. There are wild visions of survival, leaps into an unknown future. You see also how distinct pictures of time come into conflict, how they call out to or invade each other, showing you time as a thing variously personal and impersonal, concrete and fantastic, open and closed. The world of childhood becomes its own kind of maze, a time maze as well as a space maze, multiplying passageways between new and old, early and late, the vanished away and the yet-to-be. How old are these children? How old should you be?

Let each of them speak a little at the end:

I ran and they chased, and I kept running and they kept chasing.

You're free—you're free.

This is a hard letter to write.

You've no idea how confusing it is all the things being alive.

You see I don't know any stories. None of the lost boys knows any stories.

I've got an earthquake.

No fixed abode.

You and I are the same.

ACKNOWLEDGMENTS

THE LATE ANGUS Fletcher first urged me to make a book out of my fascination with these imaginary children, keeping the subject alive in many exchanges by phone and email. An early spark came also from Richard Howard, in wandering talks about Alice and Peter. Rikki Ducornet and Helen Oyeyemi, makers of their own uncanny children, were guardian spirits, sharing thoughts and questions from the beginning to the end of writing. Jim Longenbach and Joanna Scott, who know my work of old, read the manuscript with their acute and ever-generous critical eyes, helping me see much better the book I've been writing. Uli Knoepflmacher also brought his sympathetic scrutiny to my chapters, even as he helped me find my way through the vast scholarship on children's literature, to which he's contributed so much. Gordon Teskey and Rosanna Warren gave their sustaining enthusiasm for the project. Conversations and exchanges with Mark Anderson, Peter Cole, Jean D'Costa, Ishion Hutchinson, Thomas Karshan, Ellen Levy, John Michael, Esther Schor, Stephen Schottenfeld, and Froma Zeitlin opened up fresh questions, clarified doubts, and pointed me to sources I'd not otherwise have known.

I'd like to have given this book to two friends and teachers now gone, Harold Bloom and John Hollander, who taught me always to keep faith with my oldest springs of literary pleasure.

I owe an essential debt to the students in my classes on "dangerous children" at the University of Rochester, who read the books with such energy and openness, with a sense of what's urgent. Their words still resonate in my mind. These classes also brought me back, in ways I'd not predicted, to memories of my own childhood reading, prodding me to reflect on what I owe to that.

My great thanks to my editors of many years, Alan Thomas and Randy Petilos, to my splendid copyeditor, Erik Carlson, and to the many others at the University of Chicago Press who have made it possible for this book to see the light.

Zimm the cat has been the best of early morning writing partners.

Liza Lorwin talked over all of these stories as the book was being written, and read the manuscript chapter by chapter. She wondered with me about so many turns of thought and speech in my fictive children, about the precise shades of wonder in them, what in them is dangerous and endangered. These conversations are woven into every page of this study. While writing, my mind has also turned often to a stage work of which Liza was cocreator, as writer and producer: Mabou Mines's *Peter and Wendy*, a much-honored play that I saw first in 1996 at The Public Theater as part of the Henson International Festival of Puppet Theater, and then repeatedly in 2009 and 2010 at the Edinburgh Festival and the New Victory Theater in New York. It remains for me an inspiring vision of how child worlds and adult worlds can converse and play. I give this book to Liza as a small return for countless gifts.

NOTES

Quotations from my main texts are taken from the following editions:

Lewis Carroll. *Alice in Wonderland and Through the Looking-Glass*. Edited by Hugh Haughton. London: Penguin, 1998.

Carlo Collodi. *The Adventures of Pinocchio*. Translated by Geoffrey Brock. New York: NYRB, 2009. Quotations from the Italian are taken from the bilingual volume *The Adventures of Pinocchio / Le Avventure di Pinocchio*, translated and edited by Nicolas J. Perella. Berkeley: University of California Press, 1986, based on the critical edition of Ornella Castellani Pollidori, Pescia: Fondazione nazionale Carlo Collodi, 1983.

Henry James. *What Maisie Knew*. Edited by Christopher Ricks. London: Penguin, 2010.

J. M. Barrie. *Peter Pan* (*Peter and Wendy* and *Peter Pan in Kensington Gardens*). Edited by Jack Zipes. London: Penguin, 2004.

Franz Kafka. "The Cares of a Family Man." Translated by Willa and Edwin Muir, in Franz Kafka, *The Complete Stories*, 427–29. Edited by Nahum Glatzer. New York: Schocken, 1971. Quotations from the German text are from "Die Sorge des Hausvaters," in Kafka, *Drucke zu Lebzeiten: Kritische Ausgabe*, edited by Wolf Kittler, Hans-Gerd Koch, and Gerhard Neumann, 2 vols., 1:282–84. Berlin: S. Fischer, 1994.

Richard Hughes. *A High Wind in Jamaica*. New York: NYRB, 1999.

Elizabeth Bowen. *The Death of the Heart*. London: Gollancz, 1938.

Vladimir Nabokov. *Lolita*. New York: Putnam's, 1958.

PROLOGUE

2 "EITHER TOO FEW OR TOO MANY WORDS": Angus Fletcher, *Colors of the Mind: Conjectures on Thinking in Literature*, 265.

3 KILLED, MOURNED, AND CONTINUALLY RESURRECTED: See Reinhard Kuhn, *Corruption in Paradise: The Child in Western Literature*, 179.

3 "CURED OF HIS CHILDHOOD": Lucie Delarue-Mardrus, quoted in Gaston Bachelard, *The Poetics of Reverie*, 139.

3 THERE IS MORE IN THESE CHILDREN: I adapt this sentence from William Empson, *"Alice in Wonderland:* The Child as Swain," 260–61.

4 "EVERY CHILD IS THE ASTONISHING BEING": Bachelard, *The Poetics of Reverie*, 116.

4 "INSOLENT AND REMOTE": Walter Benjamin, "Old Toys," in *Selected Writings*, vol. 2, 1927–34, 101.

4 "THE IMAGINED-AWAY, OR THE PERMANENTLY TRANSLATED": Edward Snow, *Inside Bruegel: The Play of Images in "Children's Games,"* 159.

4 "CAN'T BE BETTER THAN WE ARE": Marina Warner, *Managing Monsters: Six Myths of Our Time*, 46.

5 CAN MAKE THOSE WHO FACE THEM FEEL UNEXPECTEDLY VULNERABLE: See Kuhn, *Corruption in Paradise*, 46.

5 "CHARGED WITH DEMONIC DANGER": Joe Moshenska, *Iconoclasm as Child's Play*, 175.

5 "ENTRUST THEIR OWN PHANTOMS TO CHILDREN": Giorgio Agamben, *Infancy and History: On the Destruction of Experience*, 95.

5 "KNOW HOW TO CONTAIN THEM": James Kincaid, *Child-Loving: The Erotic Child and Victorian Culture*, 79.

5 "THEY ARE SHAMELESS ABOUT IT": Adam Phillips, *The Beast in the Nursery: On Curiosity and Other Appetites*, 155.

6 AN UNEASY ALLIANCE BETWEEN INNOCENCE AND EXPERIENCE: See U. C. Knoepflmacher, *Ventures into Childland: Victorians, Fairy Tales, and Femininity*, 8–10 and passim.

6 THEIR IMAGINATIVE LIVES AS BOOKS: See Seth Lerer, *Children's Literature: A Reader's History from Aesop to Harry Potter*, 86, 166, and passim.

7 "PUT AWAY THE WRONG CHILDISH THINGS": John Hollander, personal conversation.

7 "CHILDISH THINGS CAN BE PUT ASIDE VENGEFULLY": Stanley Cavell, *In Quest of the Ordinary: Lines of Skepticism and Romanticism*, 74.

7 AN INSISTENT DOUBLING OF CHILD VOICE AND ADULT VOICE: See Perry Nodelman, *The Hidden Adult: Defining Children's Literature*, 1–82 and passim.

7 COLLABORATES WITH AND TESTS THE OTHER: See Marah Gubar, *Artful Dodgers: Reconceiving the Golden Age of Children's Literature*, 7–8 and passim.

9 DISMEMBERED AND DEVOURED BUT IN THE END REBORN: See "Hymn to Hermes," in H. G. Evelyn-White, ed. and trans., *Hesiod, The Homeric Hymns and Homerica*, 362–405; and Nonnos, *Dionysica*, book VI, lines 155–205, and books VII, VIII, and IX passim (vol. 1, pp. 245–327).

9 THE GUILEFUL CHILD KRISHNA: *Bhāgavata Purāṇa* 10.8.21–45, in Wendy Doniger, ed. and trans., *Hindu Myths*, 214–21.

9 EVEN THE YOUNG JESUS: See the Infancy Gospel of Thomas, chapters 2–5 and 14. In Ronald Hock, ed. and trans., *The Infancy Gospels of James and Thomas*, 105–11 and 133.

9 "AND HIS EYES WERE SUNS": Carl Kerényi, "The Primordial Child in Primordial Times," 50.

9 "THE ROYAL POWER IS THE CHILD'S": Heraclitus, fragment 52d. See Charles H. Kahn, *The Art and Thought of Heraclitus: An Edition of the Fragments with Translation and Commentary*, 278.

9 WISE FOOLS OR CUNNING TRICKSTERS, OR BOTH AT ONCE: See Maria Tatar, *The Hard Facts of the Grimms' Fairy Tales*, 87, 98.

9 DRINKS HER GRANDMOTHER'S BLOOD AND EATS HER FLESH: See Robert Darnton, "Peasants Tell Tales: The Meaning of Mother Goose," 10.

10 "LIKE A FIEND HID IN A CLOUD": William Blake, *The Complete Poetry and Prose*, 28.

10 "THE GHOSTLY LANGUAGE OF THE ANCIENT EARTH": William Wordsworth, "*The Prelude*" (1805), book 2, line 328, in *The Major Works, Including "The Prelude*," 400.

10 "PHANTASMAGORIA OF THE NURSERY": Ellen Moers, *Literary Women*, 99.

10 MADE LURID, EVEN MONSTROUS: See Leslie Fiedler, "The Eye of Innocence: Some Notes on the Role of the Child in Literature," 480.

11 "VICTIMS, SUMMARY EXECUTIONS, HUMAN SACRIFICES": Jean Cocteau, *The Holy Terrors* [Les enfants terribles], 5.

11 "SQUANDERS, BUNGLES, DESTROYS, MOCKS": Nathalie Sarraute, *Do You Hear Them?*, 22.

11 "THAT WHICH WE HAVE BEEN OBLIGED TO LOVE": Joyce Carol Oates, "Killer Kids," 20.

11 "BEAUTIFUL, MAGICAL BEST THING": Toni Morrison, *Beloved*, 289.

ALICE

14 "SERENE SEDUCTIVE DISCONTINUITY": Walter de la Mare, *Lewis Carroll*, 62.

16 "QUAINTLY OLD-FASHIONED": Phillips, *The Beast in the Nursery*, 149.

17 "FLAUNTED, A SKILLFUL, INCOMPETENCE": Susan Stewart, *Nonsense: Aspects of Intertextuality in Folklore and Literature*, 88.

18 "WHAT THEY CAN'T, DON'T, OR WON'T SAY": Helen Oyeyemi, letter to the author.

18 "A SORT OF RESERVE OF FORCE": Empson, "*Alice in Wonderland*: The Child as Swain," 277.

18 "ALICE HAS BECOME OUR MENTOR": Marianne Moore, *The Complete Prose*, 171.

19 "WE TOO BECOME CHILDREN AGAIN": Virginia Woolf, *The Moment, and Other Essays*, 70.

20 REAL AND IMAGINARY FOOD: See Nina Auerbach, "Alice and Wonderland: A Curious Child"; and Marina Warner, *No Go the Bogeyman: Scaring, Lulling, and Making Mock*, 136–59 and passim.

20 "UTTERLY WITHOUT PATRONIZING": Eleanor Cook, *Enigmas and Riddles in Literature*, 179.

20 "COMPLICATIONS AND REVERSIBILITIES": Kenneth Burke, *A Rhetoric of Motives*, 268.

21 TOO MUCH A MATTER OF POLITE SURFACES: See Antonin Artaud, letter to Henri Parisot, September 22, 1945, in *Selected Writings*, 448–51.

22 THE MOURNFUL, AGGRESSIVE-DEFENSIVE WORDPLAY OF HAMLET: See Empson, "*Alice in Wonderland*: The Child as Swain," 293.

25 "NO BADGER CAN GUESS A CONUNDRUM" (footnote): Lewis Carroll, *Symbolic Logic*, 123, 133.

26 "BY THY WORDS THOU SHALT BE CONDEMNED": Matthew 12:36–37 (KJV).

27 "WITHIN THIS NIMBUS OF THE IRRECOVERABLE": Gillian Beer, *Alice in Space: The Sideways Victorian World of Lewis Carroll*, 115–16.

29 SILENCE SHAPED BY ACTS OF SILENCING: See Paolo Valesio, *Ascoltare il silenzio: La retorica come teoria*, 353–96.

29 AS READERS HAVE BEEN AT PAINS TO SHOW: See Elizabeth Sewell, *The Field of Nonsense*, 115–29; and Eric Partridge, "The Nonsense Words of Edward Lear and Lewis Carroll," in *Here, There and Everywhere: Essays upon Language*, 162–88.

32 "FROM THIS TIME FORTH I NEVER WILL SPEAK WORD": William Shakespeare, *Othello*, in *The Arden Shakespeare*, 5.2.300–301.

32 "LIPS, LET FOUR WORDS GO BY AND LANGUAGE END": Shakespeare, *Timon of Athens*, 5.1.219.

32 "THE REST IS SILENCE": Shakespeare, *Hamlet*, 5.2.337.

32 "THY SILENT EARS": George Herbert, "Denial," in *The Complete English Poems*, 73.

32 "THAT NOISY SILENCE, BEFORE LANGUAGE JOINED IN": Phillips, *The Beast in the Nursery*, 42–43.

33 AT HOME IN THEIR SILENCES: See Auerbach, "Alice and Wonderland: A Curious Child," 41.

PINOCCHIO

37 AN ULTIMATELY INFERNAL PLACE: See Agamben, *Infancy and History*, 86.

39 "KICKING AT ITS COFFIN": Carmelo Bene, *Pinocchio*, 108 (my translation).

39 "THE HUMAN, ITS CHATTERING, ITS BREATHING": Bene, *Pinocchio*, 117 (my translation).

39 "THE DRY SHADOW-LIGHT": Fernando Tempesti, "Chi era il Collodi, Com'è fatto *Pinocchio*," 67 (my translation).

40 EVEN SUICIDAL IMPULSES: See Pietro Toesca, "La filosofia di Pinocchio, ovvero l'Odissea di un ragazzo per bene con la memoria di burattino," 469.

41 "INFINITELY NECESSARY AND FRIGHTENING": Giorgio Manganelli, *Pinocchio: Un libro parallelo*, 12 (my translation).

42 THE WOOD OF OUR HUMANITY: See Benedetto Croce, "Pinocchio," 350 (my translation).

44 "AND CAN MAKE VILE THINGS PRECIOUS": William Shakespeare, *King Lear*, 3.2.70–71.

48 A VISION OF A PERFECTLY ORDINARY LIFE: See Manganelli, *Pinocchio: Un libro parallelo*, 189.

48 "EVERYTHING ONLY CONNECTED BY 'AND' AND 'AND'": Elizabeth Bishop, "Over 2000 Illustrations and a Complete Concordance," in *Poems*, 58.

49 STITCHED TOGETHER WITH NIGHT SCENES: See Rodolfo di Biasio, "Il notturno in *Pinocchio*."

50 "GRAVEYARD OF GOOD PURPOSES": Daniela Marcheschi, *Collodi ritrovato*, 133 (my translation).

51 "FROM THE VERY BEGINNING AS AN INSANE WORLD": Suzanne Stewart-Steinberg, *The Pinocchio Effect: On Making Italians, 1860–1920*, 35.

51 "EXPRESSION OF A FUNDAMENTAL INERTIA" (footnote): Stewart-Steinberg, *The Pinocchio Effect*, 62.

52 THAT BECOMING THAT REAL BOY IS HIS WISH: See Rebecca West, afterword to Collodi, *Pinocchio*, trans. Geoffrey Brock, 171.

52 AMBIGUOUSLY WITCH AND PHANTASM: See Manganelli, *Pinocchio: Un libro parallelo*, 153.

53 A MOMENT OF DARK ROMANTICISM: See Italo Calvino, "Carlo Collodi, *Pinocchio*," 802.

54 "THE SON SAVES THE FATHER": Paul Auster, *The Invention of Solitude*, 135.

MAISIE

57 "HOW BEAUTIFUL FIRE IS": Percy Bysshe Shelley, "The Witch of Atlas," lines 259–64, in *Shelley's Poetry and Prose*, 375.

57 "FLUSH AND COLOUR AND ANIMATE": Henry James, *Literary Criticism*, vol. 2, *French Writers, Other European Writers, Prefaces to the New York Edition*, 1278.

58 "TROUBLE THE MIND LIKE MUSIC": Nan Shepherd, *The Living Mountain*, 42.

59 "LARGEST CHAPTER OF HUMAN ACCIDENTS": Henry James, "London," in *Collected Travel Writings: Great Britain and America*, 30, 21, 35.

59 SILENCES PATIENT, NEEDFUL, EVASIVE, SACRED, CRUEL, AND OBTUSE: See Millicent Bell, "The Language of Silence: *What Maisie Knew*," in *Meaning in Henry James*, 243–61.

59 "KNOWLEDGE—HALF-DREADED, HALF-DESIRED": Ruth Bernard Yeazell, *Language and Knowledge in the Late Novels of Henry James*, 25.

61 SHARES WITH OTHERS OF JAMES'S HEROINES: See Peter Brooks, *The Melodramatic Imagination: Balzac, Henry James, Melodrama, and the Mode of Excess*, 158.

63 "CONNECTION BETWEEN OPACITY AND PAIN": Sharon Cameron, *Thinking in Henry James*, 64n.

63 TRANSLATING THEM INTO SIMPLER TERMS: See Yeazell, *Language and Knowledge in the Late Novels of Henry James*, 1–15.

66 "THE BEGINNINGS OF STUPOR AND MELANCHOLY" (footnote): Charles Baudelaire, "The Philosophy of Toys," 20.

67 "THE MEDIUM OF RARE INAPTITUDES": Henry James, *A Small Boy and Others*, 193.

68 "INTERESTED IN ONE DIDN'T KNOW WHAT": James, *A Small Boy and Others*, 209–10.

68 "THINGS VAIN AND UNINTENDED": James, *A Small Boy and Others*, 213–14.

69 "BOTH CLEAR AND YET TOO BLURRED": T. J. Lustig, *Henry James and the Ghostly*, 174.

69 A GHOST WHOM IT MIGHT BE DANGEROUS TO DRIVE AWAY: See R. P. Blackmur, *Studies in Henry James*, 48–49.

69 "SOMEBODY'S NORMAL RELATION TO SOMETHING": James, *Literary Criticism*, 1260, 1259.

69 "ONE KNOWS THE MOST DAMNING THINGS ABOUT ONE'S SELF": Henry James, letter to H. G. Wells, December 9, 1898, in *Henry James: A Life in Letters*, 312.

71 EVEN AS SHE KEEPS HER SILENCE (footnote). See Norman Page, *Henry James: Interviews and Recollections*, 55, 134, 127.

74 "BETWEEN THE EXPLANATION OF CIRCUMSTANCES AND THE CREATION OF THEM": Yeazell, *Language and Knowledge in the Late Novels of Henry James*, 78.

75 AS IT BECKONS AND ENCLOSES US: See Angus Fletcher, *A New Theory for American Poetry: Democracy, the Environment, and the Future of the Imagination*, 22.

80 "MELODRAMA OF CONSCIOUSNESS": See Brooks, *The Melodramatic Imagination*, 153–97.

80 "SUDDEN RUPTURES AND DISSOLUTIONS": Laurence B. Holland, *The Expense of Vision: Essays in the Craft of Henry James*, 185.

83 "UNSPEAKABLE AND UNTOUCHABLE": Henry James, *The Sacred Fount*, 159.

84 "THE HOUR OF THE END OF THAT CHILDHOOD": James, letter to Mrs. John Chandler Bancroft, March 21, 1898, in *Henry James: A Life in Letters*, 299–300.

84 "A QUICKENED SENSE OF LIFE": James, *Literary Criticism*, 1285.

85 "TO SECURE STEADINESS RATHER THAN POSITION": Blackmur, *Studies in Henry James*, 233.

PETER

87 "SATIRE THAT DOESN'T QUITE COME OFF": Sir Walter Raleigh, letter to Cynthia Asquith, quoted in Janet Dunbar, *J. M. Barrie: The Man behind the Image*, 229.

87 "THE IMPOSSIBILITY OF CHILDREN'S FICTION": See Jacqueline Rose, *The Case of Peter Pan, or The Impossibility of Children's Fiction*.

88 "NO ONE HAS GROWN UP IDEAS": J. M. Barrie, from "Fairy," autograph manuscript notes for the play *Peter Pan*, dated October 14, 1903. Beinecke Library, J. M. Barrie Collection, GEN MSS 1400, box 42, folder 910.

89 "I DO NOT THINK THAT THEY WILL SING TO ME": T. S. Eliot, "The Love Song of J. Alfred Prufrock," in *The Poems of T. S. Eliot*, vol. 1, *Collected and Uncollected Poems*, 9.

91 "BRING THE DEPARTED BACK": J. M. Barrie, *The Little White Bird*, 45–46.

93 "BUT REMAINS ALONE": Kincaid, *Child-Loving*, 287.

96 "UNLEAVENED ADULTHOOD AS A LIVING DEATH": Keith Miller, "The Flight from Neverland," 16.

96 NEVER TO HAVE OVERCOME: See J. M. Barrie, *Margaret Ogilvy*, 1–20.

97 IT MIGHT HAVE BEEN A SUICIDE: See Andrew Birkin, *J. M. Barrie and the Lost Boys*, 293.

97 "DESPERATE ATTEMPT TO GROW UP BUT CAN'T": Barrie, notebook, Beinecke Library, J. M. Barrie Collection, GEN MSS 1400, box 26, folder 762. Quoted in Birkin, *J. M. Barrie and the Lost Boys*, 296–97.

97 "THE FIVE OF YOU VIOLENTLY TOGETHER" (footnote): Barrie: *The Plays of J. M. Barrie*, 489.

97 "THE PATHOLOGY OF A DREAM" (footnote): Elizabeth Bowen, *Collected Impressions*, 149.

99 "BEING A GHOST IS WORSE THAN SEEING THEM": Barrie, *Mary Rose*, act 3, scene 3, in *The Plays of J. M. Barrie*, 1146.

99 "NEVER REALLY BEEN BORN": See James Knowlson, *Damned to Fame: The Life of Samuel Beckett*, 544.

99 "BEFORE ITS TIME": Samuel Beckett, *The Collected Shorter Plays*, 216.

99 "I DON'T WANT TO BE A GHOST ANY MORE": Barrie, *Mary Rose*, act 3, scene 3, in *The Plays of J. M. Barrie*, 1146.

99 HE NEVER GOT FURTHER THAN THE DRAFT OF A SCREENPLAY: See Joseph Mc-Bride, "Alfred Hitchcock's *Mary Rose*: An Old Master's Unheard *Cri de Coeur*."

101 "AND THIS GIVES LIFE TO THEE": Shakespeare, Sonnet 18, *The Arden Shakespeare*.

101 "A BECKETTIAN FLATNESS AND ABSTRACTION": Miller, "The Flight from Neverland," 16.

ODRADEK

104 AT HOME IN THE WORLD OF CHILDREN: See Harold Bloom, *The Strong Light of the Canonical: Kafka, Freud, and Scholem as Revisionists of Jewish Culture and Thought*, 14.

104 "HEAD OF HOUSEHOLD": This is Michael Hofmann's translation in *Metamorphosis, and Other Stories*, 211–12. I've otherwise quoted from the translation of Willa and Edwin Muir in *The Complete Stories*.

104 "BEGINNING OF A LONG EXISTENCE": Walter Benjamin, "Franz Kafka," in *Selected Writings*, vol. 2, 1927–34, 799.

105 "IS AND IS NOT A DREYDL": Iris Bruce, "Kafka and Jewish Folklore," 158.

105 "COMPROMISES THE ORDINATION OF THINGS": J. H. Van den Berg, *The Changing Nature of Man: Introduction to a Historical Psychology*, 94.

106 STUDIES THE SAFETY OF BODIES: See for instance "Measures for Preventing Accidents from Wood-Planing Machines" and "Accident Prevention in Quarries," in Franz Kafka, *The Office Writings*, 109–19 and 273–300.

106 EVEN TO THE POINT OF ESTRANGEMENT: See Wilhelm Emrich, *Franz Kafka: A Critical Study of His Writings*, 103; and Marek Nekula, *Franz Kafka and His Prague Contexts: Studies in Language and Literature*, 37–38.

106 "LITTLE RED FEET STRETCHED OUT FOR TENDER PITY" (footnote): Franz Kafka, *Letters to Friends, Family, and Editors*, 17.

108 "THE FORM WHICH THINGS ASSUME IN OBLIVION": Benjamin, "Franz Kafka," 810, 811.

108 "COUNTLESS UNCERTAIN AND CHANGING COMPOUNDS": Benjamin, "Franz Kafka," 810.

108 "OR A PIECE OF STRING?": Dennis Silk, "The Marionette Theater," 240.

108 UNRECOGNIZABLE, SINGULAR, UPROOTED, ECSTATIC: See Stanley Corngold, *Lambent Traces: Franz Kafka*, 11 and passim.

108 "THE INSECT ITSELF CANNOT BE DEPICTED": Kafka, letter to Kurt Woolf, October 25, 1915, in *Letters to Friends, Family, and Editors*, 115.

108 "I FIND KS UGLY, ALMOST REPUGNANT": Franz Kafka, diary entry from May 27, 1914, quoted in Roberto Calasso, *K.*, 20.

109 "AS SILENT AS THE WOOD": Franz Kafka, "The Worries of a Head of Household," in *Metamorphosis, and Other Stories*, 212.

109 THE DOUBLED LETTERS K. K. APPEAR OFTEN (footnote): See, for instance, "On the Examination of Firms by Trade Inspectors," in Kafka, *The Office Writings*, 121–40.

109 "THE IMPOSSIBILITY OF CROWS" (footnote): Franz Kafka, *The Zürau Aphorisms*, 32.

110 "OF THE MOST DISTANT, OF THE MOST UTTERLY DISTANT, VOICES": Franz Kafka, *The Castle*, 20.

111 THE SILENCE ATTENDING THE GROTESQUE EXECUTION: See Danielle Allen, "Sounding Silence," 332.

111 "WITH GESTURES THAT SAY 'NO'": Rainer Maria Rilke, *Book of Images*, 85.

111 "NOR THE SMOKE-DRIFT OF PUFFED-OUT HEROES, NOR HUMAN CRY": Wallace Stevens, *The Palm at the End of the Mind: Selected Poems and a Play*, 367.

111 MAY STAY FOREVER CONCEALED FROM US: See Kafka, *The Zürau Aphorisms*, 51.

112 "UNEXPECTED, UNINVITED, INESCAPABLE": Kafka, letter to Max Brod, December 1917, in *Letters to Friends, Family, and Editors*, 174.

112 THE VAST RESPONSIBILITY WE OWE THEM: See Kafka, *The Zürau Aphorisms*, 91.

112 "NEXUS OF CENTRIFUGAL AND CENTRIPETAL MOTIONS": Calasso, *K.*, 63.

112 "ON THE THRESHOLD OF A HIDDEN WORLD": Calasso, *K.*, 10.

112 CALLED "FATELESSNESS": See Imre Kertész, *Fatelessness*.

113 "THEY, AND THEIR CHILDREN, AND THEIR CHILDREN'S CHILDREN": Ezekiel 37:25 (Jewish Publication Society Translation).

113 "WHICH DOESN'T CREATE BUT CALLS": Franz Kafka, diary entry from October 18, 1921, quoted in Calasso, *K.*, 305.

EMILY

116 HISTORY OF RESISTANCE AND REBELLION: See Vincent Brown, *Tacky's Revolt: The Story of an Atlantic Slave War*, 1–43.

116 STORIES TOLD HIM BY HIS MOTHER (footnote): See Louise Morgan, "Richard Hughes, Artist and Adventurer," 328.

116 "THE DETAIL OF FLORA, FAUNA, LANDSCAPE, PEOPLE" (footnote): Jean D'Costa, personal communication.

116 "DOZENS OF EARLY NINETEENTH-CENTURY TRAVEL BOOKS" (footnote): See Morgan, "Richard Hughes, Artist and Adventurer," 328.

116 THE REAL AND IMAGINED VIOLENCE OF SLAVERY (footnote): See Monique Allewaert, *Ariel's Ecology: Plantations, Personhood, and Colonialism in the American Tropics*, 66–82, 93–104.

120 "MUST STIFLE UNRELENTING INTERNALIZATION": Susan Howe, *The Quarry*, 116.

124 "LIKE THE VERY SEA BREEZE ITSELF": Oates, "Killer Kids," 17.

125 "IN THE BACK OF SOMEONE'S MIND": John Ashbery, "For John Clare," in *Collected Poems 1956–1987*, 198.

125 "AN UNQUENCHABLE FIRE WITHIN": Roger Caillois, "The Myth of Secret Treasures in Childhood," 257.

125 "THE NATURAL HERO OF ROMANCE": Angus Fletcher, introduction to *Treasure Island*, by Robert Louis Stevenson, xxxi.

125 "BASIC HUMAN SURVIVAL": Fletcher, introduction to *Treasure Island*, xvii.

129 REENTERING THE MEMORY OF WHAT THREATENED HER: See Cathy Caruth, *Unclaimed Experience: Trauma, Narrative, and History*, 60–63 and passim.

PORTIA

133 "WHAT QUESTIONS TO PUT TO OUR OWN HEARTS": Elizabeth Bowen, review of *Overtures to Death*, by C. Day Lewis, in *The Weight of a World of Feeling: Reviews and Essays*, 76.

134 VIVID AND SOLIDIFIED SHADOWS: See Maud Ellmann, *Elizabeth Bowen: The Shadow across the Page*, 128–43.

134 "ALMOST A WALKING ENTROPY": Neil Corcoran, *Elizabeth Bowen: The Enforced Return*, 107.

134 "THAT IT WAS THEY WHO WERE LACKING IN SOME FACULTY": Elizabeth Bowen, *Eva Trout, or Changing Scenes*, 172.

135 "CONCEALED FROM US BECAUSE IT IS TOO BAD TO BE TOLD": Elizabeth Bowen, preface to *Uncle Silas*, by Joseph Sheridan Le Fanu, in *Collected Impressions*, 15.

136 "OUR BUSINESS TO LOSE INNOCENCE": Bowen, *Collected Impressions*, 265.

136 "STILL INTENSELY PHYSICAL" PRESENCE: Corcoran, *Elizabeth Bowen: The Enforced Return*, 108.

136 "THE HUMAN ORDER SEEMED TO HAVE LAPSED" (footnote): Elizabeth Bowen, *Collected Stories*, 649.

136 "ENGAGED INNOCENTLY IN SOME ACT OF DESTRUCTION" (footnote): Elizabeth Bowen, *The Heat of the Day*, 234.

138 "SAVAGE CLUTTER": Hermione Lee, *Elizabeth Bowen: An Estimation*, 108.

138 "SALVAGE CLUTTER": Susan Howe, *Concordance*, 23.

139 SOMETHING OF THE "HOWL": See Victoria Glendinning, *Elizabeth Bowen: A Biography*, 137.

139 STRIPPED, DESOLATING FORCE OF THE WORDS: See Sinéad Mooney, "Unstable Compounds: Bowen's Beckettian Affinities."

139 "DISTURBS THE CHASTITY OF THE MIND" (footnote): Elizabeth Bowen, *The Weight of a World of Feeling*, 88.

145 "PORTIA AS THE CHILDBRIDE OF DEATH": Lee, *Elizabeth Bowen: An Estimation*, 124.

145 THE STRANGE WORK OF PHONE CALLS: See Ellmann, *Elizabeth Bowen: The Shadow across the Page*, 167–68.

146 SHAKESPEARE'S PORTIA: See Corcoran, *Elizabeth Bowen: The Enforced Return*, 124–25.

LOLITA

151 "BACK TO THE LOVE-PLAY ALWAYS": John Hollander, "The Perilous Magic of Nymphets: *Lolita* by Vladimir Nabokov," 559.

153 HALF CAPTURE, HALF ESCAPE: On the life of imagined orphans, lost and found, flying and in flight, stolen and stealthy, waif and wraith, see Karl Miller, *Doubles: Studies in Literary History*, 39–55.

154 "EXILIC VELOCITY": Michael Seidel, "Stereoscope: Nabokov's *Ada* and *Pale Fire*," 244.

155 "CAN RECORD BUT HARDLY SEE": Michael Wood, *The Magician's Doubts: Vladimir Nabokov and the Risks of Fiction*, 168.

158 "WE ARE MOST ARTISTICALLY CAGED": Vladimir Nabokov, *Pale Fire*, 37.

159 STUDIOUS OF DEATH: See Vladimir Nabokov, *Bend Sinister*, 115–16.

159 "SPHERICAL AND WITHOUT EXITS": Vladimir Nabokov, *Speak, Memory*, 20.

159 "AT WORK ON SOME TOTALLY DIFFERENT MATTER": Nabokov, *Bend Sinister*, 176.

159 "THE IMPRISONED HUM OF ONE OF MY OWN SEASIDE SUMMERS": Nabokov, *Speak, Memory*, 259.

159 A CHILD LOLITA FULL OF THE ENERGY OF PLAY: See Thomas Karshan, *Vladimir Nabokov and the Art of Play*, 169–82.

162 "THOROUGHLY, PAINFULLY OR ECSTATICALLY IMAGINED": Wood, *The Magician's Doubts*, 54.

165 "A PAINFUL BIRTH, A DIFFICULT BABY": Nabokov, *Speak, Memory*, 65.

165 AIMS TO REMIND US OF FRIEDRICH SCHILLER (footnote): See Karshan, *Vladimir Nabokov and the Art of Play*, 170.

169 "A PALPABLE REFLECTION OF HIS DEATHLY CONDITION": Ellen Pifer, *Nabokov and the Novel*, 37.

170 "MAWKISH AND SELF-REGARDING": Wood, *The Magician's Doubts*, 140.

170 SKIRTING "THE EDGE OF KITSCH": Kevin Ohi, *Innocence and Rapture: The Erotic Child in Pater, Wilde, James, and Nabokov*, 158.

171 "A MOMENTARY VACUUM": Nabokov, *Speak, Memory*, 139.

172 "THAT FLUTTERING THINGS HAVE SO DISTINCT A SHADE": Stevens, "Le Monocle de Mon Oncle," in *The Palm at the End of the Mind*, 44.

CODA

174 LIKE DOUBLE AGENTS: See Christine Roth, "Looking through the Spyglass: Lewis Carroll, James Barrie, and the Empire of Childhood," 23.

READINGS

Aasgaard, Reidar. "Paul as a Child: Children and Childhood in the Letters of the Apostle." *Journal of Biblical Literature* 126, no. 1 (2007): 129–59.

Agamben, Giorgio. *Infancy and History: On the Destruction of Experience.* Translated by Liz Heron. London: Verso, 2007.

Allen, Danielle. "Sounding Silence." *Modernism/Modernity* 8, no. 2 (2001): 325–34.

Allewaert, Monique. *Ariel's Ecology: Plantations, Personhood, and Colonialism in the American Tropics.* Minneapolis: University of Minnesota Press, 2013.

Anderson, Mark, editor. *Reading Kafka: Prague, Politics, and the Fin de Siècle.* New York: Schocken, 1989.

Ariès, Philippe. *Centuries of Childhood: A Social History of Family Life.* Translated by Robert Baldick. New York: Random House, 1962.

Artaud, Antonin. *Selected Writings.* Edited by Susan Sontag. Translated by Helen Weaver. New York: Farrar, Straus & Giroux, 1976.

Ashbery, John. *Collected Poems 1956–1987.* New York: Library of America, 2008.

Auerbach, Nina. "Alice and Wonderland: A Curious Child." *Victorian Studies* 17, no. 1 (1973): 31–47.

Auerbach, Nina, and U. C. Knoepflmacher, editors. *Forbidden Journeys: Fairy Tales and Fantasies by Victorian Women Writers.* Chicago: University of Chicago Press, 1992.

Auster, Paul. *The Invention of Solitude.* New York: Sun, 1982.

Bachelard, Gaston. *The Poetics of Reverie.* Translated by Daniel Russell. New York: Orion 1969.

Barrie, J. M. *The Little White Bird.* London: Hodder and Stoughton, 1902.

———. *Margaret Ogilvy.* London: Hodder and Stoughton, 1896.

———. *Peter Pan (Peter and Wendy and Peter Pan in Kensington Gardens).* Edited by Jack Zipes. London: Penguin, 2004.

———. *The Plays of J. M. Barrie.* Edited by A. E. Wilson. Rev. ed., London: Hodder and Stoughton, 1942.

Baudelaire, Charles. "The Philosophy of Toys." Translated by Paul Keegan. In *On Dolls*, edited by Kenneth Gross, 11–21. London: Notting Hill Editions, 2012.

Bauer, Esther K. "The Power of the Look: Franz Kafka's 'The Cares of a Family Man.'" In Lucht and Yarri, *Kafka's Creatures*, 157–73.

Bazzocchi, Marco. "I territori di Pinocchio." *Il Verri* 9, nos. 1–2 (1992): 147–50.

Beckett, Samuel. *The Collected Shorter Plays*. New York: Grove Weidenfeld, 1984.

Beer, Gillian. *Alice in Space: The Sideways Victorian World of Lewis Carroll*. Chicago: University of Chicago Press, 2016.

Bell, Millicent. *Meaning in Henry James*. Cambridge, MA: Harvard University Press, 1991.

Bene, Carmelo. *Pinocchio*. Milan: Usher, 1981.

Benjamin, Walter. "A Glimpse into the World of Children's Books." In *Selected Writings*, vol. 1, *1913–26*, edited by Marcus Bullock and Michael W. Jennings, 435–43. Cambridge, MA: Harvard University Press, 1996.

———. "Old Toys," "A Cultural History of Toys," "Toys and Play," "Children's Literature," and "Franz Kafka." In *Selected Writings*, vol. 2, *1927–34*, edited by Michael W. Jennings, Howard Eiland, and Gary Smith, translated by Rodney Livingstone and others, 98–102, 113–16, 117–21, 250–56, 794–818. Cambridge, MA: Harvard University Press, 1999.

Biasio, Rodolfo di. "Il notturno in *Pinocchio*." In Panteri, *Studi collodiani*, 263–71.

Birkin, Andrew. *J. M. Barrie and the Lost Boys*. New Haven: Yale University Press, 2003.

Bishop, Elizabeth. *Poems*. Edited by Saskia Hamilton. New York: Farrar, Straus & Giroux, 2011.

Blackmur, R. P. *Studies in Henry James*. Edited by Veronica A. Makowsky. New York: New Directions, 1983.

Blake, Kathleen. *Play, Games, and Sport: The Literary Works of Lewis Carroll*. Ithaca: Cornell University Press, 1974.

Blake, William. *The Complete Poetry and Prose*. Edited by David Erdman. Rev. ed., Berkeley: University of California Press, 1982.

Bloom, Harold. *The Strong Light of the Canonical: Kafka, Freud, and Scholem as Revisionists of Jewish Culture and Thought*. New York: City College, 1987.

———, editor. *Vladimir Nabokov: Modern Critical Views*. New York: Chelsea House, 1987.

Blumenberg, Hans. *Shipwreck with Spectators: Paradigm of a Metaphor for Existence*. Translated by Steven Rendall. Cambridge, MA: MIT Press, 1997.

Boas, George. *The Cult of Childhood*. London: Warburg Institute, 1966.

Bold, Valentina, and Andrew Nash. *Gateway to the Modern: Resituating J. M. Barrie*. Edinburgh: Scottish Literature International, 2014.

Bowen, Elizabeth. *Collected Impressions*. New York: Knopf, 1950.

———. *The Collected Stories*. New York: Knopf, 1981.

———. *The Death of the Heart*. London: Gollancz, 1938.

———. *Eva Trout, or Changing Scenes*. New York: Knopf, 1968.

———. *The Heat of the Day*. London: Jonathan Cape, 1948.

———. *The House in Paris*. New York: Knopf, 1935.

———. *The Little Girls*. New York: Knopf, 1963.

———. *The Weight of a World of Feeling: Reviews and Essays*. Edited by Allan Hepburn. Evanston: Northwestern University Press, 2017.

Brooker, Will. *Alice's Adventures: Lewis Carroll in Popular Culture.* New York: Continuum, 2004.

Brooks, Peter. *The Melodramatic Imagination: Balzac, Henry James, Melodrama, and the Mode of Excess.* New Haven: Yale University Press, 1976.

Brown, Vincent. *Tacky's Revolt: The Story of an Atlantic Slave War.* Cambridge, MA: Harvard University Press, 2020.

Bruce, Iris. "Kafka and Jewish Folklore." In *The Cambridge Companion to Kafka,* edited by Julian Preece, 150–68. Cambridge, UK: Cambridge University Press, 2002.

Burke, Kenneth. *A Rhetoric of Motives.* New York: Prentice-Hall, 1952.

Caillois, Roger. *Man, Play, and Games.* Translated by Meyer Barash. New York: Free Press, 1961.

———. "The Myth of Secret Treasures in Childhood." In *The Edge of Surrealism: A Roger Caillois Reader,* edited by Claudine Frank, translated by Claudine Frank and Camille Naish, 252–61. Durham: Duke University Press, 2003.

Calasso, Roberto. *K.* Translated by Geoffrey Brock. New York: Knopf, 2005.

Calvino, Italo. "Carlo Collodi, *Pinocchio*" [original title, "*Ma Collodi non esiste*"]. In *Saggi 1945–85,* edited by Mario Barenghi, 2 vols., 2:801–7. Bologna: Einaudi, 1995.

Cameron, Sharon. *Thinking in Henry James.* Chicago: University of Chicago Press, 1989.

Camporesi, Piero. *Bread of Dreams: Food and Fantasy in Early Modern Europe.* Translated by David Gentilcore. Chicago: University of Chicago Press, 1989.

Carroll, Lewis. *Alice in Wonderland and Through the Looking-Glass.* Edited by Hugh Haughton. London: Penguin, 1998.

———. *The Letters of Lewis Carroll.* Edited by Morton N. Cohen. 2 vols. New York: Oxford University Press, 1979.

———. *Symbolic Logic: Part I, Elementary.* Rev. 4th ed. London: Macmillan, 1897.

Caruth, Cathy. *Unclaimed Experience: Trauma, Narrative, and History.* Baltimore: Johns Hopkins University Press, 1996.

Cavell, Stanley. *In Quest of the Ordinary: Lines of Skepticism and Romanticism.* Chicago: University of Chicago Press, 1988.

Chaney, Lisa. *Hide-and-Seek with Angels: A Life of J. M. Barrie.* New York: St. Martin's, 2005.

Chessman, Harriet S. "Women and Language in the Fiction of Elizabeth Bowen." *Twentieth Century Literature* 29, no. 1 (1983): 69–85.

Cocteau, Jean. *The Holy Terrors* [Les enfants terribles]. Translated by Rosamond Lehmann. New York: New Directions, 1966.

Cohen, Morton N. *Lewis Carroll: A Biography.* New York: Knopf, 1995.

Collodi, Carlo. *The Adventures of Pinocchio / Le Avventure di Pinocchio.* Translated and edited by Nicolas J. Perella. Berkeley: University of California Press, 1986.

———. *The Adventures of Pinocchio.* Translated by Geoffrey Brock. New York: NYRB, 2009.

Connolly, Julian W. *A Reader's Guide to Nabokov's "Lolita."* Boston: Academic Studies Press, 2009.

Cook, Eleanor. *Enigmas and Riddles in Literature.* Cambridge, UK: Cambridge University Press, 2006.

Coover, Robert. *Pinocchio in Venice.* New York: Simon & Schuster, 1991.

Corcoran, Neil. *Elizabeth Bowen: The Enforced Return.* Oxford: Oxford University Press, 2004.

Corngold, Stanley. *Lambent Traces: Franz Kafka*. Princeton: Princeton University Press, 2004.

Coveney, Peter. *The Image of Childhood: The Individual and Society; A Study of a Theme in English Literature*. Rev. ed., Harmondsworth: Penguin, 1967.

Croce, Benedetto. "Pinocchio." In *La letteratura della nuova Italia*, vol. 5, 3rd ed., 346–50. Bari: Laterza, 1950.

Curreri, Luciano, editor. *Pinocchio in Camicia Nera: Quattro "Pinocchiate" Fasciste*. Cuneo: Nerosubianco, 2008.

Darnton, Robert. "Peasants Tell Tales: The Meaning of Mother Goose," in *The Great Cat Massacre and Other Episodes in French Cultural History*, 9–74. New York: Basic, 1984.

de la Mare, Walter. *Lewis Carroll*. London: Faber and Faber, 1932.

Deleuze, Gilles. *The Logic of Sense*. Edited by Constantin V. Boundas. Translated by Mark Lester with Charles Stivale. New York: Columbia University Press, 1990.

Deleuze, Gilles, and Félix Guattari. *Kafka: Toward a Minor Literature*. Translated by Dana Polan. Minneapolis: University of Minnesota Press, 1986.

Doniger, Wendy, editor and translator. *Hindu Myths*. London: Penguin, 1975.

Douglas-Fairhurst, Robert. *The Story of Alice: Lewis Carroll and the Secret History of Wonderland*. Cambridge, MA: Harvard University Press, 2015.

Dunbar, Janet. *J. M. Barrie: The Man behind the Image*. London: Collins, 1970.

Dusinberre, Juliet. *Alice to the Lighthouse: Children's Books and Radical Experiments in Art*. Basingstoke: Macmillan, 1987.

Eisen, George. *Children and Play in the Holocaust: Games among the Shadows*. Amherst: University of Massachusetts Press, 1988.

Eliot, T. S. *The Poems of T. S. Eliot*. Vol. 1, *Collected and Uncollected Poems*, edited by Christopher Ricks and Jim McCue. New York: Farrar, Straus & Giroux, 2015.

Ellmann, Maud. *Elizabeth Bowen: The Shadow across the Page*. Edinburgh: Edinburgh University Press, 2003.

Empson, William. "*Alice in Wonderland*: The Child as Swain." In *Some Versions of Pastoral*, 253–94. New York: New Directions, n.d.

Emrich, Wilhelm. *Franz Kafka: A Critical Study of His Writings*. Translated by Sheema Zeben Buehne. New York: Ungar, 1968.

Evelyn-White, H. G., editor and translator. *Hesiod, The Homeric Hymns and Homerica*. Loeb Classical Library. Cambridge, MA: Harvard University Press, 1927.

Fiedler, Leslie. "The Eye of Innocence: Some Notes on the Role of the Child in Literature." In *Collected Essays of Leslie Fiedler*, 2 vols., 1:471–511. New York: Stein and Day, 1971.

Fletcher, Angus. *Colors of the Mind: Conjectures on Thinking in Literature*. Cambridge, MA: Harvard University Press, 1991.

———. Introduction to *Treasure Island*, by Robert Louis Stevenson, xv–xli. New York: Barnes and Noble, 2005.

———. *A New Theory for American Poetry: Democracy, the Environment, and the Future of the Imagination*. Cambridge, MA: Harvard University Press, 2004.

Freud, Sigmund. *Three Essays on the Theory of Sexuality*. Translated and edited by James Strachey. New York: Basic Books, 1962.

———. *The Uncanny*. Translated by David McLintock. London: Penguin, 2003.

Frosch, Thomas R. "Parody and Authenticity in *Lolita*." In Bloom, *Vladimir Nabokov*, 127–42.

Gabriele, Mino. "Il burattino e lo specchio." In Pierotti, *C'era una volta un pezzo di legno*, 43–46.

Gagliardi, Antonio. *Il burattino e il labirinto: Una lettura di Pinocchio*. Turin: Tirrenia-Stampatori, 1980.

Genot, Gérard. "Le corps de Pinocchio." In Panteri, *Studi collodiani*, 299–313.

Gildersleeve, Jessica. *Elizabeth Bowen and the Writing of Trauma: The Ethics of Survival*. Amsterdam: Rodopi, 2014.

Glendinning, Victoria. *Elizabeth Bowen: A Biography*. New York: Random House, 1977.

Goodenough, Elizabeth, Mark Heberle, and Naomi B. Sokoloff, editors. *Infant Tongues: The Voice of the Child in Literature*. Detroit: Wayne State University Press, 1994.

Graves, Richard Perceval. *Richard Hughes: A Biography*. London: André Deutsch, 1994.

Greenway, Betty, editor. *Twice-Told Children's Tales: The Influence of Childhood Reading on Writers for Adults*. New York: Routledge, 2005.

Grenby, M. O., and Andrea Immel, editors. *The Cambridge Companion to Children's Literature*. Cambridge, UK: Cambridge University Press, 2009.

Gubar, Marah. *Artful Dodgers: Reconceiving the Golden Age of Children's Literature*. Oxford: Oxford University Press, 2009.

Harrison, Robert Pogue. *Juvenescence: A Cultural History of Our Age*. Chicago: University of Chicago Press, 2014.

Hartman, Geoffrey. *Wordsworth's Poetry: 1787–1814*. New Haven: Yale University Press, 1964.

Heller-Roazen, Daniel. *The Enemy of All: Piracy and the Law of Nations*. New York: Zone, 2009.

Herbert, George. *The Complete English Poems*. Edited by John Tobin. London: Penguin, 1991.

Higonnet, Anne. *Pictures of Innocence: The History and Crisis of Ideal Childhood*. London: Thames and Hudson, 1998.

Hock, Ronald, editor and translator. *The Infancy Gospels of James and Thomas*. Santa Rosa: Polebridge, 1995.

Holland, Laurence B. *The Expense of Vision: Essays on the Craft of Henry James*. Princeton: Princeton University Press, 1964.

Hollander, John. "The Perilous Magic of Nymphets: *Lolita* by Vladimir Nabokov" (book review). *Partisan Review* 23, no. 4 (1956): 557–60.

Hollindale, Peter. Introduction to *Peter Pan in Kensington Gardens and Peter and Wendy*, vii–xxviii. Oxford: Oxford World's Classics, 1991.

Hollingsworth, Christopher, editor. *Alice beyond Wonderland: Essays for the Twenty-First Century*. Iowa City: University of Iowa Press, 2009.

Howe, Susan. *Concordance*. New York: New Directions, 2020.

———. *The Quarry*. New York: New Directions, 2015.

Hughes, Richard. *A High Wind in Jamaica*. New York: NYRB, 1999.

———. *In Hazard*. New York: NYRB, 2007.

Huizinga, Johan. *Homo Ludens: A Study of the Play-Element in Culture*. Boston: Beacon, 1955.

Hynes, Samuel. *The Edwardian Turn of Mind*. Princeton: Princeton University Press, 1968.

Inglesby, Elizabeth C. "'Expressive Objects': Elizabeth Bowen's Narrative Materializes." *Modern Fiction Studies* 53, no. 2 (2007): 306–33.

Jack, R. D. S. *The Road to the Never Land: A Reassessment of J. M. Barrie's Dramatic Art.* Aberdeen: Aberdeen University Press, 1991.

James, Henry. *Collected Travel Writings: Great Britain and America.* New York: Library of America, 1993.

———. *The Complete Notebooks of Henry James.* Edited by Leon Edel and Llyall H. Powers. Oxford: Oxford University Press, 1987.

———. *Henry James: A Life in Letters.* Edited by Philip Horne. New York: Viking Penguin, 1999.

———. *Literary Criticism.* Vol. 2, *French Writers, Other European Writers, Prefaces to the New York Edition.* New York: Library of America, 1984.

———. *The Sacred Fount.* New York: New Directions, 1995.

———. *A Small Boy and Others.* New York: Scribner's, 1913.

———. *The Turn of the Screw.* Edited by David Bromwich. London: Penguin, 2011.

———. *What Maisie Knew.* Edited by Christopher Ricks. London: Penguin, 2010.

Jaques, Zoe. *Children's Literature and the Posthuman: Animal, Environment, Cyborg.* London: Routledge, 2015.

Johnson, D. Barton. *Worlds in Regression: Some Novels of Vladimir Nabokov.* Ann Arbor: Ardis, 1985.

Kafka, Franz. *The Castle.* Translated by Mark Harman. New York: Schocken, 1998.

———. *The Complete Stories.* Edited by Nahum Glatzer. New York: Schocken, 1971.

———. *Diaries, 1914–1923.* Edited by Max Brod. Translated by Martin Greenberg, with the cooperation of Hannah Arendt. New York: Schocken, 1948.

———. *Letters to Friends, Family, and Editors.* Translated by Richard Wilson and Clara Wilson. New York: Schocken, 1977.

———. *Metamorphosis, and Other Stories.* Translated by Michael Hofmann. London: Penguin, 2008.

———. *The Office Writings.* Edited by Stanley Corngold, Jack Greenberg, and Benno Wagner. Translations by Eric Patton and Ruth Hein. Princeton: Princeton University Press, 2009.

———. "Die Sorge des Hausvaters." In *Drucke zu Lebzeiten: Kritische Ausgabe,* edited by Wolf Kittler, Hans-Gerd Koch, and Gerhard Neumann, 2 vols., 1:282–84. Berlin: S. Fischer, 1994.

———. *The Zürau Aphorisms.* Introduction and afterword by Roberto Calasso. Translated by Michael Hofmann. Calasso's commentary translated by Geoffrey Brock. London: Harvill Secker, 2006.

Kahn, Charles H. *The Art and Thought of Heraclitus: An Edition of the Fragments with Translation and Commentary.* Cambridge, UK: Cambridge University Press, 1979.

Karshan, Thomas. *Vladimir Nabokov and the Art of Play.* Oxford: Oxford University Press, 2011.

Kerényi, C. "The Primordial Child in Primordial Times." In *Essays on a Science of Mythology: The Myth of the Divine Child and the Mysteries of Eleusis,* by C. J. Jung and C. Kerényi, translated by R. F. C. Hull, 33–94. New York: Pantheon, 1949.

Kertész, Imre. *Fatelessness.* Translated by Tim Wilkinson. New York: Random House, 2004.

Kincaid, James R. "Alice's Invasion of Wonderland." *PMLA* 88, no. 1 (1972): 92–99.

———. *Child-Loving: The Erotic Child and Victorian Culture.* New York: Routledge, 1992.

Klein, Melanie. *Narrative of a Child Analysis*. London: Hogarth Press and the Institute of Psycho-Analysis, 1961.

Knoepflmacher, U. C. "Revisiting Wordsworth: Lewis Carroll's 'The White Knight's Song.'" In *Victorians Reading the Romantics: Essays by U. C. Knoepflmacher*, edited by Linda M. Shires, 144–61. Columbus: Ohio State University Press, 2016.

———. *Ventures into Childland: Victorians, Fairy Tales, and Femininity*. Chicago: University of Chicago Press, 1998.

Knoepflmacher, U. C., and Mitzi Myers. "From the Editors: 'Cross-Writing' and the Reconceptualization of Children's Literary Studies." *Children's Literature* 25 (1997): vii–xvii.

Knowlson, James. *Damned to Fame: The Life of Samuel Beckett*. New York: Simon & Schuster, 1996.

Kristeva, Julia. "Place Names." Translated by Tom Gora and Alice Jardine. *October* 6 (1978): 93–111.

Kuhn, Reinhard. *Corruption in Paradise: The Child in Western Literature*. Hanover, NH: University Press of New England, 1982.

Kuznets, Lois. *When Toys Come Alive: Narratives of Animation, Metamorphosis, and Development*. New Haven: Yale University Press, 1994.

Lecercle, Jean-Jacques. *Philosophy of Nonsense: The Intuitions of Victorian Nonsense Literature*. London: Routledge, 1994.

Lee, Hermione. *Elizabeth Bowen: An Estimation*. London: Vision, 1981.

Lerer, Seth. *Children's Literature: A Reader's History from Aesop to Harry Potter*. Chicago: University of Chicago Press, 2008.

Locke, Richard. *Critical Children: The Use of Childhood in Ten Great Novels*. New York: Columbia University Press, 2011.

Lucht, Marc, and Donna Yarri, editors. *Kafka's Creatures: Animals, Hybrids, and Other Fantastic Beings*. Lanham, MD: Lexington Books, 2010.

Lurie, Alison. *Don't Tell the Grown-ups: Subversive Children's Literature*. Boston: Little, Brown, 1990.

Lustig, T. J. *Henry James and the Ghostly*. Cambridge, UK: Cambridge University Press, 1994.

Mallarmé, Stéphane. *Recueil de "Nursery Rhymes."* Edited by Carl Paul Barbier. Paris: Gallimard, 1964.

Manganelli, Giorgio. *Pinocchio: Un libro parallelo*. Milan: Adelphi, 2002.

Manolescu, Monica. "'I Speak like a Child': Orality in Nabokov." In *Nabokov Upside Down*. Edited by Brian Boyd and Marijeta Bozovic, 85–98. Evanston: Northwestern University Press, 2017.

Marcheschi, Daniela. *Collodi ritrovato*. Pisa: ETS, 1990.

McBride, Joseph. "Alfred Hitchcock's *Mary Rose*: An Old Master's Unheard *Cri de Coeur*." *Cinéaste* 26, no. 2 (2001): 24–28.

McGavran, James Holt, editor. *Literature and the Child: Romantic Continuations, Postmodern Contestations*. Iowa City: University of Iowa Press, 1999.

———, editor. *Romanticism and Children's Literature in Nineteenth-Century England*. Athens: University of Georgia Press, 1991.

Miller, David Lee. *Dreams of the Burning Child: Sacrificial Sons and the Father's Witness*. Ithaca: Cornell University Press, 2002.

Miller, Karl. *Doubles: Studies in Literary History*. Oxford: Oxford University Press, 1985.

Miller, Keith. "The Flight from Neverland." *Times Literary Supplement* 4942, January 2, 1998, 16.

Moers, Ellen. *Literary Women*. New York: Doubleday, 1976.

Mooney, Sinéad. "Unstable Compounds: Bowen's Beckettian Affinities." *Modern Fiction Studies* 53, no. 2 (2007): 238–56.

Moore, Marianne. *The Complete Prose*. Edited by Patricia Willis. New York: Viking, 1986.

Moretti, Franco. "Kindergarten." In *Signs Taken for Wonders: Essays in the Sociology of Literary Forms*, translated by Susan Fischer, David Forgacs, and David Miller, 157–81. London: Verso, 1983.

Morgan, Louise. "Richard Hughes, Artist and Adventurer" [interview], *Everyman*, April 9, 1931, 327–29.

Morgan, Paul. *The Art of Richard Hughes: A Study of the Novels*. Cardiff: University of Wales Press, 1993.

Morrison, Toni. *Beloved*. New York: Everyman's Library, 2006.

Moshenska, Joe. *Iconoclasm as Child's Play*. Stanford: Stanford University Press, 2019.

Nabokov, Vladimir. *Bend Sinister*. New York: Henry Holt, 1947.

———. *Invitation to a Beheading*. Translated by Dimitri Nabokov. New York: Putnam's, 1959.

———. *Lolita*. New York: Putnam's, 1958.

———. *Nabokov's Butterflies: Unpublished and Uncollected Writings*. Edited by Brian Boyd and Robert Michael Pyle. New translations from the Russian by Dmitri Nabokov. Boston: Beacon, 2000.

———. *Pale Fire*. New York: Putnam's, 1962.

———. *Speak, Memory: An Autobiography Revisited*. Rev. ed., New York: Putman's, 1966.

Natov, Roni. *The Poetics of Childhood*. London: Routledge, 2003.

Nekula, Marek. *Franz Kafka and His Prague Contexts: Studies in Language and Literature*. Translated by Robert Russell and Carly McLaughlin. Prague: Charles University in Prague Karolinum Press, 2016.

Newton, Michael. *Savage Girls and Wild Boys: A History of Feral Children*. London: Faber and Faber, 2002.

Nietzsche, Friedrich. *The Birth of Tragedy*. Translated by Shaun Whiteside. Edited by Michael Tanner. London: Penguin, 1993.

Nodelman, Perry. *The Hidden Adult: Defining Children's Literature*. Baltimore: Johns Hopkins University Press, 2008.

Nonnos. *Dionysica*. Translated by W. H. D. Rouse. Loeb Classical Library. 3 vols. Cambridge, MA: Harvard University Press, 1940.

Oates, Joyce Carol. "Killer Kids." *New York Review of Books* 44, no. 17 (1997): 17–20.

Ohi, Kevin. *Innocence and Rapture: The Erotic Child in Pater, Wilde, James, and Nabokov*. New York: Palgrave Macmillan, 2005.

Opie, Iona, and Peter Opie. *Children's Games in Street and Playground: Chasing, Catching, Seeking, Hunting, Racing, Duelling, Exerting, Daring, Guessing, Acting, Pretending*. Oxford: Oxford University Press, 1969.

———. *The Lore and Language of Schoolchildren*. Oxford: Oxford University Press, 1959.

Ozick, Cynthia. *What Henry James Knew, and Other Essays on Writers*. London: Jonathan Cape, 1984.

Page, Norman, editor. *Henry James: Interviews and Recollections*. New York: St. Martin's, 1984.

————, editor. *Nabokov: The Critical Heritage*. London: Routledge and Kegan Paul, 1982.

Panteri, Mosfero, et al., editors. *Studi collodiani: Atti del I Convegno Internazionale, Pescia, 5–7 Ottobre 1974*. Pescia: Casa di Risparmio di Pistoia e Pescia, 1976.

Partridge, Eric. *Here, There and Everywhere: Essays upon Language*. London: Hamish Hamilton, 1950.

Phillips, Adam. *The Beast in the Nursery: On Curiosity and Other Appetites*. New York: Vintage, 1998.

————. "Edward Lear's Nonsense and British Psychoanalysis." *Raritan: A Quarterly Review* 35, no. 2 (2015): 31–44.

Phillips, Robert, editor. *Aspects of Alice: Lewis Carroll's Dreamchild as Seen through the Critics' Looking-Glasses, 1865–1971*. New York: Vanguard, 1971.

Piaget, Jean. *The Construction of Reality in the Child*. Translated by Margaret Cook. New York: Basic Books, 1954.

Pierotti, Gian Luca, editor. *C'era una volta un pezzo di legno: La simbologia di Pinocchio*. Milan: Emme, 1981.

Pifer, Ellen. *Demon or Doll: Images of the Child in Contemporary Writing and Culture*. Charlottesville: University Press of Virginia, 2000.

————. *Nabokov and the Novel*. Cambridge, MA: Harvard University Press, 1980.

Pitcher, George. "Wittgenstein, Nonsense, and Lewis Carroll." *Massachusetts Review* 6, no. 3 (1965): 591–611.

Plotz, Judith. *Romanticism and the Vocation of Childhood*. New York: Palgrave, 2001.

Posnock, Ross. *The Trial of Curiosity: Henry James, William James, and the Challenge of Modernity*. New York: Oxford University Press, 1991.

Prose, Francine. Introduction to Hughes, *A High Wind in Jamaica*, v–xii.

Rackin, Donald. *Alice in Wonderland and Through the Looking-Glass: Nonsense, Sense, Meaning*. New York: Twayne, 1991.

Rampton, David. *Vladimir Nabokov: A Critical Study of the Novels*. Cambridge, UK: Cambridge University Press, 1984.

Rennie, Neil. *Treasure Neverland: Real and Imaginary Pirates*. Oxford: Oxford University Press, 2013.

Reynolds, Kimberley. *Radical Children's Literature: Future Visions and Aesthetic Transformations in Juvenile Fiction*. Houndmills: Palgrave Macmillan, 2007.

Richardson, Alan. "Romanticism and the End of Childhood." In McGavran, *Literature and the Child*, 23–43.

Rilke, Rainer Maria. *The Book of Images*. Translated by Edward Snow. San Francisco: North Point, 1991.

Rorty, Richard. *Contingency, Solidarity, and Irony*. Cambridge, UK: Cambridge University Press, 1989.

Rose, Jacqueline. *The Case of Peter Pan, or The Impossibility of Children's Fiction*. London: Macmillan, 1984.

Roth, Christine. "Looking through the Spyglass: Lewis Carroll, James Barrie, and the Empire of Childhood." In Hollingsworth, *Alice beyond Wonderland*, 23–36,

Sarraute, Nathalie. *Do You Hear Them? [Vous les entendez?]*. Translated by Maria Jolas. New York: Braziller, 1973.

Schiller, Friedrich. *On the Aesthetic Education of Man, in a Series of Letters*. Translated by Reginald Snell. New York: Ungar, 1965.

Scholem, Gershom, editor. *The Correspondence of Walter Benjamin and Gershom Scholem: 1932–1940*. Translated by Gary Smith and Andre Lefevere. New York: Schocken, 1989.

Seidel, Michael. "Stereoscope: Nabokov's *Ada* and *Pale Fire*." In Bloom, *Vladimir Nabokov*, 235–57.

Sewell, Elizabeth. *The Field of Nonsense*. London: Chatto and Windus, 1952.

———. *Lewis Carroll: Voices from France*. Edited by Clare Imholtz. Lewis Carroll Society of North America, 2008.

Shakespeare, William. *The Arden Shakespeare Complete Works*. Edited by Ann Thompson, David Scott Kastan, and Richard Proudfoot. London: Bloomsbury, 2011.

Shavit, Zohar. *Poetics of Children's Literature*. Athens: University of Georgia Press, 1986.

Shelley, Percy Bysshe. *Shelley's Poetry and Prose*. Edited by Donald H. Reiman and Neil Freistat. 2nd ed., New York: Norton, 2002.

Shepherd, Nan. *The Living Mountain*. Edinburgh: Canongate, 2014.

Silk, Dennis. "The Marionette Theater." In *William the Wonder-Kid: Plays, Puppet Plays and Theater Writings*, 238–49. Riverdale-on-Hudson: Sheep Meadow, 1997.

Simms, Eva M. *The Child in the World: Embodiment, Time, and Language in Early Childhood*. Detroit: Wayne State University Press, 2008.

Snow, Edward. *Inside Bruegel: The Play of Images in "Children's Games."* New York: North Point, 1997.

Sokel, Walter H. *The Myth of Power and the Self: Essays on Franz Kafka*. Detroit: Wayne State University Press, 2002.

Spariosu, Mihai I. *Dionysus Reborn: Play and the Aesthetic Dimension in Modern Philosophical and Scientific Discourse*. Ithaca: Cornell University Press, 1989.

Steedman, Carolyn. *Strange Dislocations: Childhood and the Idea of Human Interiority, 1780–1930*. Cambridge, MA: Harvard University Press, 1995.

Stevens, Wallace. *The Palm at the End of the Mind: Selected Poems and a Play*. Edited by Holly Stevens. New York: Knopf, 1971.

Stewart, Garrett. "Death Bequeathed." In Bloom, *Vladimir Nabokov*, 191–208.

Stewart, Susan. *Nonsense: Aspects of Intertextuality in Folklore and Literature*. Baltimore: Johns Hopkins University Press, 1978.

Stewart-Steinberg, Suzanne. *The Pinocchio Effect: On Making Italians, 1860–1920*. Chicago: University of Chicago Press, 2007.

Stirling, Kirsten. *Peter Pan's Shadows in the Literary Imagination*. New York: Routledge, 2012.

Stockton, Kathryn Bond. *The Queer Child, or Growing up Sideways in the Twentieth Century*. Durham: Duke University Press, 2009.

Stokes, Adrian. *The Game That Must Be Lost: Collected Papers*. London: Carcanet, 1973.

Suchoff, David. *Kafka's Jewish Languages: The Hidden Openness of Tradition*. Philadelphia: University of Pennsylvania Press, 2012.

Sutton-Smith, Brian. *The Ambiguity of Play*. Cambridge, MA: Harvard University Press, 1997.

Švankmajer, Jan, director. *Alice* [Něco z Alenky]. Film. 1988.

Tamen, Miguel. *What Art Is Like, in Constant Reference to the Alice Books*. Cambridge, MA: Harvard University Press, 2012.

Tatar, Maria. *The Hard Facts of the Grimms' Fairy Tales*. 2nd ed., Princeton: Princeton University Press, 2003.

Tempesti, Fernando. "Burattini in piazza del Granduca." In *Pinocchio fra i burattini*, edited by Fernando Tempesti, 101–7. Florence: La Nuova Italia, 1993.

———. "Chi era il Collodi, Com'è fatto *Pinocchio*." Introduction to *Pinocchio*, edited by Fernando Tempesti. Milan: Feltrinelli, 1972.

Toesca, Pietro. "La filosofia di Pinocchio, ovvero l'Odissea di un ragazzo per bene con la memoria di burattino." *Forum Italicum* 33, no. 2 (1997): 459–86.

Valesio, Paolo. *Ascoltare il silenzio: La retorica come teoria*. Bologna: Il Mulino, 1986.

Van den Berg, J. H. *The Changing Nature of Man: Introduction to a Historical Psychology*. Translated by H. F. Croes. New York: Dell, 1975.

Van Duyn, Mona. "Pattern and Pilgrimage: A Reading of *The Death of the Heart*." *Critique: Studies in Contemporary Fiction* 4, no. 2 (1961): 52–66.

Warner, Marina. *From the Beast to the Blonde: On Fairy Tales and Their Tellers*. New York: Farrar, Straus & Giroux, 1995.

———. *Managing Monsters: Six Myths of Our Time (The Reith Lectures 1994)*. London: Vintage, 1994.

———. *No Go the Bogeyman: Scaring, Lulling, and Making Mock*. New York: Farrar, Straus & Giroux, 1998.

West, Rebecca. Afterword to Collodi, *The Adventures of Pinocchio*, translated by Geoffrey Brock, 163–189.

Wilson, Robin. *Lewis Carroll in Numberland: His Fantastical Mathematical Logical Life*. London: Allen Lane, 2008.

Winnicott, D. W. *Playing and Reality*. London: Tavistock, 1971.

Wood, Michael. *The Magician's Doubts: Nabokov and the Risks of Fiction*. Princeton: Princeton University Press, 1994.

Woolf, Virginia. *The Moment, and Other Essays*. London: Hogarth, 1947.

Wordsworth, William. *The Major Works, Including "The Prelude."* Edited by Stephen Gill. Oxford: Oxford University Press, 1994.

Yeazell, Ruth Bernard. *Language and Knowledge in the Late Novels of Henry James*. Chicago: University of Chicago Press, 1976.

Yeung, Heather H. *On Literary Plasticity: Readings with Kafka in Ecology, Voice, and Object-Life*. London: Palgrave Macmillan, 2020.

Ziolkowski, Eric. *Evil Children in Religion, Literature, and Art*. Houndmills: Palgrave, 2001.

Zipes, Jack. *Fairy Tales and the Art of Subversion: The Classical Genre for Children and the Process of Civilization*. New York: Routledge, 1991.

INDEX

Ingelow, Jean, 10
innocence, 1–2, 3, 5, 6, 10, 11, 19–20, 34, 64,
66, 69–70, 72, 75, 101, 109, 112, 135–38,
140, 143, 147

James, Henry: "The Beast in the Jungle,"
61; *The Golden Bowl*, 61; *The Portrait
of a Lady*, 78; *The Sacred Fount*, 83; *A
Small Boy and Others*, 67–68; *The Turn
of the Screw*, 5, 68–69; *What Maisie
Knew*, 1, 6, 12, 57–85, 133, 164, 173, 175;
The Wings of the Dove, 61
Jesus Christ, 9, 26, 54
Joyce, James, 139n, 146
Jung, C. G., 99

Kafka, Franz: "The Cares of a Fam-
ily Man," 1, 6, 12, 103–13, 133, 173, 175;
The Castle, 109n, 110; diaries, 109, 113;
"Josephine the Singer, or The Mouse
Folk," 112; letters, 105n, 108; *Metamor-
phosis*, 104, 108; office writings, 106,
109n; *The Trial*, 109, 113; *The Zürau
Aphorisms*, 111–12
Kafka, Ottla, 111–12
Karshan, Thomas, 159, 165n
Kerényi, Carl, 9
Kertész, Imre, 112
Kincaid, James, 5, 93
Kingsley, Charles, 10
Klee, Paul, 108
Knoepflmacher, U. C., 180n
Krishna, 9
Kuhn, Reinhard, 179n, 180n

language, 2, 5, 6–7, 11, 15–19, 20–30, 32, 35,
38, 47–48, 55, 59, 65, 106, 109–10, 113,
120, 122, 129–30, 151–52, 154, 165, 174.
See also names and naming; nonsense;
silence
Lee, Hermione, 145, 187n
Le Fanu, Sheridan, 187n
Lerer, Seth, 180n
Lessing, Doris, 11
Lewis, Matthew, 116n
Llewelyn-Davies (family), 96n
Llewelyn-Davies, Michael, 96–97

Lolita. See under Nabokov, Vladimir
Lustig, T. J., 69
Lyne, Adrian, 170

MacDonald, George, 10
Mackail, Denis, 97n
magic, 9, 15, 34, 38, 39, 52, 87, 111, 113, 151–
52, 155, 160, 171
Manganelli, Giorgio, 41, 52
Marcheschi, Daniela, 182n
McBride, Joseph, 185n
memory (and forgetting), 3, 26–27, 28, 34,
48–49, 55, 67, 78, 86, 91, 95–97, 102, 105,
116, 120, 123, 129–31, 133, 135, 144, 155,
157, 158–59, 161–63, 170, 175
metamorphosis, 3, 5, 15, 37, 52, 154. *See
also* Ovid
Miller, Karl, 188n
Miller, Keith, 96, 185n
Milton, John, 14
Moers, Ellen, 181n
Mooney, Sinéad, 187n
Moore, Marianne, 18
Morrison, Toni, 11
myth, 8–9

Nabokov, Vladimir: *Bend Sinister*, 159;
Invitation to a Beheading, 158–59;
Lolita, 1, 6, 150–72, 173, 175; *Pale Fire*,
158; *Speak, Memory*, 75, 159, 188n
names and naming, 1, 4, 18, 21, 23, 40, 43,
44, 45, 60, 90, 91, 95, 101, 106, 109–10,
113, 120, 123, 132, 153, 161, 165, 168, 171,
174. *See also* language; nonsense
Nekula, Marek, 185n
Nodelman, Perry, 180n
nonsense, 2, 6, 15, 17, 21–29, 32–33, 48, 62,
109, 139n, 168. *See also* language; names
and naming; play; silence

Oates, Joyce Carol, 11, 124
objects, 3, 14, 17–18, 28, 33, 38, 39, 44,
103–5, 107–8, 112, 114, 126, 127, 134, 136n,
162, 174. *See also* dolls; puppets; toys
Ohi, Kevin, 188n
Ovid, 15, 37
Oyeyemi, Helen, 18